New Perspectives in Special Education

'This book should be read by everyone who wants to understand special education today.'

James M. Kauffman, Ed.D, Professor Emeritus of Education, University of Virginia

New Perspectives in Special Education opens the door to the fascinating and vitally important world of theory that informs contemporary special education. It examines theoretical and philosophical orientations such as 'positivism', 'poststructuralism' and 'hermeneutics', relating these to contemporary global views of special education.

Offering a refreshingly balanced view across a broad range of debates, this topical text guides the reader through the main theoretical and philosophical positions that may be held with regard to special education, and critically examines positions that often go unrecognised and unquestioned by practitioners and academics alike. It helps the reader to engage with and question the positions taken by themselves and others, by providing thinking points and suggestions for further reading at the end of each chapter.

Perspectives covered include:

- positivism and empiricism
- phenomenology and hermeneutics
- historical materialism and critical theory
- holism and constructivism
- structuralism and poststructuralism
- pragmatism and symbolic interactionism
- psychoanalysis
- postmodernism and historical epistemology

Anyone wishing to gain a fuller understanding of special education should not be without this stimulating and much-needed text.

Michael Farrell is a widely published private special education consultant. He works with children, families, schools, local authorities, voluntary organisations, universities and government ministries. He has published extensively with Routledge, with recent titles including *Debating Special Education*, *Educating Special Children, Second Edition*, and second edition titles in the whole *Effective Teacher's Guide* series.

'At last, a book that critically unpacks the theory behind practices in special education . . . this book complements the ongoing quest for teaching and support strategies that maximize learning and engagement in people with additional support needs of all types. Highly recommended.'

Michael Arthur-Kelly, Ph.D., Associate Professor and Director, Special Education Centre, The University of Newcastle, NSW, Australia

'A unique text that challenges special educators to examine critical issues and practices in the field.'

Lyndal M. Bullock, Regents Professor, Special Education, University of North Texas

'*New Perspectives in Special Education* provides a much-needed analysis of the theoretical and philosophical underpinnings of the current practice of inclusive and special education. Farrell clearly examines positions and practices in the field that typically go unquestioned by practitioners and academics. In so doing he has produced a text that should be essential reading for all teachers, psychologists, other practitioners, administrators and lecturers involved in inclusive and special education.'

Professor Garry Hornby, College of Education, University of Canterbury, Christchurch, New Zealand

'A much awaited book, it offers a balanced and debated view of Special Education and inclusion. Farrell provides the learner with a clear understanding of integration and inclusion and full inclusion. In addition, it offers the educator learner an insight into inclusive education and pedagogy. The author carefully presents special education from varying theoretical perspectives, which is uncommon and refreshing. A book that clearly challenges rethinking about how we could be thinking about Special Education and inclusion for the 21st century.'

Dr Karen P. Nonis, Associate Professor of Early Childhood & Special Needs Education, The National Institute of Education, Nanyang Technological University, Singapore

'The text builds on a growing interest in applying a more deeply theorised approach to undersanding the field of special education, and it does so by offering a succinct but comprehensive overview.'

Dr Kristine Black-Hawkins, Faculty of Education, University of Cambridge, England

'Dr Michael Farrell succeeds in making the ideas of the various philosophies accessible and understandable, and does so in a vivid and practical manner.'

Dr Gary O'Reilly, Deputy Director, Doctoral Programme in Clinical Psychology, School of Psychology, University College Dublin, Ireland

New Perspectives in Special Education

Contemporary philosophical debates

Michael Farrell

Routledge
Taylor & Francis Group

LONDON AND NEW YORK

First published 2012
by Routledge
2 Park Square, Milton Park, Abingdon, Oxon OX14 4RN

Simultaneously published in the USA and Canada
by Routledge
711 Third Avenue, New York, NY 10017

Routledge is an imprint of the Taylor & Francis Group, an informa business

© 2012 Michael Farrell

British Library Cataloguing in Publication Data
A catalogue record for this book is available from the British Library

Library of Congress Cataloging in Publication Data
Farrell, Michael, 1948–
New perspectives in special education : contemporary philosophical
debates / Michael Farrell.
p. cm.
1. Special education–Philosophy. I. Title.
LC3965.F38 2013
371.901–dc23
2011049163

ISBN: 978-0-415-50421-8 (hbk)
ISBN: 978-0-415-50422-5 (pbk)
ISBN: 978-0-203-12845-9 (ebk)

Typeset in Bembo
by Keystroke, Station Road, Codsall, Wolverhampton

MIX
Paper from
responsible sources
FSC® C004839
www.fsc.org

Printed and bound in Great Britain by
CPI Antony Rowe, Chippenham, Wiltshire

Contents

About the author

Michael Farrell was educated in the United Kingdom. After training as a teacher at Bishop Grosseteste College, Lincoln, and obtaining an honours degree from Nottingham University, he gained a Masters Degree in Education and Psychology from the Institute of Education, London University. Subsequently, he carried out research for a Master of Philosophy degree at the Institute of Psychiatry, Maudsley Hospital, London, and for a Doctor of Philosophy degree under the auspices of the Medical Research Council Cognitive Development Unit and London University.

Professionally, Michael Farrell worked as a head teacher, a lecturer at London University and as a local authority inspector. He managed a national psychometric project for City University, London and directed a national teacher education project for the United Kingdom Government Department of Education. His present role as a private special education consultant includes work with children and families, schools, local authorities, voluntary organisations, universities, and government departments in Britain and elsewhere.

His many books, translated into European and Asian languages, include:

- *Educating Special Children: An Introduction to Provision for Pupils with Disabilities and Disorders*, Second edition (Routledge, 2012)
- *Foundations of Special Education: An Introduction* (Wiley, 2009)
- *The Special Education Handbook* (Fourth edition) (David Fulton, 2009).

Preface

This book provides, in one volume, an overview of the main philosophical positions informing special education. Other books focus on one or a few such perspectives but none, so far as I have been able to ascertain, takes a similar broad view. Positivism and empiricism, phenomenology, hermeneutics, historical materialism, critical theory, holism, constructivism, structuralism, poststructuralism, pragmatism, symbolic interactionism, Freudian psychoanalysis, Lacan's theories, postmodernism and historical epistemology are all examined. While seeking to give each perspective a fair hearing, the book recognises the preeminent place of positivism in special education.

I welcome comments from readers that might strengthen future editions.

Michael Farrell
Herefordshire
dr.m.j.farrell@btopenworld.com

Acknowledgements

I am very happy to acknowledge the generous help of many colleagues who read chapters or drew my attention to material I might otherwise have overlooked. In particular I wish to warmly thank the following:

Professor Ellen Brantlinger, Professor in Curriculum and Instruction, Indiana University Bloomington kindly read and commented on the chapter on 'Historical materialism and critical theory'.

Professor Scot Danforth, Associate Professor and Department Chair in the Division of Teaching and Learning, University of Missouri–St. Louis provided insightful comments on an early draft of the chapter on 'Holism and constructivism'.

Professor Mary Poplin, Associate Professor of Education, Claremont Graduate School, California helpfully drew my attention to much useful information on the area of constructivism.

Professor Thomas Skrtic, Professor of Special Education, University of Kansas helpfully clarified several points about his own interpretation of critical pragmatism in connection with the chapter on pragmatism.

Professor James M. Kauffman, University of Virginia kindly commented on the chapter concerning 'Positivism'.

Professor Simo Vehmas, Jyväskylä University, Finland read the chapter on 'Positivist special education and other perspectives' and provided invaluable comments.

The support of these colleagues undoubtedly strengthened the book. However, there is no implication that they necessarily agree with its views. Any shortcomings are of course entirely my own responsibility.

I am also deeply appreciative of the support of Alison Foyle and all the staff at Routledge.

Chapter outlines

Chapter I   Differing roadmaps: special education, disability and inclusion

In this chapter I propose the content, aims and readers of the book. I then explain briefly the nature of perspectives and their concomitants, theory and research. I discuss special education, legal definitions of disability and other understandings of the term. I consider inclusion in three senses: including pupils already attending regular schools; integration, inclusion as mainstreaming, and full inclusion; and inclusion as pupil participation. The chapter looks at inclusive education and inclusive pedagogy.

I examine relationships between views of disability and attitudes to inclusion. Some criticisms of inclusion as mainstreaming are examined. These concern inclusion: as a primary aim of schooling; as liberation from oppression; as the pursuit of equal opportunity; as a human right; and as fairness. I then consider relationships between criticisms of special education and claims for inclusion.

Chapter 2   Creative tensions? Contemporary special education and its critics

This chapter describes contemporary special education as reflected in legislation and practice in the United States and the United Kingdom. In doing so, it elaborates on: education in general; disabilities and disorders; and special education provision in terms of curriculum, pedagogy, school and classroom organisation, resources, and therapy. It discusses what is distinctive about special education; describes its foundational disciplines such as neuropsychology; and points out the importance of academic progress and personal and social development. I discuss the location of special education, and its aims and methods.

Next, the chapter briefly discusses criticisms of special education and responses to these. The focus is on: sociological criticisms of an individual perspective; rights-based criticisms and contested values; criticisms of categorical classification; criticisms of assessment; and negative labelling.

Chapter 3 A scientific stance: positivism and empiricism

This chapter introduces and evaluates positivism (and earlier empiricism) and logical positivism. Positivism is suggested to be the predominant theoretical basis of special education. Applications of a positivist approach to special education are explained including notions of classification and identification and assessment of disabilities and disorders. Positivism informs provision including behavioural interventions. The relationships between positivism and 'evidence-based practice' and professional knowledge are outlined. Evaluations of positivism and its application in special education are presented. The strengths of positivism include its potential to guide provision in terms of better outcomes for special children. Foundations of special education comprise predominantly disciplines with an individual and positivist orientation – for example, neuropsychology and developmental psychology, but also include other orientations, including social ones. Criticisms include that it can lead to overly scientific approaches taking insufficient account of the complexity of individuals.

Chapter 4 Being and interpretation: phenomenology and hermeneutics

This chapter outlines two perspectives having historical interconnections: phenomenology and hermeneutics. Phenomenology is approached through the ideas of Husserl and the early work of Martin Heidegger. The main emphasis is the work of Merleau-Ponty. This leads to an explanation of Iwakuma's exploration of the implications of Merleau-Ponty's ideas of the body and embodiment. Phenomenology and its applications to special education are evaluated, including insights into 'embodiment'.

Hermeneutics is introduced by brief reference to the approaches of Schleiermacher and Dilthey. The main emphasis however is on the philosophical hermeneutics of Gadamer. The chapter examines the applications to special education of philosophical hermeneutics by Gallagher, for example in *Challenging Orthodoxy in Special Education: Dissenting Voices* (Gallagher *et al.*, 2004, Love Publishing). The views of Iano are also considered. An evaluation of hermeneutics and its applications is presented.

Chapter 5 Economic forces and suspicion: historical materialism and critical theory

This chapter first considers historical materialism and then critical theory that was influenced by aspects of Marxism. Historical materialism is introduced and evaluated. Historical materialist applications to understandings of disability and the development of a social model are explained. An evaluation is offered of the social model.

Critical theory is introduced and its development in relation to Marxism explained through a brief account of the Frankfurt School. Particular attention is given to the work of Habermas. Tomlinson's work as an early advocate of critical theory in a rather broad sense is mentioned. The chapter examines the more recent writings of Brantlinger in *Who Benefits From Special Education? Remediating (Fixing) Other People's Children* (2006, Lawrence Erlbaum). An evaluation is made of the application of critical theory to special education, including the potential for questioning apparently benign commercial forces and the difficulty of establishing the grounding for a perspective purporting to see 'hidden' forces in society.

Chapter 6   Seeing the big picture and making knowledge: holism and constructivism

This chapter considers the related perspectives of holism and constructivism. Holism is explained through Smuts' coining of the term in *Holism and Evolution* (1926, Sierra Sunrise). Other related views of holism are touched on. Holism in relation to special education is examined through the work of Lous Heshusius. For example, her 1989 article 'The Newtonian Paradigm, Special Education, and Contours of Alternatives: An Overview' and more recent reflections *Challenging Orthodoxy in Special Education: Dissenting Voices* (Gallagher, Heshusius, Iano and Skrtic, 2004, Love Publishing). Constructivism is introduced. Brief mention is made of the aspects of the work of Piaget. The chapter considers the constructivist aspects of the work of Vygotsky in *Mind in Society: The Development of Higher Psychological Processes* (1978, Harvard University Press). Applications of constructivism to special education is presented through the writing of Poplin and her later views and the views of Danforth and Smith.

Chapter 7   Understanding structure and its dismantling: structuralism and poststructuralism

This chapter traces structuralism from the particular emphasis placed on aspects of Saussure's 1915 *Course in General Linguistics*. Jacobson's analysis of phonology is presented as compatible with Saussure's notion that language comprises a system of differential signs. Applications to special education draw on the work of Piaget, as influenced by Lévi-Strauss. The applications of Piaget's sensorimotor stage to understanding the development and learning of learners with profound cognitive impairments is examined. The contribution of structuralism and its application to special education is evaluated, including briefly the criticisms of poststructuralism and the difficulties of transferring developmental observations relating to infants to older learners with cognitive impairments.

Poststructuralism is defined. The focus is on Derrida's early development of deconstruction especially *Of Grammatology*. Applications to special education refer to Silvers's suggestion that 'normalcy' and 'disability' need not be antithetical and to Titchkosky's questioning of the disabled body as a life constituted out of the negation of able-bodiedness. The main source is Danforth and Rhodes's attempt to deconstruct the binary pair 'ability' and 'disability'.

Chapter 8 Working things out and bestowing meaning: pragmatism and symbolic interactionism

The chapter introduces the work of Dewey and American pragmatism. Criticisms of pragmatism are presented including Russell's rejection of Dewey's doctrine of 'substituting inquiry for truth as the fundamental concept of logic and theory of knowledge'. Mention is made of the neo-pragmatism of Richard Rorty. Applications of pragmatism to special education are considered, especially Skrtic's *Disability and Democracy: Reconstructing (Special) Education for Post-modernity* (1995, Teachers College Press). Pragmatism and its contribution to special education is evaluated, including the cohesive nature of Skrtic's arguments but the difficulty of developing approaches to pedagogy in an adhocratic way.

Symbolic interactionism is outlined with reference to the work of George Herbert Mead and Herbert Blumer. Symbolic interactionism has informed medical sociology and qualitative research methods. In addressing subjective questions such as the subjective experiences of individuals with disabilities and the perceptions of disability of others who are not disabled it is not always clear how such perspectives might be extended more widely than the samples reported. Where individuals debate and contest views and interpretations of reality, there may be major differences between perspectives. In such circumstances, social interaction itself is considered to provide the rational structures to mediate and resolve different interpretations. This raises the difficulties of how particular interpretations will be judged more adequate than others. At the theoretical level, the approach might offer little to extend historical analysis beyond a reductionist focus on social interaction.

Chapter 9 Psyche and language: psychoanalysis – Freud and Lacan

This chapter explains some aspects of psychoanalysis developed by Sigmund Freud. It describes the theories of Jacques Lacan and his attempt to reinterpret aspects of Freud's theories in the light of structuralist and poststructuralist interests. Next, I examine the development of Freud's theories in applications for children with reference to the ideas and practice of psychoanalysts Melanie Klein, Donald Winnicott and John Bowlby. The chapter describes applications of psychoanalysis and derived approaches to special educational provision. It then considers various therapies, the work of schools whose approach is informed by psychoanalytic concepts, and nurture groups. I evaluate the application of psychoanalysis to understanding disability and special education.

The chapter next describes applications of psychoanalysis and derived therapeutic approaches to special educational provision. It does this with reference to observations made by Deborah Marks concerning possible psychoanalytic perspectives of children's difficult behaviour in schools and the possible unconscious motivations of some helping professionals. I also look at how Lacan's theories have been interpreted in relation to disability. The chapter then considers focal psychodynamic psychotherapy, arts therapies and play therapy, and the work of schools whose approach is informed by psychoanalytic concepts; and nurture groups. Finally, the chapter gives an evaluation of psychoanalysis and Lacan's theories and their application to understandings of disability and special education.

Chapter 10   Shifting sands and power/knowledge: postmodernism and historical epistemology

A postmodern view of science is suggested by Lyotard in *The Postmodern Condition: A Report on Knowledge* (1984, Manchester University Press). Postmodern science concerns 'undecidables' and paradoxes and evolves in a discontinuous way. Its 'model of legitimation' is based on reasoning that contradicts logical rules. Heshusius, in criticising curriculum-based assessment and direct instruction, in special education, suggests their underlying assumptions are parallel to the 'mechanistic, Newtonian paradigm'. More recently, Heshusius has stated that the procedures of science were not 'divine intervention' but science is a 'historically and socially embedded construction'. An evaluation is presented. Postmodernism has been criticised by Sokal and Bricmont. It has been described as a form of 'antirealist doctrine' antipathetic towards 'objectivity and knowledge'. Aspects of the work of the French philosopher Gilles Deleuze are briefly considered. I look at attempts to relate his work to inclusion and by implication to criticisms of special education. An evaluation is made of the application of postmodernism to special education.

Historical epistemology is explained in relation to the views of Michel Foucault with particular reference to knowledge and power. The chapter describes adaptations of Foucault's ideas to disability and to special education. This includes a consideration of Tremain's interpretations of Foucault's themes in relation to impairment, and Allan's consideration of Foucault's views for special educational procedures. Foucault's ideas and their application to special education are evaluated including Shorter's criticisms of the historical accuracy and therefore the historical interpretations in Foucault's *The History of Madness* (2006, Routledge). Applications to special education lead to potentially useful questioning of the roles of professionals. But if the matrix of power-knowledge pervades every aspect of social life, there needs to be some further justification of why one set of power-knowledge relationships might be challenged rather than others.

Chapter 11   Taking stock: positivist special education and other perspectives

This chapter examines the perspectives discussed in the book in relation to positivist special education. It considers whether there can be any areas of productive contact between an essentially positivist special education and other viewpoints.

Chapter 12   Different thinking and reviewing provision: implications for special education of different perspectives

The final chapter examines the implications for special education of the different perspectives. It looks at the different ways of thinking that the perspectives generate. The chapter considers what the perspectives have to say with regard to curriculum and assessment, pedagogy, resources, organisation and therapy.

Chapter 1

Differing roadmaps

Special education, disability and inclusion

Content, aims and readers

New Perspectives in Special Education examines major theoretical positions informing special education. It comprises twelve chapters, a bibliography, and a combined author and subject index. Aiming to help readers engage with and question perspectives they or others may take, the book offers a guide to the main positions held in contemporary special education. The volume is intended for students (and lecturers using the book as a course text) and professionals wishing to consider major underlying perspectives in special education. It has an international remit, as it does not focus on the laws and procedures of any one country. Although the book concerns theory, it also refers to implications for practice.

Perspectives and their concomitants

Perspectives

Perspectives, theory and research methods are related. A 'perspective' may imply particular beliefs about the world, the nature of knowledge, society, individuals, and mental states and processes.

For a sociologist such perspectives might be views of 'humankind', 'society', and 'the interrelation between the individual and society' (Meighan and Harber, 2007, p. 282). A perspective could include a view of what should be considered crucial properties conditioning 'human conduct and experience in social order'. It might be concerned with what it is to know or understand the 'properties of those aspects of social life under investigation'. It may embrace a view of the relationship between what might be seen as 'academic' explanations of social life and the development of policies that may be used to 'direct the everyday affairs of members of society' (ibid.). In a sociological context, a perspective may be defined as 'a frame of reference, a series of working rules by which a person is able to make sense of complex and puzzling phenomena' (ibid. p. 281).

Individuals may hold a perspective because they believe it reflects a 'true' position of the world, society, or some other area of discussion. They may consider it is logical or sensible to take a particular perspective. The consequences of doing so might be beneficial for the individual or others, suggesting a moral justification. A perspective may be held through custom in an unreflecting manner because others hold a similar view. It may be a passive interpretation of the world or may inspire acting in particular ways so consequences follow. Perspectives may be justified on their own account or may be ways of criticising the views held by others.

Theory

The term 'theory' derives from the Greek 'theōria', meaning viewing, speculation, or contemplation. Theory has been defined as 'a set of propositions which provides principles of analysis or explanation of subject-matter' (Mautner, 2000, p. 563). A common distinction is made between 'practice', associated with activity and doing, and 'theory', as more concerned with contemplation and passivity (ibid. p. 454, paraphrased).

In physics, a theory is a 'high level explanation' bringing together many facts and it points observations towards further not yet observed phenomena (Townsend, 1997, p. 3). If observations are in line with the theory it is confirmed, although this does not necessarily mean that it will never be disconfirmed. However, one incontrovertible fact that contradicts a theory will require that the theory is modified or replaced. Whether a theory is correct or incorrect (or perhaps it is better to say the extent to which a theory is adequate) depends on 'the truth or falsity of the observations that they include and that they predict' (ibid.).

Since the 1980s, the term 'theory' has been used in cultural studies and elsewhere to refer to a particular kind of theory informed by writers such as Derrida, Foucault, and Lacan. This usage tends to suggest relativism towards knowledge and interpretation. Writing of 'critical theory' in a broad sense, Macey (2000, p. v) suggests the modern view of theory emerged from 'an impatience with what passed for common sense and empiricism'. Such theory also constitutes a political demand emerging from the view that theories are 'never politically innocent'. Theories are considered to express and reproduce political prejudices 'even when they deny it'. The critical theory of the Frankfurt School aimed to reveal and then neutralise such prejudices (ibid.).

Research

Particular perspectives may influence research methods in the social sciences. A distinction is sometimes made between the assumptions that may underlie the use of quantitative and qualitative methods.

Quantitative methods are often linked with philosophical positions including postpositivism, pragmatism and constructivism and include traditional approaches to ethnography and anthropology (Alexander, 2009, p. 283). These provide 'structures of determining the nature of reality, the nature of knowing and what constitutes knowledge' (ibid.). These structures are linked to methodological procedures that dictate particular ways of 'doing' and 'knowing' and the 'meaningfulness of the known in social science research'. The structures shape the nature of values and ethics and the process of determining them (ibid.).

On the other hand, qualitative methods may be associated with 'more liberatory philosophical perspectives and methods of analysis that are grounded in a close scrutiny of human experience'. Among such approaches are poststructuralism (Alexander, 2009, p. 283). These methods emphasise 'the variability of human experience, the articulation of voice and the social construction of knowledge'. They maintain the view that reality is socially constructed through the 'communal nature of human contact'. They speak of 'embodied presence and articulated lived experience' and the ways these 'help shape the reality for self and others' (ibid.).

Overall, perspectives of special education are important because they help orientate different views of what special education is about or what adherents to various perspectives consider it should to be about.

Special education

Special education is defined and discussed at some length in a subsequent chapter of this book. However, a brief definition may be useful before related matters are discussed. Special education has been briefly described as 'specially designed instruction . . . to meet the unique needs of a child with a disability' (United States Department of Education, 1999, pp. 124–125). But special education is broader than instruction, and the term 'provision' is perhaps more fitting. For example in *Foundations of Special Education* (Farrell, 2009) the following definition is proposed:

> Special education refers to distinctive provision, including education, for pupils with disabilities and disorders. It is informed by a range of foundational disciplines and encourages academic progress and personal and social development. Special education has identifiable aims and methods.
>
> (Farrell, 2009, p. 1)

Legal definitions of special education tend to relate it to what is considered to be required if a child has a disability or disorder. For example, in England, in the Education Act 1996 is: 'a child has special educational needs . . . if he has a learning difficulty which calls for special educational provision to be made for him' (Section 312).

Disability

International and legal definitions of disability

The World Health Organisation (2001) seeks to provide a common language and a shared framework for describing health and health-related matters. It defines disability and functioning and lists environmental factors that interact with them:

- Functioning refers to all bodily functions.
- Disability refers to impairments (problems in body function or structure such as a significant deviation or loss), activity limitations and participation restrictions.

(ibid. p. 3)

Legal definitions of disability (more often considered as disabilities and disorders) relate to a positivist notion. Positivism will be considered in a later chapter but essentially it takes a scientific view. Disabilities are not seen as predominantly social phenomena, for example. They are able to be classified. Individuals with disabilities and disorders can be identified and assessed and provision can be made to ensure they make good progress in their learning and development.

Types of disabilities and disorders (Farrell, 2008) relate to legal and quasi-legal classifications. In the United States, pupils considered to need special education as it is covered by federal law have a defined disability, and the disability has an adverse educational impact. Categories of disability under federal law as amended in 1997 (20 United States Code 1402, 1997) are reflected in the following 'designated disability codes':

01 Mentally Retarded
02 Hard-of-hearing
03 Deaf
04 Speech and Language Impaired
05 Visually Handicapped
06 Emotionally Disturbed
07 Orthopedically Impaired
08 Other Health Impaired
09 Specific Learning Disability
10 Multi-handicapped
11 Child in Need of Assessment
12 Deaf/Blind
13 Traumatic Brain Injury
14 Autism.

In England, a similar classification (Department for Education and Skills, 2005, *passim*) comprises:

- Specific learning difficulties (e.g. dyslexia, dyscalculia, dyspraxia)
- Learning difficulty (moderate, severe, profound)
- Behavioural, emotional and social difficulty
- Speech, language and communication needs
- Autistic spectrum disorder
- Visual impairment
- Hearing impairment
- Multi-sensory impairment
- Physical disability.

Similar classifications are used in numerous developed countries. The types, as can be seen, include disorders such as 'orthopaedic impairment and motor disorder', 'disruptive behaviour disorders', 'anxiety disorders and depressive disorders', 'attention deficit hyperactivity disorder', 'communication disorders', 'developmental co-ordination disorder', 'reading disorder', 'disorder of written expression', and 'mathematics disorder'. 'Deafblindness' is an impairment of both hearing and vision. Autism is sometimes located on a supposed continuum of 'autistic spectrum disorder'. The categories include impairments for example, 'profound, 'moderate to severe' and 'mild cognitive impairment', 'hearing impairment', 'visual impairment' and 'health impairment'. 'Traumatic brain injury' can lead to impairments and disorders depending on the site and extent of the injury.

The term 'disability' is sometimes used (for example in the United States) to refer in a general way to all these disorders, impairments and injuries.

In England, the legal definition of special education distinguishes between 'disability' and 'difficulty in learning'. The definition of 'special educational needs' in the Education Act 1996 is: 'a child has special educational needs . . . if he has a learning difficulty which calls for special educational provision to be made for him' (Section 312). The Act then defines 'learning difficulty' stating that a child has a learning difficulty if:

(a) he has a significantly greater difficulty in learning than the majority of children of his age;
(b) he has a disability which either prevents or hinders him from making use of educational facilities of a kind generally provided for children of his age in schools within the area of the local education authority; or
(c) he is under the age of five and is, or would be if special educational provision were not made for him, likely to fall within paragraph (a) or (b) when of, or over, that age.

(Education Act 1996, Section 312 (2))

It will be seen that in this legal definition, a disability is one of the features (the other being 'difficulty in learning') that can lead to a 'learning difficulty' which might in turn 'call for' special educational provision to be made.

In the Disability Discrimination Act 1995, a disabled person is defined as one who has 'a physical or mental impairment which has a substantial and long-term adverse effect on his ability to carry out normal day-to-day activities'. (The expression 'physical and mental impairment' is taken to include sensory and learning impairment.)

Other understandings of disability

Definitions and understandings of disability have not always been legal ones. Other ways of envisaging disability have emerged, as later chapters will show. Below is a very brief outline of some of these perspectives. Later chapters explain the terms and the perspectives much more fully.

From a phenomenological standpoint, Merleau-Ponty ([1945] 1982; [1948] 1973) rejects a separation of the experiencing person and the, as it were, external object. That is, he does not accept subject–object dualism. Merleau-Ponty rather takes the view that the body functions as a whole, with perception being the primary mode of embodied consciousness. This view has influenced those theorising about bodily existence and disability. Shildrick (2009) seeks to celebrate the fluidity, unpredictability and connectivity associated with disability, focusing on a view of disability as integral to human differences. The aim is to see disability as a mark of the possibilities of becoming. Instability might be a catalyst for different modes of inter subjectivity. Iwakuma (2002) suggests Merleau-Ponty's ideas can help one understand 'disability experiences' including the process of becoming a 'fully fledged' person with a disability (p. 85).

Oliver (1990) develops a historical-materialist account of disablement, suggesting disabled people 'experience disability as social restriction' (p. xiv). Oliver's (1996) definition of disabled people involves: 'the presence of an impairment', the 'experience of externally imposed restrictions', and 'self-identification as a disabled person' (p. 5). All phenomena it is claimed, including social categories, 'are produced by the economic and social forces of capitalism itself' (ibid. p. 131). The category of disability is 'produced' in the particular form it appears by economic and social forces. Barnes (1998) views the social model of disability as 'a focus on the environmental and social barriers which exclude people with perceived impairments from mainstream society'. It distinguishes between impairment and disability. Impairment is seen as 'biological characteristics of the body and mind'. Disability is presented as 'society's failure to address the needs of disabled people'. The model offers a 'framework within which policies can be developed' focusing on 'aspects of disabled people's lives which can and should be changed' (ibid. p. 78).

Postmodern approaches can encourage a re-examination of opposites such as 'disabled' and 'able-bodied'. Definitions of disability do not necessarily have to imply that all the experience of disability has to be viewed as a negation of ability. The experience of disability has its own realities. Titchkosky (2002) states 'it is still common to regard the disabled body as a life constituted out of the negation of able-bodiedness and, thus, as nothing in and of itself' (p. 103). Poststructuralism questions this sole perspective that disability is inevitably the negative opposite of normality. Also, Danforth and Rhodes (1997) suggest the acceptance of concepts such as 'disabled' hinders efforts to move towards more inclusive schooling. This in their view is because the concept 'disability' already assumes the identification and separation of one group of children from another. For Danforth and Rhodes, disability is a social construct that should be challenged. By developing an approach questioning the term 'disability', it becomes possible to better advocate inclusion (1997, p. 357).

Albrecht (2002) characterises symbolic interactionism as highlighting 'subjective experience and the interpretation of social reality' (p. 27). In disability studies, the perspective has been used to enquire about the subjective experience of disability and how others perceive, define and react to disabled people. Social interactionism is deemed 'well equipped to analyse how social problems, behaviour and institutions are socially constructed' (ibid. p. 28). Cheu (2002, p. 209) takes this view to its logical extreme when he states 'If you do not believe there is a disability, if you do not believe there is anything that needs to be "cured" or genetically prevented – that disability is indeed little more than a social construction – then you will likewise be freed from the need for cure'.

In the field of psychoanalysis, attempts have been made to relate the ideas of the French psychoanalyst Lacan to the study of disability. The focus is on what Lacan says about the body. Shildrick (2009) recalls Lacan's discussion of very early development, namely the early 'imaginary' and his mention of 'a fragmented image of the body' (Lacan, [1949, 1966] 2006, p. 78). She refers to Lacan's mention of 'imagos' of 'castration, emasculation, mutilation, dismemberment, dislocation, evisceration, devouring and bursting open of the body' (Lacan, [1948, 1966] 2005, p. 85). Shildrick (2009) suggests such images can remind us of the 'socio-cultural fantasies that have always surrounded disability' (p. 91). Shildrick considers implications for the disabled body, one that persists in its 'manifestation of dis-integration and disunity' (ibid.).

Foucault's ideas ([1963] 2003; [1976] 1998) have been used to examine views of impairment as simply a natural material phenomenon. Tremain (2002) states that Foucault sees the materiality of the body as associated with the 'historically contingent practices that bring it into being'. These practices make impairment an object of knowledge and 'objectivize' impairment (Tremain, 2002, p. 34). The materiality of impairment and impairment itself are 'naturalised *effects* of disciplinary knowledge/power' (ibid. p. 34, italics in original). 'Impairment' may be uncritically seen as 'non-historical (biological) matter of the body'. But this matter it is said is in fact 'moulded by time and class' (ibid. pp. 34–35). Where impairment has continued to be seen as politically neutral, it has stayed as an unexamined underpinning of discourse. In challenging this it is possible to 'identify and resist the ones that have material-*ized* it' (Tremain, 2002, p. 35, italics in original).

Inclusion

Inclusion is a very wide term yielding many definitions. It may refer for example to social or educational inclusion. It may refer to any social groups that are considered to be excluded or at risk of exclusion. It may refer to particular locations or to participation in various settings. In the present context, I consider inclusion as it concerns special pupils. Below I consider:

- including pupils already attending regular schools
- integration, inclusion as mainstreaming, and full inclusion
- inclusion as pupil participation.

Including special pupils already in regular schools

One aspect of inclusion is that of including special pupils who are already in mainstream schools. This seems to be the purpose of the *Index for Inclusion* (Booth, Ainscow and Black-Hawkins, 2000). The document concerns the inclusion of all those connected with the school, adults as well as children, not only special pupils. It addresses three dimensions of schooling: creating inclusive cultures, producing inclusive policies, and evolving inclusive practices. Each dimension is exemplified by a number of indicators that may be used to assess the current situation, as well as planning to be, in the *Index*'s terms, more inclusive in the future.

In general, including pupils already in mainstream school involves developing a culture in mainstream schools for inclusion. Teachers would develop opportunities to consider new ways of involving pupils and employ experimentation and reflection. Teachers will probably have values providing a rationale for inclusive practice, believing that special pupils belong in mainstream classes. As well as a commitment to reviewing performance there would be a commitment to change. Teachers would draw on various teaching approaches. Collaborative problem solving would help teachers and others to seek solutions to challenges arising when teaching a diverse group of pupils.

To the extent that special pupils are included in the school ethos and in lessons, it would be expected that they would be likely to learn more than if they were not included. As learning normally equates with better attainment and progress, it would be expected that improving the inclusion of a pupil in the appropriate learning environment would raise attainment. Put another way, this approach to inclusion could be justified on the grounds of raising attainment and improving psychosocial development.

Developing an inclusive ethos and inclusive approaches may increase the school's capacity to include pupils who are presently not in mainstream or who otherwise might be considered to be better placed in a special school. This leads to a further aspect of inclusion, the relative proportion of pupils in mainstream schools and special schools. Inclusion may involve systematically looking at three aspects of school life:

- an inclusive ethos
- inclusive policies
- inclusive practices (Farrell, 2005, p. 94).

Integration, inclusion as mainstreaming, and full inclusion

Distinguishing between inclusion and integration

Notions of 'integration' preceded ideas of inclusion. Integration may be under-stood as the principle of educating special pupils and other children together. It was seen as 'an aspect of the broader aim of "normalisation" which advocates people with special needs having equal opportunities to everyone else and being integrated into community life' (Farrell, Kerry and Kerry, 1995, p. 119). In England, as long ago as 1978, the 'Warnock Report' (1978) identified three forms of integration in relation to education. These were:

1   Locational integration, in which a special unit or class was provided in an ordinary school;
2   Social integration, in which the disabled pupil participates in broadly social activities in school, such as assemblies and break times;
3   Functional integration, in which the disabled pupil takes part in the academic curriculum.

These three forms are listed in ascending order of completeness of integration. The Report envisaged a continuing role for special schools. (For a fuller summary of the Report, see Farrell, 1995, p. 310. For the full text, see www. educationengland.org.uk/documents/warnock/).

Inclusion may be compared with 'integration' and applied to provision for special pupils in mainstream schools. Integration can be said to assume that the mainstream school system remains the same but that extra arrangements are made to provide for special pupils. Inclusion is presented as encouraging schools to reconsider their structure, pedagogy, pupil grouping and use of support so that the school responds to the perceived needs of all its pupils. Teachers collaboratively seek new ways of involving all pupils drawing on experimentation and reflection. It implies planned access to a broad and balanced curriculum developed from its foundations as a curriculum for all pupils.

Inclusion as mainstreaming

Inclusion has been described as provision for all students including those with disabilities and disorders, giving 'equitable opportunities to receive effective educational services'. These opportunities would be offered in 'age-appropriate classes in neighbourhood school'. As deemed necessary, it would include 'supplemental aids and support services' (National Center on Inclusive Education and Restructuring, 1995, p. 6). Antia, Stinson and Gaustad (2002) describe inclusion as involving a student with a disability belonging to and having full membership of a regular classroom, in an ordinary school in the local community.

Inclusion may result in increasing the proportion of pupils in mainstream schools in relation to special schools. For some, including some so-called 'disability theorists', the aim is that no pupils would be educated in special schools and that all special pupils would be educated in mainstream schools. Some commentators such as Ballard (1995) and Barton (1995) conceive of inclusion as a political struggle against negative attitudes, structures and approaches in the education system. Inclusion is seen as a process through which schools develop responses to value diversity. For Bailey (1998) inclusion involves 'being in an ordinary school with other students, following the same curriculum all the time in the same classrooms, with the full acceptance of all, and in a way which makes the student feel no different from other students'.

Full inclusion

Full inclusion implies that all children are educated together in the same mainstream classrooms, following the same curriculum at the same point in time, and experiencing essentially the same teaching as other children. This would preclude the need for special education. There would be no need for separate provision in special schools or units because all children would be educated in mainstream classes. Identification, assessment, classification, or distinctive provision associated with special education would be unnecessary because nothing different would be provided for special children than for other children. They would follow the same curriculum with essentially the same pedagogy. Classroom support and resources might be different but this would be seen as part of the variation that might be made for any child. Therapy provision tends to be ignored in this scenario.

The expression 'full inclusion' as it applies to special pupils maintains that all special pupils should be educated in mainstream schools. A range of provision such as mainstream school, separate units based in mainstream, and special schools would not be acceptable. It would be better to have increased support and resources in mainstream schools in proportion to the severity and complexity of the disability or disorder (Gartner and Lipsky, 1989).

Inclusion as pupil participation

Participation in a range of settings

At first inclusion seems to have been associated with mainstream schools as a euphemism for mainstreaming. It was possible to say in the late 1990s:

It is interesting that few are heard speaking of inclusion into special schools. If ordinary schools are associated with inclusion then special school are presumably associated with exclusion. Yet many special schools offer inclusion into the educational system which ordinary schools could not achieve. To over-emphasise inclusion may give the impression, if one is not very careful, that special schools are poor relations in educational provision.

(Farrell, 1999, p. 101)

Other definitions of inclusion emphasise participation. Pupils may be educated in various settings including special schools, separate units on a mainstream school campus, part-time support in a resources room, or full participation in a mainstream classroom. All these settings would be seen as being equally able to provide inclusive environments.

Participation applied to special schools and mainstream schools

Some definitions of inclusion emphasise participation. Pupils may be educated in a range of settings including special schools, separate units based on a mainstream school campus, part-time support in a resources room, or full participation in a mainstream classroom. All these settings would be seen as being equally able to provide inclusive environments and special schools would also be inclusive (Farrell, 2000). In this understanding inclusion is about 'securing appropriate opportunities for learning, assessment and qualifications to enable the full and effective participation of all pupils in the process of learning' (Wade, 1999).

Inclusive pedagogy concerns approaches to teaching and learning that emphasise and try to ensure the participation of all pupils. The term reflects the differences found in definitions of inclusion itself. For some, inclusive pedagogy is equally appropriate for special schools and mainstream schools. For others, it is associated with educating special children in a mainstream classroom and seeking to ensure the fullest participation.

Inclusive education/pedagogy

A fuller understanding of what might be meant by inclusion in relation to education may be formed by asking the questions: who, what, where, how, why and when (Farrell, 2004, pp. 88–92).

- Who is included?   All pupils, pupils with disabilities and disorders?
- What is intended?   Participation? Mainstreaming?
- Where are they included? Regular schools? Special Schools? Elsewhere?
- How are they included?   Through curriculum flexibility? Different pedagogy?

- Why are they included?   Moral reasons? Educational reasons?
- When are pupils included?   When existing provision is shown to fail?

Inclusive pedagogy concerns mainly the question of 'how' inclusion is to occur.

A practical example of inclusive pedagogy is 'adapted physical education' (APE) an individualised programme provided by people who have studied the requirements of physical education instruction for children with disabilities. In the United States, the APE teacher concentrates on fundamental motor skills and physical performance of individual pupils and may work with students for a specified number of hours per week (Gabbard, LeBlanc and Lowry, 1994). The classroom teacher and APE teacher work together to develop and teach programmes of physical education as well as leisure and recreation. While some strategies can be effective in encouraging participation, it is not always established if they are effective in enabling a special child to learn and develop better. If this is demonstrated, then of course the pedagogy becomes not just inclusive pedagogy but effective pedagogy.

Relationships between views of disability and attitudes to inclusion

This chapter has looked at different views of what 'disability' might be and at various conceptions of 'inclusion'. It is now possible to examine how the views of disability relate to views of inclusion. In particular in this section, I focus on inclusion as mainstreaming. Legal definitions of disability as already suggested tend to be positivist. But other views of disability may lead to different responses. Perhaps disability can be taken to mean something else, other than what it means in legal definitions and in everyday understanding.

For example, disability might be a social constraint. Disabled individuals may be seen as experiencing 'disability as social restriction' (Oliver, 1990, p. xiv) in a historical-materialist account of disablement. An impairment is 'present' and 'externally imposed restrictions' are 'experienced' (Oliver, 1996, p. 5). But the category of disability is 'produced' in the particular form it appears by economic and social forces (ibid. p. 131). Anyone believing this is likely to see special education and special schools as part of society's response to the disabilities that capitalism has 'produced'. Removing supposed barriers will be the approach that is preferred. Accordingly, Barnes (1998) applauds the 'focus on the environmental and social barriers which exclude people with perceived impairments from mainstream society'. The model distinguishes between impairment as 'biological characteristics of the body and mind' and disability as 'society's failure to address the needs of disabled people'.

Postmodern approaches place great responsibility on the power of words. It is thought these approaches can encourage a re-examination of opposites such as 'disabled' and 'able-bodied'. Danforth and Rhodes (1997) suggest the acceptance of concepts such as 'disabled' hinders moves towards more inclusive schooling because the concept 'disability' already assumes the identification and separation of one group of children from another. For Danforth and Rhodes (1997) disability is a social construct that should be challenged. By developing an approach questioning the term 'disability', it becomes possible to better advocate inclusion (ibid. p. 357). Again, for those who believe that disability might have some basis in everyday reality, this is a difficult approach. If you can shape language so that disability and being able-bodied are blurred you can argue better for mainstreaming, seems to be the point. Again the notion of what disability might be informs the action that seems appropriate.

The view of disability that seems to emerge from the work of the French historian of ideas Michel Foucault ([1963] 2003; [1976] 1998) is one that questions the notion of impairment as a natural phenomenon. Tremain (2002) states that Foucault sees the materiality of the body as associated with the 'historically contingent practices that bring it into being'. In challenging this and its consequences it is possible to 'identify and resist the ones that have material-*ized* it' (Tremain, 2002, p. 35, italics in original). But even if any of this is accepted, once those that have materialized the body have been challenged, then what? The answer might of course be that there should be more inclusion. If disability is historically brought into being then perhaps its generation can be avoided.

Some criticisms of inclusion as mainstreaming

Criticisms have been made of inclusion as mainstreaming which are set out in detail elsewhere (Farrell, 2010, pp. 105–114). These concern inclusion as:

- a primary aim of schooling
- liberation from oppression
- the pursuit of equal opportunity
- a (usually basic) human right
- fairness.

Consider inclusion as a primary aim of education. This can run counter to judgements about the best education for the child. Although inclusion may be an important secondary aim (Barrow, 2001) the primary aim of schools is education not inclusion (Farrell, 2006). To decide whether a child in a mainstream school will benefit from special education is an educational decision. It is based on judgements and evidence that the child will attain and progress better in learning and development. The issue of whether this special education is given partially in separate classes is an educational one in the broadest sense. A judgement that a child will be better educated and will develop better in a separate special school is similarly educational. Once this is agreed in a decision involving the child, parents, teachers and others, then the aim of inclusion in the sense of the fullest participation in whatever setting is suitable can be an important consideration.

Inclusion as liberation from oppression can only be convincing if it can be demonstrated that special educational provision including provision in special schools is constraining or limiting of freedom. Therefore inclusionists point to the supposed oppressive nature of special education. Among those discussing possible oppression are Vlachou (1997, pp. 22, 24); Reiser and Mason (1992, p. 27) and Fulcher (1995, p. 9). Such deliberations on normalisation as a concept and a process raise some worthwhile points. But any link between special education, labels, and external or internal oppression seems wide of the mark for many. Special students stubbornly fail to recognize they are being degraded and treated inhumanly as they enjoy activities with their friends and learn and develop well. They (and their parents) see special education as liberating rather than oppressive. Being able to learn well and enjoy participating with other children counts for more than being forced into a mainstream classroom. One person's oppression is another's liberation.

Perhaps a special child would necessarily have equality of opportunity for a good education or participation if placed in a mainstream classroom. Regarding ethnicity there would be no grounds on which a student should not be admitted. Once in the school there would be no grounds for expecting that he would not progress as well as others. For a special child, the situation may be different. The child may be thought to be 'entitled' to a place in a mainstream classroom. But the difference between the levels at which the child is working and that at which others are working may be very wide (for example because of profound cognitive impairment). It would be impracticable for a typical teacher to teach to that range of attainment. Therefore being a member of that class group is not the same as having an equal opportunity to learn and participate as other children. A similar situation may be envisaged for a child with autism, or conduct disorder. The child would not be 'included' in any generally accepted meaning of the term, but would simply be physically present in the classroom.

Regarding rights, Kundera (1991) argues 'the more the fight for human rights gains in popularity the more it loses any concrete content'. Everything has become a right. 'The desire for love the right to love' and so on (ibid. p. 154). Glendon (1991) maintains 'there is very little agreement regarding *which* needs, goods, interests, or values should be characterised as "rights", or concerning what should be done when . . . various rights are in tension or collision with one another' (p. 16, italics in original). Rights rhetoric is bound up with 'a near silence concerning responsibility, and a tendency to envision the rights-bearer as a lone autonomous individual' (p. 45). Similarly, in Benn and Peters' (1959, pp. 88–89) perception of the reciprocal nature of rights and duties, a right implies a correlative duty on others. Rights rhetoric sees a right not as a rule-bound normative phenomenon but as something an individual somehow owns. In special education, among supposed rights is the 'right' to be educated in an ordinary school claimed by those equating inclusion with mainstreaming. The parents of a child who is deaf can claim the 'right' for the child to be educated in a mainstream classroom because he is considered part of an oppressed group. At the same time, parents argue for the 'right' for a deaf child to be educated in a special school where he can learn deaf sign language if he is regarded as a member of a linguistic minority.

While inclusion is supposedly informed by the principle of fairness, this means different things to different people. A principle of fairness is that 'it is morally wrong, in itself, to treat individuals differently without providing relevant reasons for doing so'. However, it has to be clear what the 'relevant reasons' are. This is because they depend on context and have to be established by independent reasoning. Whether behaviour is 'fair' is determined with reference to other substantive moral values and the facts of a situation. Fairness can be part of a coherent moral viewpoint, but if taken as a principle of school practice, inclusion can lead to unfairness (Barrow, 2001, pp. 236–240). The term 'fairness' may be 'under extended' when arguing for mainstreaming (Farrell, 2009, ch. 3). It may be maintained it is not 'fair' to exclude pupils from mainstream education when they do not differ from other children in the school. Here, the concept of 'fairness' assumes there are no relevant differences between special pupils and others. However, the concept of fairness can be extended to apply to the degree to which it is 'fair' to educate pupils in ordinary schools, where there *is* a relevant difference, between special pupils and others. Recognising that the concept of fairness can apply to both circumstances may lead to a clearer consideration of issues. These include whether there is any point at which it can be agreed that differences between a special student and a student without a disability or disorder are relevant to the place where the child is predominantly educated. Such differences might include very wide differences in cognitive abilities or behaviour. This enables disputants to examine further issues rather than be deadlocked because of an unacknowledged difference in the use of the concept of 'fairness'.

Empirical evidence regarding inclusion is equivocal (e.g. Marston, 1996; Manset and Semmel, 1997, p. 177; Mills *et al.,* 1998; Stanovich, Jordan and Perot, 1998; Salend and Duhaney, 1999; Vaughan and Klinger, 1998; Powers, Gregory and Thoutonhoofd, 1999; Peetsma *et al.,* 2001). Lindsay (2003) reviewing overviews and reviews, concluded they 'cannot be said to be ringing endorsements' and 'fail to provide clear evidence for the benefits of inclusion' (p. 6). Kavale and Mostert (2003, abstract) speak of 'full inclusion spin' having influence 'disproportionate to its claims for efficacy'. They argue caution because at best, evidence is mixed.

Given all this, some commentators detect a lack of progress towards inclusion. Allan (2006) refers to 'Frustration with the faltering rate of progress toward full inclusion' (pp. 27–28). Furthermore, 'we continue to mythologize progress towards inclusion' (p. 28). Malign reasons have been proposed. It is suggested that 'Much of the failure to make progress with inclusion has been recognised as lying with the continued malevolent influence of special needs paradigm, with its medical and charity discourses, and which engenders deficit orientated practices' (ibid. p. 28). What is not considered is that the arguments for inclusion might be being ignored because they are wrong.

Back in 2001, Dyson stated there was an 'inclusion backlash' (2001, p. 26). England educates tens of thousands of children in special schools (Farrell, 2006, 2008) and arguments for inclusion as mainstreaming exert decreasing influence. Michael Gove, as shadow education secretary in 2007, stated, 'In the last ten years, the failed ideology of inclusion and the drop in special school places have left the more vulnerable more exposed' (www.publicservice.co.uk/news_story.asp?id=3463).

In the United States, the focus on evidence-based practice has led to further questioning of inclusion as mainstreaming. If the evidence has to indicate the academic progress and psychosocial development of pupils, it becomes harder to argue for inclusion as the central value of education.

Relationships between criticisms of special education and claims for inclusion

Relationships between the supporters of inclusion and dissenters are not always warm. Allan (2008) accuses Kauffman and Sasso (2006, p. 65) of using 'venomous language' to denounce postmodernism and complains this is 'hardly likely to promote dialogue' (Allan, 2008, p. 147). Yet Allan seems unable to resist a bit of venomous language herself. She recognises 'Even Mary Warnock, hailed as the "architect of inclusion" . . . argues that inclusion was a big mistake' (2008, p. 2). However, Warnock's language is 'deeply offensive' for example referring to 'a Down syndrome girl' whereas Allan would presumably prefer to speak of 'a girl with Down syndrome'. Warnock's confusion, says Allan, is therefore 'considerable' (ibid.). Warnock 'swings her ideology handbag' (Allan, 2008, p. 13). Warnock visited Scotland where she was 'dining out' on her pamphlet praising special schools. Misprinted publicity material stated that her talk concerned 'exclusion' rather than 'inclusion' and an audience member suggested the cat was out of the bag, making Warnock a 'hapless victim'. Similarly, for Barton (2005) Warnock's change of view is 'naive and politically reactionary' (p. 4) as well as 'ignorant and offensive' (p. 3).

Where inclusion as mainstreaming is supported, in parallel, criticisms of special education are likely to be made. If special education was accepted as a good thing, then why would it be necessary to argue for mainstreaming?

It follows that criticisms of special education can be seen as endorsements of inclusion. Elsewhere, I have argued that some criticisms of special education are ill-informed and unsustainable (Farrell, 2010, *passim*). Special education may be depicted as entrenched in a medical and individual model when it takes account of many perspectives (Farrell, 2009, *passim*). Rights-based criticisms suggest the value system of special education is wrong, depicting inclusion as the answer because it is seen as responding to the very rights that special education is said to be denying. But the claim that only inclusionists have moral values and that anything counter to inclusion is unjust, divisive or demeaning seems increasingly like prejudice (Farrell, 2010, pp. 20–29). The idea that the knowledge base of special education was limited to a bit of behavioural psychology and scraps of medicine and psychiatry, as for example Thomas and Loxley (2007) seem to suggest, proves equally muddled. The very wide base on which special education draws has always been apparent to those working in the area. Therefore it is naïve to depict special education as resting precariously on an impoverished knowledge base and needing only a bit more common humanity (Farrell, 2010, pp. 41–50).

From an inclusion perspective, classification would be seen as unnecessary as there is nothing essentially different to classify. But the idea that classification is of itself restrictive and divisive ceases to carry much credibility if classifications are recognized to be about disabilities and disorders and not children. The useful links with evidence-based provision further erode the negative view of classification (Farrell, 2010, pp. 51–62). For supporters of inclusion, assessment might be seen as irrelevant and constraining. But claims that assessments, especially those of intelligence, are biologically reductionist seem to be wide of the mark (Farrell, 2010, pp. 63–73).

If all children were uniformly educated in a mainstream classroom, there would be no need for labelling, which is seen by some inclusionists as purely negative. Yet the positive implications of identification and the deployment of positive labels seem to run counter to this view (Farrell, 2010, pp. 74–83). Those pressing for the closure of special schools might think professionals are out to gain self-aggrandisement. But this seems to jar with the perceptions of parents and children who daily see professionals going far beyond the call of duty to educate and care for special children (Farrell, 2010, pp. 84–94).

If advocates of mainstreaming were correct in their perceptions, it would be recognised that there are no grounds for supposing a special provision for special children. Therefore there would be no argument for any kind of separate provision. All pupils could and should be educated in a mainstream classroom together. However, the suggestion that special educators are doing nothing different to mainstream teachers because children all learn according to the same principles does not bear serious scrutiny (Farrell, 2010, pp. 95–104).

Thinking points

- Is inclusion as mainstreaming adequately represented when considered in terms of: including pupils already attending regular schools; integration, inclusion as mainstreaming, and full inclusion; and inclusion as pupil participation?
- To what extent do you agree or disagree with the criticisms of inclusion outlined?

Key texts

Farrell, M. (2004) *Inclusion at the Crossroads: Special Education – Concepts and Values,* London: David Fulton Publishers. This book illustrates how aspects of special education can be better understood when seen in the context of certain ideas and values that partly underpin those aspects. Chapter 8, 'Including Pupils with SEN: Rights and Duties' may be of interest.

Farrell, M. (2009) *Foundations of Special Education: An Introduction,* New York and London: Wiley-Blackwell. This text sets out the disciplinary foundations of contemporary special education and gives examples of how each influences special education. It covers: legal/typological, terminological, social, medical, neuropsychological, psychotherapeutic, behavioural/observational, developmental, psycholinguistic, and technological foundations.

Chapter 2

Creative tensions?

Contemporary special education and its critics

What is special education?

The United States Department of Education defines special education as 'specially designed instruction . . . to meet the unique needs of a child with a disability' (United States Department of Education, 1999, pp. 124–125). But, it has been suggested, special education is broader than instruction, and the term 'provision' is more fitting. Other features of special education may also be included in a broader definition. Such an approach is taken for example in *Foundations of Special Education* (Farrell, 2009) where the following definition is proposed:

> Special education refers to distinctive provision, including education, for pupils with disability/disorder. It is informed by a range of foundational disciplines and encourages academic progress and personal and social development. Special education has identifiable aims and methods.
>
> (Farrell, 2009, p. 1)

Education

Education is defined as 'the process of giving or receiving systematic instruction' (Soanes and Stevenson, 2003) and to educate someone is to provide 'intellectual, moral and social instruction' (ibid.). Education clearly concerns not just intellectual progress but also social and personal development. More broadly, instruction is considered as only one way of teaching, and elements of pedagogy include: modelling, questioning, and task structuring (Tharp, 1993, pp. 271–272).

The concept of education implies that 'something worthwhile is being or has been intentionally transmitted in a morally acceptable manner' (Peters, 1966). Views of what is worthwhile may be different in different cultures and may change over time in any one culture. One interpretation of what might be 'worthwhile', is that it is the skills, knowledge, attitudes and values a society endorses (Farrell, Kerry and Kerry, 1995, p. 70). The 'intentional' aspect of

Peters' definition distinguishes education from incidental learning, and suggests education involves structured experiences aimed at facilitating learning. The 'morally acceptable manner' element of education concerns the process by which worthwhile content is transmitted. Education implies freedom to consider differing views and information, and coming to a reasoned conclusion. It consequently differs from indoctrination, although the two are not always as easily separable as might be supposed (ibid. pp. 70–71).

It is suggested that to be 'educated' implies that the individual 'has been changed by the experience of education in terms of behaviors towards others, ability to understand the world (or aspects of it) and in ability to do things in the world'. Also, the transformation is 'integrally related to the concepts of knowledge and understanding' (Barrow and Woods, 1982).

Types of disabilities and disorders

Types of disabilities and disorders are discussed more extensively elsewhere (Farrell, 2008) and related to legal and quasi-legal classifications used in the United States and in England. Similar classifications are used in numerous developed countries. The types are:

- Profound cognitive impairment
- Moderate to severe cognitive impairment
- Mild cognitive impairment
- Hearing impairment
- Visual impairment
- Deafblindness
- Orthopaedic impairment and motor disorder
- Health impairment
- Traumatic brain injury
- Disruptive behaviour disorders (including conduct disorder)
- Anxiety disorders and depressive disorders
- Attention deficit hyperactivity disorder
- Communication disorders (speech, grammar, comprehension, semantics, pragmatics)
- Autism
- Developmental co-ordination disorder
- Reading disorder
- Disorder of written expression
- Mathematics disorder.

Recognising types of disabilities and disorders implies that they can be justified as a way of viewing reality. This is debated more with regard to some types of disorders and disabilities such as attention deficit hyperactivity disorder than with others – for example, profound cognitive impairments (Farrell, 2008, ch. 1 and *passim*). Also, recognising different types of disabilities and disorders implies some means of classification and identification.

This may involve the application of criteria such as those set out for some disorders and disabilities in the *Diagnostic and Statistical Manual of Mental Disorders Fourth Edition Text Revision (DSM-IV-TR)* (American Psychiatric Association, 2000). It may include paediatric screening or the use of an agreed benchmark of typical development. Detailed assessment of the child's capabilities and the effect of the disability or disorder enables parents, teachers and others to begin to consider implications there might be for learning and development.

In the Commonwealth of Australia, one may take the example of the Government of South Australia and the *Disability Support Program–2007 Eligibility Criteria* (Government of South Australia Department of Education and Children's Support Services, 2007). This included the following 'disabilities':

- Autistic disorder or Asperger's disorder
- Global developmental delay
- Intellectual disability
- Physical disability
- Sensory disability (hearing)
- Sensory disability (vision)
- Speech and/or language disability.

Provision

Provision that promotes the learning and development of special children was the subject of the book, *Educating Special Children* (Farrell, 2012), which discussed the following elements of provision:

- Curriculum
- Pedagogy
- School and classroom organisation
- Resources
- Therapy.

The curriculum has been defined as 'the formal and informal content and process by which learners gain knowledge and understanding, develop skills, and alter attitudes, appreciations and values under the auspices of that school' (Doll, 1996, p. 15). Curriculum includes the aims and objectives of teaching and learning, and the design and structure of what is taught in relation to areas of learning and programmes within those areas. It may be envisaged and organised by subjects (such as mathematics or art) or areas (for example, communication and personal education). Some aspects permeate the whole curriculum, such as literacy, numeracy, computer skills and problem-solving skills.

Levels of all or some subjects may be lower than age-typical. The balance of subjects and areas of the curriculum may be different to what is usual. The balance of components of subjects could be atypical. The content of certain areas of the curriculum may be different to those for most children. Assessment may involve very small steps to indicate progress in areas of difficulty (Farrell, 2008, ch. 1).

'Pedagogy' concerns a teacher's efforts to promote and encourage pupils' learning and may include individualised learning, group work, discussion, audiovisual approaches, and whole-class teaching (Farrell, Kerry and Kerry, 1995, p. 4). The teacher may emphasise certain sensory modalities in presenting information or encourage the pupil to use particular senses. A child who is blind may write in Braille, interpreting by touch rather than sight. Pedagogy may involve distinctive approaches for a particular disability or disorder, such as 'Structured Teaching' for children with autism (Schopler, 1997). Alternatively, pedagogy may emphasise approaches used also with children who do not have a disorder or disability, for example slower lesson pace for pupils with mild cognitive impairment. Such teaching may be regarded as essentially being 'more intensive and explicit' examples of approaches used with all children (Lewis and Norwich, 2001, pp. 5–6). However, it is recognised that teaching intended for pupils with cognitive impairment could be 'inappropriate for average or high attaining pupils' (ibid. p. 6).

School organisation may involve flexible arrival and departure times for lessons for some pupils with orthopaedic impairment. Safety considerations also influence organisational aspects. Flexible arrangements for pupil absences from school can include home tuition and emailed work supporting home study. Classroom organisation for pupils with profound or severe cognitive impairment may include the technique of 'room management' (Lacey, 1991). Regarding a pupil with hearing impairment, the classroom may be organised to optimise his seeing other speakers for lip-reading.

Resources can include aspects of school building design such as those aiding access for pupils with orthopaedic impairment. Classroom design embraces available space, lighting, acoustics, and potential distractions and facilitators to learning. Furniture adaptations include adjustable tables and adapted seating. Among physical and sensory aids are alternative keyboards and tracker balls. Computer technology can enable links to be made between the child's behaviour and what happens in the environment. Resources also include those for augmentative and alternative communication. The former involves ways to augment partially intelligible speech, while the latter concern communication other than speech or writing (Bigge et al., 1999, p. 130). Cognitive aids include: computer software encouraging responses; symbols used for communication; and computer programmes breaking tasks into very small steps.

'Therapy' may refer to provision intended to help promote skills and abilities or well-being. For special students, these may include elements that are predominantly: physical (e.g. aspects of occupational therapy and physiotherapy);

psychological (e.g. psychotherapy); communicative (e.g. speech and language therapy); and medical (e.g. drugs). Therapy and aspects of care are educational to the extent they are intended to lead to changes in behaviour; attitudes and self-valuing, similar to some of the aspirations of education.

Distinctiveness

Lewis and Norwich (2001) consider what is distinctive about provision for special children. In doing so they look at:

- Needs common to all children
- Needs specific to a particular group
- Needs unique to individual children.

They focus on the second and third positions. The second position which they call a 'general difference position' concerns the group-specific needs of pupils with different types of disabilities and disorders. The third position they call a 'unique differences position'.

In the *general difference* position, 'group-specific needs' of pupils with a disability or disorder are brought to the fore. At the same time, needs common to all learners and needs unique to individual learners remain important (Lewis and Norwich, 2001, pp. 3–4). The *unique difference* position de-emphasises the common pedagogic needs of all children. It emphasises unique differences of pupils, and rejects group-specific needs.

Lewis and Norwich (2001) favour a unique difference position. They suggest that the usually accepted categories of 'special needs' are of limited use with regard to 'pedagogic *principles*' (p. 216, italics added). These limitations concern the 'context of planning, or monitoring, teaching and learning in most areas' (p. 220).

However, it can also be argued that it is justifiable to maintain a 'group difference position' for all types of disability and disorder with regard to profiles of provision including pedagogy. That is, it is possible to identify distinctive provision effective with different types of disability or disorder (Farrell, 2008, *passim*). This provision, as already indicated, concerns the curriculum, pedagogy, school and classroom organisation, resources and therapy.

Foundations of special education

Foundations of special education are underpinning aspects of contemporary special education (Farrell, 2009, *passim*). These contribute to the understanding and practice of special education and to provision for different types of disabilities and disorders, for example, psychotherapeutic underpinnings have particular relevance for pupils with disorders of conduct. At the same time, psychotherapeutic foundations may have relevance for other types of disabilities and disorders, and provision for pupils with conduct disorder may be informed by other disciplines. Foundational areas are:

- Legal/typological
- Terminological
- Social
- Medical
- Neuropsychological
- Psychotherapeutic
- Behavioural/observational
- Developmental
- Psycholinguistic
- Technological
- Pedagogical.

Academic progress and personal and social development

Special educational provision, like general educational provision, seeks to enhance learning and development. Academic progress includes progress in school subjects such as mathematics, literacy, science or art as well as progress in areas of the curriculum like problem-solving skills, computer skills or communication. Personal and social development refers to the wide range of development that education seeks to encourage such as personal and social skills, compassion and high self-esteem.

Where special education is effective, progress in learning and psychosocial development are encouraged. It may not always be possible to show that a pupil is progressing and developing. For example, the child may have a debilitating illness, and here the aspiration might be to maintain levels of current functioning or to slow the rate of deterioration. The importance of academic progress and personal and social development is discussed more fully in *Standards and Special Educational Needs* (Farrell, 2001) and in *Key Issues in Special Education* (Farrell, 2005).

Location

Special education places great importance on progress and personal development. The venue in which special education is provided is viewed in terms of its contribution to such progress and development. The range of venues includes ordinary school classrooms, resource rooms within ordinary schools, units offering predominantly separate provision in ordinary schools, and special schools (Farrell, 2006).

The aims and methods of special education

The aims of special education include, with regard to pupils with disabilities and disorders:

- Identifying and assessing special pupils and evaluating whether their disability or disorder is likely to hinder learning and development;
- Identifying the distinctive provision that best promotes learning and development;
- Identifying foundational disciplines that contribute to promoting learning and development;
- Ensuring that elements of provision informed by these foundations promote learning and development.

Many methods that are already used aid the learning and development of special students. Tactile methods may be employed for blind students and behavioural strategies for children with conduct disorder. Such methods may be kept under review to ensure they are benefiting the student.

Any newer promising methods that are tried may be observed, carefully described and analysed to identify which aspects are important and effective. Attempts are made to explain why the approach works and to widen its application. The strategy may have been tried in certain circumstances and may be attempted more widely. It may have been used with a small number of pupils and may be tried with more pupils. Hypotheses may be formed relating to such findings. These may be tested and evaluated leading to accounts of evidence-based practice. Methodology can range from observation and description used for critical reflection (induction) to hypotheses and theory (deduction).

For *reading disorder*, strategies may relate to suggested underlying problems such as phonological deficit or visual difficulties. As well as working on associated difficulties, interventions directly tackle reading. This often involves teaching phonological skills necessary for using a phonemic code, and sound–symbol correspondences (Swanson, Harris and Graham, 2003). Where an intervention involves using a phonemic code and sound–symbol correspondences, implementation will be observed and described as accurately as possible. Researchers and others will try to explain which elements appear successful; aiming to ensure the approach will work for at least some other pupils with reading disorder.

Based on this information, a hypothesis is framed. This might be 'For pupils with reading disorder, where the main difficulty appears to be phonological, the use of a specified phonic-based intervention for ten minutes per day for 6 months will lead to a 12-month gain in measured reading ability.' This could be further refined. The educator might specify the particular program and any adaptations to the curriculum and assessment, pedagogy, or other aspects of provision.

In the United States, an enactment of the *No Child Left Behind Act 2002* is relevant to the present discussion. The enactment is that all students including special students will demonstrate annual yearly progress and perform at a proficient level on state academic assessment tests. Identifying scientific methods and evidence-based practices can contribute to this aspiration. But identifying, implementing and evaluating a range of valid, effective practices is not straightforward. Also, families and professionals have to decide on the suitability of an intervention or approach for a particular child looking at various options.

Simpson (2005), considering autism, makes observations relevant to disabilities and disorders more generally. Ideally, evidence will involve peer review and the validation of products and materials through research designs using random samples and control and experimental groups (pp. 141–142 paraphrased). Other methods may be appropriate in different circumstances for various reasons. For example, student sample size might be small, and clinic education programmes can be very different to one another. Also it may be necessary to be flexible in 'matching research designs to specific questions and issues' and instead use single-subject design validation or correlational methods (ibid. p. 142).

Parents and professionals will require a range of information to make informed decisions. The efficacy and anticipated outcomes of interventions are important. They will need to know whether anticipated outcomes are in line with student needs. Potential risks need to be anticipated, including risks to family cohesion of long-term very intensive interventions. The most effective means of evaluation will need to be discussed (ibid. p. 143 paraphrased). In the light of all this, clearly, decisions are informed not only by evidence-based practice but also professional judgment and the views of the child and family.

Disciplines and perspectives underpinning special education are considered, critically examining their relevance for understanding and practice. The foundational discipline of medicine may be related to special education in various ways. Medicine informs classifications and procedures for seizures and epilepsy, for the implications of traumatic brain injury, and the use of medication for attention deficit hyperactivity disorder. Developmental perspectives relating to typically developing infants may inform provision for older pupils with profound cognitive impairment.

Some criticisms of special education

In an area as important as the education, development and well-being of some of the most vulnerable children in society, it is not surprising that there is interest in special education and sometimes criticism. Where special education can engage with pertinent criticisms, it can improve and do better for special children. The criticisms outlined below are discussed much more fully in *Debating Special Education* (Farrell, 2010). That book discusses:

- sociological criticisms
- rights-based criticisms and contested values
- postmodern criticisms
- concerns about the special education knowledge base
- classification
- assessment
- labelling
- professional limitations
- the question of special provision
- inclusion.

This section touches on a few of these issues: sociological criticisms of an individual perspective, rights-based criticisms and contested values, criticisms of categorical classification, criticisms of assessment, and negative labelling.

Sociological criticisms of an individual perspective

Where special education is seen as taking an exclusively or very predominantly individual view – sometimes said to be a 'within child' view – of disability and disorder, sociological criticisms are sometimes heard. These involve proposing an alternative view, such as a social model, as well as directly criticising the perceived limitations of an individual perspective. Social views tend to attribute disabilities and disorders to environmental factors such as the supposed negative attitudes of educators and the use of unsuitable pedagogy. 'Disability' is regarded as a socially created or constructed phenomenon additional to a person's impairment (Shakespeare, 2006, p. 12–13) involving interaction between impairment and social influences.

Supporters of a social model sometimes caricature an individual perspective as a 'medical model' (e.g. Hurst, 2000, p. 1083), ignoring that the individual perspective transcends medicine. Special education is informed not only by disciplines taking an individual approach, but also by perspectives taking account of group, family and social influences. Also medical sociology has long recognised the social context of disabilities and disorders (Bury, 2000). Nevertheless, there are legitimate concerns about a medical orientation where it might lead to the possible overuse of medication – for example, for attention deficit hyperactivity disorder (Lloyd, Stead and Cohen, 2006).

In criticism of the social model it is suggested that an initially useful insight into the role of social factors in the experiences of disabled people has developed into an 'increasingly ideological' view (Shakespeare, 2006, p. 13). Shakespeare (2006, p. 53) maintains 'it hardly matters whether the social model is a system, model, paradigm, idea, definition or even tool. What matters is that the social model is wrong'.

In practice, an understanding of disabilities and disorders and of special education is developed by regarding perspectives as interrelated layers of analysis and by developing related approaches to assessment and practice. The approach maintains an individual view, but draws also on other perspectives.

Rights-based criticisms and contested values

Where special education involves the separate education of children – for example in special schools – it is sometimes claimed that it is denying a 'right' to education in the mainstream. It is claimed that special education generally and special schools in particular deny rights, run counter to equality of opportunity, and are socially unjust.

In recent years the language of rights has been used to argue for particular positions. It is claimed that the moral basis for 'inclusion', in the sense of mainstreaming education, is one of rights (Gallagher, 2001). It is said that when pupils are educated in special schools a basic human right to be educated with others is denied. Accordingly, special schools should be closed and all education should take place in schools for all children. UNESCO's *Salamanca Statement* and 'Framework for Action on Special Needs Education' is sometimes misrepresented as providing unequivocal support for inclusive (mainstream) education. Yet Section 3, paragraph 2 qualifies the enrolment of children in regular schools by stating this is to be done only if there are no compelling reasons to act otherwise (for example practicability, cost, and the incompatibility of inclusion with the educational needs of all children). Numerous parents and pupils prefer to exercise their 'right' that their child be educated in a special school and parents fight for the continuation of their local special schools for this reason (Farrell, 2006).

The term 'equal opportunities' may be used to suggest that all ought to have a chance to be educated in a mainstream school and that special schools deny equality of opportunity to be included in mainstream classrooms. Separate provision may be presented as denying an equal opportunity for special children to participate with peers not having a disability or disorder. This might therefore reduce opportunities to learn social and personal skills from others. Where it is meaningful to speak of equality of opportunity, then the expectation is that outcomes are improved for the children offered that equal opportunity. Where outcomes are unaffected or negative, then providing an equal opportunity to supposedly benefit from provision is meaningless. The imagined equality of opportunity in mainstream may be leading to poorer outcomes than a special school, leading parents to comment favourably on a change from mainstream to special school (Farrell, 2006, pp. 27–28).

The notion of social justice is sometimes associated with 'fairness'. It may be stated it is 'fair' to educate all children in mainstream classrooms, and unfair to educate them separately. Yet inclusion as a principle of school practice can lead to unfairness. A class may be designated and designed for pupils who have specified prior knowledge, skills or understanding, effectively making them criteria for admission. To take into such a class pupils who do not meet these criteria is unfair because pupils are being treated identically for no good reason, which is as unfair as treating pupils differently for no good reason.

Criticisms of categorical classification

Special education involves categorising disabilities and disorders, and this is sometimes criticised. The validity and reliability of some categories of disability and disorder may be questioned. If a category is clear and well defined, one expectation is that there would be a considerable degree of agreement about how many children are identified in different localities and by different people. These would be expected to be similar, unless there were reasons to assume otherwise. Yet, sometimes there are very wide variations in the supposed prevalence of conditions such as oppositional defiant disorder and conduct disorder (American Psychiatric Association, 2000). The prevalence of oppositional defiant disorder varies from 2% to 16%. Such a wide variation shakes confidence that what is being identified and classified is valid or that the assessment is reliable. The variation may reflect the nature of the population sample and the methods of assessment. It may also relate to difficulty determining whether apparent oppositional defiant disorder is a justifiable category or whether the behaviour in school arises predominantly from poor teaching and inadequate behaviour management. Such differences suggest caution when using the category.

Many of the classifications used in relation to special education are part of the *Diagnostic and Statistical Manual of Mental Disorders Fourth Edition Text Revision (DSM-IV-TR)*. This is a categorical classification that divides mental disorders into types 'based on criteria sets with defining features' (p. xxxi). The editors of *DSM-IV-TR* (American Psychiatric Association, 2000) do not assume each category is a 'completely discrete entity' with 'absolute' boundaries separating it from other mental disorders or from no mental disorder (p. xxxi). Professional judgement is also needed. The editors recognise the range and differences of clinical presentation. Consequently, *DSM-IV* often includes 'polythetic' criteria sets in which the individual is diagnosed using only a subset of items from a fuller list.

There is debate about which disorders should be included and the optimal method of their organisation (American Psychiatric Association, 2000, p. xxxii).

Dimensional systems of classifying health and capacity are available such as those developed by the World Health Organisation (2002, 2007). It is suggested these might be more justifiable than categorical classifications such as 'conduct disorder' (American Psychiatric Association, 2000). A dimensional model might beneficially shift the unit of classification from diagnosis to the functional characteristics of the child, in keeping with a 'holistic and non-stigmatising' approach to disability (Simeonson, Simeonson and Hollenweger, 2008, p. 217). This assumes that non-dimensional disability classifications are inevitably fragmentary and stigmatising. The *International Classification of*

Disability, Functioning and Health (World Health Organisation, 2001) might ultimately be used to construct a classification of educational disability with greater relevance to 'curriculum and teaching decisions and practices' but currently it 'may not have specific relevance to educational provision, defined in curriculum and pedagogic terms' (Norwich, 2008, p. 147).

Principles of classification are important (Fletcher, Morris and Lyon, 2003, pp. 34–35). The validity and reliability of categories can be tested, leading to clearer and more robust categories. For classification to be useful, terminology has to be clear. Equally important is the relationship between constructs and forms of assessment, and between assessment and interventions (Larkin and Cermac, 2002, p. 90). Despite the challenges of delineating disorders, much that is useful to teachers and others can be identified in research and professional practice referring to categorical classifications to provide for children with such disorders. This includes useful practical implications for provision and prognosis (Fletcher, Shaywitz and Shaywitz, 1999). Categorical classification allows generalisations to be made about the disorder or disability that can contribute to evidence-based practice.

Criticisms of assessment

Where assessments used in special education are criticised, the measurement of intelligence may be discussed. An aspect of the debate about intelligence is the relationships between intelligence and the respective contributions of heredity and the environment. Evidence is often cited from twin studies, such as the Minnesota Study of Twins Reared Apart (Bouchard *et al.*, 1990). Extensive evidence from such research suggests that a very conservative estimate of genetic influence on intelligence differences would be about 50%. Such studies have not been without critics. For example in adopted twin experimental designs, it may be assumed that related individuals are being brought up in dissimilar environments but this may not be known (Richardson, 1999, p. 71).

Such criticisms may be speculative in that they may not re-examine the evidence but simply raise the possibility of the contaminating effects of the environment on findings. Richardson (1999) proposes that there is a 'genetic determinism at the core of IQ theory' forming a 'highly simplistic picture of human intelligence'. This has pervaded the minds of psychologists and those operating 'the institutions of education and employment' (p. 199). In response, Richardson calls for the banning of IQ testing (p. 201). There may be a concern that teachers and others could interpret the contribution of heredity as limiting. They might therefore make less effort to encourage the education and development of children including those with lower measured intelligence. However, the interaction between heredity and the environment is surely too complex to justify such a scenario.

It is apparent why intelligence testing is criticised by those supporting educational mainstreaming. It has been claimed that assumptions about the

effectiveness of separate special schools 'largely built on notions of the importance of nature over nurture' rested on a view of 'inherited and immutable
intelligence' (Thomas and Loxley, 2007, pp. 36–37). A historical affinity is
claimed between perceived student educability and separate schooling. In this
view, students' educability – seen as 'fundamentally circumscribed by a global,
determinate intellectual capacity' – is related to 'policy regimes which construct a differentiated system of schooling, in which some students are denied
access to high-status forms of provision' (Skidmore, 2004, p. 114). However, the
idea that educability is circumscribed by intellectual 'capacity' is difficult to
maintain, based on the heritability evidence of intelligence tests. Also, policy
regimes with differentiated schools are not necessarily typified by 'denying'
provision, whether it is high-status or not. For example, in the United States
and elsewhere there are differentiated schools of many kinds (disability, sex,
religious belief) but they are not necessarily seen as a denial of choice, often
the opposite. The assumption that a separate school is a lower-status school is
unexplained. For example, parents and pupils may see a special school with
small classes, expert staff, rich resources, specialist curricula, supportive organisation, distinctive pedagogy and expensive facilities as high-status (Farrell,
2006).

Negative labelling

Special education may be depicted as negatively labelling children to their detri-
ment. A charity pressing for mainstreaming lists reasons against 'segregated'
schooling. 'Segregated schooling appeases the human tendency to *negatively label*
and isolate those perceived as different' (Centre for Studies in Inclusive
Education, 2003, italics added). The negative labelling of special schools may
reflect elements of ideology outlined by Minogue (1995, p. 17). The past history
of provision for special children may be presented as the oppression of these
pupils. Instead of seeking to tackle any particular examples of dissatisfaction with
special schools in the real world, specific discontents might be gathered into a
vision of structurally determined 'oppression'. Supporters might seek to mobilise
adults with disabilities into a struggle against the perceived oppressive system.
Liberation would be achieved when all pupils attend mainstream schools.

This is not to deny some adults look back on their education in special
schools with unhappiness. There are undoubtedly adults with disabilities or
disorders who were educated in mainstream schools who respond similarly.
But the rational response is surely to examine particular special schools or
particular experiences in them and seek to change what was not good. It is less
justifiable to assume all special schools must be malign and ignore anyone with
a different experience or a different view. Yet pupils in special schools have
very different accounts of their experiences.

Taking the example of England, this is indicated in comments reported by a
government working group (Department for Education and Skills, 2003, pp.

152–170). Pupils who had moved from mainstream to special schools commented that special school was: 'Friendlier', 'Nicer, my mum's really pleased I am here now', 'Doesn't get so wound up about the way I behave', 'I get my therapy now – I never got it at Y school', 'More friends – I can walk to school with them'. Elsewhere, the voice of pupils from special schools has been reported (Farrell, 2006, pp. 41–43). A survey carried out and analysed by pupils in a special school demonstrated that 55 of the 62 pupils would not want to return to mainstream schools. In another school, pupils speak very positively of the provision (ibid. p. 41). Others, writing as adults, give powerful accounts of the transformation their special school made to their lives (ibid. pp. 42–43).

Labelling is a complex and paradoxical process (Shakespeare and Erickson, 2000) and single-dimensional accounts emphasising only negative aspects and stigma do not do it justice. MacMillan, Jones and Aloia (1974) reviewed research literature concerning five areas of possible negative labelling in relation to children then considered 'mentally retarded'. These were the child's self-concept, and his future vocational adjustment, rejection by peers, attitudes of his family, and the expectations of teachers. They found little support for the view that children were stigmatised by being labelled 'retarded' (ibid.). Kurtz et al. (1977) conducted a study comparing labelled and non-labelled preschool children. The label was found to produce a positive effect in terms of teachers showing less social distance. Gottleib (1986) maintained that the observable behaviour of children could lead to them being negatively regarded by peers, irrespective of whether a child was labelled as 'retarded' by the school. If inappropriate behaviour is more noticeable in an ordinary school, attempts to include pupils with mental retardation would be likely to lead to them being ostracised by peers than would education in separate provision (ibid.). Even when labelling is shown to have a positive effect, researchers can be reluctant to accept the findings or the consequences. Vlachou (1997, p. 41), after reviewing some of the research demonstrating that the majority shows positive effects of labelling, concludes 'The notion of positive effects . . . is quite disturbing'. She asks 'How "positive" can interactions be that include notions of pity, over-protectiveness, dependency, "special dispensation" and the perpetuation of "sick roles"?'

Perspectives

As well as the criticisms that have been touched on and that are discussed more fully elsewhere (Farrell, 2010) there are debates about special education framed in terms of different perspectives. The purpose of the present book is to discuss these and consider the extent to which they might inform special education. The perspectives discussed in this book are (in chapter order):

- Phenomenology and hermeneutics
- Historical materialism and critical theory

- Holism and constructivism
- Structuralism and poststructuralism
- Pragmatism and symbolic interactionism
- Psychoanalysis: Freud and Lacan
- Postmodernism and historical epistemology
- Positivism.

Thinking points

- In the overview of some criticisms of special education, are there any you find more convincing than others?
- What is it that appeals to you about your preferred criticism?

Key texts

Farrell, M. (2012) *Educating Special Children: An Introduction to Provision for Pupils with Disabilities and Disorders* (second edition), New York and London: Routledge. This sets out, for different disabilities and disorders, evidence-based practice and professionally informed approaches in terms of curriculum, pedagogy, resources, therapy, and school and classroom organisation.

Farrell, M. (2009) *Foundations of Special Education*, New York and London: Wiley & Sons. This book examines the contribution to special education of different foundational disciplines: legal/typological, terminological, social, medical, neuropsychological, psychotherapeutic, behavioural/observational, developmental, psycholinguistic, technological, and pedagogical.

Kauffman, J. M. and Hallahan, D. P. (2005) *Special Education: What It Is and Why We Need It*, Boston: Pearson/Allyn & Bacon. This introductory book, in a short space, presents a strong case for special education and explains some of its main features.

Further reading

Farrell, M. (2005) *Key Issues in Special Education: Raising Pupils' Achievement and Attainment*, New York and London: Routledge. This book argues that raising standards of educational achievement and encouraging better personal and social development can guide many aspects of special education, from identification and assessment to funding and provision. It uses the England context to illustrate this.

Lewis, A. and Norwich, B. (eds) (2005) *Special Teaching for Special Children? Pedagogies for Inclusion*, Maidenhead: Open University Press. This suggests there is no special pedagogy for special children and that what appear to be distinctive approaches are variations of ordinary mainstream teaching and learning.

Farrell, M. (2009b) *The Special Education Handbook* (Fourth edition), London and New York: Routledge. This A–Z guide concerns special education particularly in the context of the United States and England. It includes entries on concepts and terms used in special education, descriptions of the main types of disability and disorder and related provision, the foundational disciplines of special education, and other areas. A thematic index guides those wishing to read more systematically.

Farrell, M., Kerry, T. and Kerry, C. (1995) *The Blackwell Handbook of Education*, Oxford: Blackwell. In A–Z format and with a thematic index to help more systematic reading, the book concerns the very broad area of general education including basic concepts. The thematic index has similar headings to those used in *The Special Education Handbook* mentioned above.

Mitchell, D. (ed.) (2004a) *Special Educational Needs and Inclusive Education: Major Themes in Education, Volume 1: Systems and Contexts*, London and New York: RoutledgeFalmer. A selection of previously published articles from various journals indicating a range of themes, which are well brought out in the editors' introduction. The themes are: perspectives on the identity of students with special educational needs, normalisation and social role valorisation, the overrepresentation of different groups in special education, financing of provisions, the impact of educational reforms on provisions, and international and national perspectives.

Reynolds, C. R. and Fletcher-Janzen, E. (eds) (2004) *Concise Encyclopaedia of Special Education: A Reference for the Education of Handicapped and Other Exceptional Children and Adults* (Second Edition), Hoboken, NJ: John Wiley & Sons. This reference work includes reviews of assessment instruments, biographies, teaching approaches, and overviews of learning disabilities.

Chapter 3

A scientific stance
Positivism and empiricism

A precursor of positivism, empiricism is a theory of epistemology (the way knowledge is gained). Empiricism may be contrasted with rationalism. Broadly speaking, rationalists consider that knowledge emerges from the operations of the faculty of reason, while empiricists hold the view that knowledge is based on experience.

Among those grouped as empiricists are the English philosopher (and physician) John Locke, the Anglo-Irish philosopher Bishop George Berkeley, and the Scottish philosopher and historian David Hume. Among those grouped as rationalists are the French philosopher René Descartes, the Dutch-Jewish philosopher Baruch Spinoza, and the German philosopher and mathematician Gottfried Wilhelm Leibniz. Indeed, the position taken by empiricists such as Locke, Berkeley and Hume is sometimes contrasted with the view taken by rationalists such as Descartes, Spinoza and Leibniz (e.g. Russell, [1912] 2001, p. 46) although there are similarities as well as differences in the views expounded by these philosophers. Empiricism then maintains that all knowledge is based on experience or is derived from experience. The notion of pre-existing knowledge is rejected.

Writing in the period after the Revolution of 1688, Locke with works such as *Essay Concerning Human Understanding* (1690) and *Education* (1693) is regarded as the founder of empiricism. Russell ([1946] 1996) considers him 'the founder of philosophical liberalism as much as of empiricism in the theory of knowledge' (ibid. p. 552). Locke's political views are incorporated into the Constitution of the United States of America. In Berkeley's counter-intuitive empiricism, expressed in *Treatise Concerning the Principles of Human Knowledge* (Berkeley, [1710] 1982) things are said to exist as a result and only as a result of their being perceived or because they are the entity doing the perceiving. (A further American connection is the naming of the city of Berkeley in California after Bishop Berkeley). Hume ([1748] 2004) in *An Enquiry Concerning Human Understanding* distinguished 'relations of ideas' (for example logical and mathematical propositions) and 'matters of fact' (for example that the moon orbits the earth).

Russell ([1946] 1996) describes empiricism as 'the doctrine that all our knowledge (with the possible exception of logic and mathematics) is derived from experience' (p. 556). Locke's first book, *Essay Concerning Human Understanding* (Locke, [1690] 1979), argues that there are no innate ideas or principles. The second book seeks to demonstrate how experience furnishes different kinds of ideas. The mind is supposed to be like a 'white paper' and 'all the materials of reason and knowledge' derive from experience (ibid. bk 2, ch. 1, s. 2). Ideas are derived from sensation and from a perception of the operation of our own mind. Locke therefore rejects the notion that there is a-priori knowledge, which somehow precedes perception. There is no knowledge for Locke, except by intuition; by reason, examining the agreement or disagreement of two ideas; and by sensation perceiving the existence of particular things (Locke, [1690] 1979, bk 4, ch. 3, s. 2).

In the philosophy of science, empiricism has a related meaning. It concerns aspects of science that are based on evidence derived, for example, from replicable experiments. A-priori speculation is rejected. Scientific method requires that hypotheses are tested and disconfirmed or verified (or at least replicated) through observations of the natural world. The method of science is therefore empirical. Scientific evidence is not acquired by intuition, for example, although in the process of developing ideas and theories there may be moments of inspired intuition. However, this is then tested against experience, not taken as evidence.

Empiricism appears to offer a way of avoiding superstition and irrationality. However, among the difficulties of the position are how empiricism accounts for the principles of space, time and causation. These have been argued (for example by the German philosopher Immanuel Kant) to be a-priori, that is, existing prior to any experience yet necessary for empirical knowledge.

It is not difficult to see the relationships between empiricism and positivism. Empiricism attaches great importance to sense experience and the development of the information that is provided by sense data through reason. Positivism is an epistemological theory associated with a scientific approach to the world. Three widely accepted central aspects of positivism have been summarised (Mautner, 2000). First, in principle, scientific methods must be applied 'in all fields of inquiry in order to gain knowledge' (p. 248). Secondly, the method of the physical sciences is considered to be 'the ideal paradigm'. Finally, facts are to be explained causally and such explanations 'consist in subsuming individual cases under general laws' (ibid.).

Auguste Comte coined the term 'positivism' in philosophy. In *Plan de travaux scientifiques nécessaires pour réorganiser la société* (*Plan of scientific studies necessary for reorganizing society*) published in 1822, Comte outlined stages of the individual and historical development of the human mind. These were, in what he considered to be the ascending order of evolutionary development and value, 'theological', 'metaphysical' and 'positive'. The theological stage is essentially superstitious. The metaphysical stage concerns abstract speculation. The positive stage is scientific.

As one of the founders of sociology, Comte sought to discover the laws governing human society, in an effort to bring sociology toward the pinnacle of positive science. His use of the term 'positive' indicates the importance of establishing laws only on the basis of experiential data. It also reflects optimism about intellectual and moral progress.

Sociological positivism and its application to social research were further developed by Émile Durkheim who developed a method bringing together sociological theory and social research.

In *Les règles de la méthode sociologique* (*The rules of sociological method*) Durkheim ([1895] 1982) sets out conditions by which he believes sociology can be a positivist social science. Sociology must have an object of study, which he proposes is the social 'fact'. It must apply objective scientific methods, bringing it as close as possible to the methods of the non-human sciences. Subjective judgement and prejudice must be rigorously avoided.

Briefly, positivism, or positivist philosophy, refers to a worldview considered compatible with science. It rejects superstition and religion. It spurns metaphysics in the sense of the notion that there is an ultimate 'transcendental' reality beyond the limits of ordinary knowledge and experience. Superstition, religion and metaphysics are seen as pre-scientific and are expected to decline as, in the wake of progress, positive science displaces them. In the positivist view, knowledge is based on sense experience and there cannot be different kinds of knowledge. Enquiry involves describing empirical facts, seeking regularities in them and making predictions. In principle, therefore, there is no difference between the methods of physical and social sciences (Mautner, 2000, p. 438).

Positivist research is characterised by a scientific approach. Observation, gathering data, interpreting and evaluating data and coming to demonstrable conclusion are typical strategies. Procedures, findings and applications are intended to be replicable. Mostert and Kavale (2001) state 'The positivist research tradition, assuming a real and objective world beyond the self, seeks to understand phenomena through observation, which provides objective factual knowledge that is then used to establish law–like relations' (p. 54).

In the twentieth century, an adaptation of positivist ideas was logical positivism (and relatedly logical empiricism). Like nineteenth-century positivism, logical positivism rejects metaphysics. It sees the task of philosophy as the logical clarification of basic concepts expressed in ordinary and in scientific language. Through logical analysis, a unity of science could be reached expressed in a common language. This would involve a clarification of the statements used in different sciences.

Two kinds of statements were considered meaningful and formed a verifiability principle. One kind is those statements whose truth or falsehood could be tested through perceptual experience. The second kind is analytic statements and their negations, which are true by virtue of their meaning, for example that 'all bachelors are unmarried men'. Logical and mathematical statements were accepted as meaningful although they were not verifiable through perceptual experience, hence the 'logical' part of the 'logical positivism' term to distinguish it from earlier forms of positivism.

Logical positivism is associated with the Vienna Circle group of philosophers and scientists including Rudolph Carnap, Otto Neurath, and Herbert Freigl. Ayer's *Language Truth and Logic* (Ayer, [1936] 2001) sets out the logical positivist position. Logical positivism intermingles with the development in the mid-twentieth century of linguistic and analytical philosophy.

Evaluation of positivism and empiricism

As indicated, for Locke, there is no knowledge except by intuition; by reason, examining the agreement or disagreement of two ideas; and by sensation perceiving the existence of particular things (Locke, [1690] 1979, bk 4, ch. 3, s. 2). Russell ([1946] 1996) identifies problems with this position. Locke assumes one can know that the mental occurrences he calls 'sensations' have causes outside themselves. He also assumes these causes resemble the sensations, which are their effects.

But if we are to adopt the principles of empiricism it is unclear how this is to be known. We experience the sensations not their causes. If the sensations were to arise spontaneously, the experience would be just the same. We can believe that sensations have causes and that the sensations resemble these causes. But such beliefs are not maintained on the grounds of experience. They are maintained on grounds that are completely independent of experience (Russell, [1946] 1996, p. 558, paraphrased).

One criticism of empiricism (and positivism) relates to the view that knowledge is based on experience or derived from it. But it can be argued that areas of human knowledge do not seem to be empirical but a-priori, that is, given. For example, principles of space and time seem to be essential prerequisites for empirical knowledge and therefore cannot themselves be empirical.

Sokal and Bricmont ([1997] 1999) give a clear outline of a scientific position, related strongly to positivism. In doing so they reject epistemic relativism, which they see as associated with much of postmodern thought. They use the term 'relativism' to refer to any philosophy 'that claims that the truth or falsity of a statement is relative to an individual or to a social group' (ibid. p. 50). Cognitive or epistemic relativism is relativism that concerns statements of fact, that is, what exists or is claimed to exist. They do not deal with scientificity in the social sciences, but refer mainly to physics.

They accept that there can be no proof that the world exists as we think it does, but that to assume so is a 'perfectly reasonable hypothesis' (Sokal and Bricmont [1997] 1999, p. 52). The most natural way of explaining the persistence of our sensations is to suppose they are 'caused by agents outside our consciousness'. This does not refute solipsism, the view that one's mind is all that exists and that to suppose knowledge of anything beyond this is unjustified. But the authors state as a principle that 'the mere fact that an idea is irrefutable does not imply that there is any reason to believe it is true' (ibid.).

Radical scepticism poses a challenge for the scientific position. Radical scepticism accepts the existence of the external world but argues that it is impossible for one to obtain any reliable knowledge of it. Where such scepticism is applied to all knowledge, the universality of the position is its weakness. This is because in everyday life, the best way to account for 'the coherence of our experience is to suppose that the outside world corresponds, at least approximately, to the image of it provided by our senses' (Sokal and Bricmont [1997] 1999, pp. 53–54).

Scientific method is not seen as greatly different to the rational attitude to everyday life. All human beings use induction, deduction and the assessment of evidence. (Induction is a way of reasoning from specific instances to general conclusions, while deduction is a form of reasoning in which the premises of an argument lead logically to the conclusion.) Scientists use these methods more systematically than others. Well-developed scientific theories are 'well supported by good arguments' although these arguments must be analysed case by case (Sokal and Bricmont [1997] 1999, p. 56). There is no 'absolutist' criterion of rationality so there can be no general justification of induction. But some inductions are more reasonable and others less reasonable. No statement about the real world can be absolutely proven but some can be proven 'beyond all reasonable doubt' (ibid. p. 58).

There have been criticisms of some attempts to formulate a scientific method, for example those of Popper (1967). However, Sokal and Bricmont ([1997] 1999) argue that these 'do not undermine the rationality of the scientific enterprise' (p. 58). For them, science is 'a rational enterprise, but difficult to codify' (ibid. p. 64).

With regard to logical positivism, the verifiability principle of the Vienna Circle was criticised because it appeared not to be meaningful as a factual claim by its own criteria. It was argued however, that the principle was not intended as a factual assertion, but as a call for the clearer use of language.

In the philosophy of science, the notion that science progresses in an incremental way through the gathering of data, its interpretation and subsequent predictions and theories has been questioned. Lyotard ([1979] 1984) suggests the spread of secularism and the diminution of political authority are challenging the dominance of scientific knowledge. Scientific knowledge, he believed, gains its unjustified prestige and seeks its legitimation from philosophical narratives (from German idealism typified by Kant) and political narratives (from the French Enlightenment). Yet in the view of science, these philosophical and political narratives do not constitute knowledge at all. Lyotard argues this contradiction demonstrates science to be interrelated to other discourses over which it has no privileged status. Postmodern science would embrace paralogy and not be bound to rational ways of thinking and proceeding.

However, Lyotard's view that scientific thinking is losing its legitimacy is weakened when one considers the comparative stability of scientific empirical laws. Where scientific theories are disputed, they are developed or changed, not by non-rational means, but by better science.

With regard to the social sciences, critical theorists may argue that positivism insufficiently recognises that social facts are not merely external in the objective world but are a product of socially mediated human consciousness. The role of the observer in the social sciences can also distort observations and events.

The so-called 'positivism debate' in Germany in the 1960s is an indication of issues relating to scientific approaches to social sciences. Under discussion were the social and political role of the social sciences, objectivity and value freedom, and methods appropriate to the social sciences. Debate involved those supporting critical rationalism (for example Karl Popper) and Frankfurt School advocates of critical theory (Adorno and Habermas). The nature of the debate can be seen in the collected contributions published in German in 1969 and subsequently in English in 1976 as *The Positivism Dispute in German Sociology* (Adorno *et al.*, 1976). Issues relating to positivist approaches to social sciences are further discussed later in the present chapter in the section on 'Evaluation of positivism in special education'.

Positivism and special education

Special education is essentially a positivist endeavour, as Chapter 2 indicates. Many aspects of special education can be associated with a positivist stance. Special education assumes that disorders and disabilities are describable as individual phenomena. It also recognises of course that social and other factors can be influential. Furthermore, it is maintained that disabilities and disorders can be meaningfully identified and classified. Special education concerns approaches that it is said can be linked to particular disabilities and disorders in evidence-based practice. It seeks and uses what it considers evidence of approaches that lead to academic progress and better personal and social development. All this is in line with a positivist perspective (Kauffman, 1999; Sasso, 2001; Kauffman and Sasso, 2006).

In special education, an attempt at a scientific approach is evident in seeking to identify children and young people considered to have disabilities and disorders. These disabilities and disorders are defined with reference to norms of development and behaviour, which imply measurement, assessment and judgements about deviations from an agreed norm.

For example, profound cognitive impairment is defined according to norms of cognitive development and functioning. In the United States of America, 'profound mental retardation' in the *Diagnostic and Statistical Manual of Mental Disorders Fourth Edition Text Revision* (American Psychiatric Association, 2000, p. 42) is defined according to limitations in both intellectual functioning and in adaptive behaviour. It is associated with an intelligence quotient (IQ) range of below 20 or 25, although IQ levels are interpreted with care, not being the sole criterion. Most children with profound mental retardation have an 'identified neurological condition' that accounts for the condition (p. 44). In early childhood, impairments of sensory neural function are evident. The diagnostic criteria for mental retardation also include 'co-current deficits or impairments in present adaptive functioning . . . in at least two of the following areas: communication, self-care, home living, social/interpersonal skills, use of community resources, self-direction, functional academic skills, work, leisure, health and safety' (p. 49).

In England, a definition of 'profound and multiple learning difficulties' in government guidance states:

> In addition to very severe learning difficulties, pupils have other significant difficulties, such as physical disabilities, sensory impairment or a severe medical condition. Pupils require a high level of support, both for their learning needs and for their personal care. They are likely to need sensory stimulation and a curriculum broken down into very small steps. Some pupils communicate by gesture, eye pointing or symbols, others by very simple language.
>
> (DfES, 2003, p. 4)

The guidance adds that, throughout their school careers, the attainments of these students is likely to remain in a range typified by the lowest levels of widely used 'performance scales' (P-scales). The relevant levels (P1–4) begin with generic aspects of development such as that pupils 'encounter' and 'show emerging awareness' of activities and experiences, and extend to emerging understanding relatable to areas such as mathematics and communication, for example that they are aware of cause and effect in familiar mathematical activities (Qualifications and Curriculum Authority, 2001a, 2001b, 2001c and later amendments).

Even with regard to disabilities that may seem clearer to identify than others – physical and sensory disabilities, for example – definitions are not always straightforward. Deafblindness is defined in relation to visual and hearing impairment although it is not seen as simply the co-occurrence of these. Indeed, 'deafblind' is often written as a single word, which may be taken to suggest the combined effect of being deaf and blind is greater than the sum of its parts. The different definitions that are found for deafblindness are associated with a range of possible interventions that may work for pupils in the remit of one definition but may not work for pupils covered under another definition. For example, many aspects of provision associated with deafblindness relate to children who are congenitally deafblind and without other disabilities.

A document by the former UK Qualifications and Curriculum Authority states: 'Pupils who are deafblind have both visual and hearing impairments that are not fully corrected by spectacles or hearing aids. They may not be completely deaf and blind. But the combination of these two disabilities on a pupil's ability to learn is greater than the sum of its parts' (Qualifications and Curriculum Authority, 1999, p. 7). A child who is deafblind may or may not have other difficulties or disabilities such as: profound cognitive impairment /

profound learning difficulties; severe cognitive impairment / severe learning difficulties; mild to moderate cognitive impairment / moderate learning difficulties; physical or motor difficulties. Some functional definitions emphasise the effects of deafblindness on communication, mobility and gaining information. Such an emphasis in functional assessment reflects that assessment of vision and hearing impairment generally does not lead to suggestions for interventions, which functional assessment is designed to do.

In the United States, the *Individuals with Disabilities Act 1997* uses the following definition,

> 'Deaf-blind' means concomitant visual and hearing impairments, the combination of which causes such severe communication and other developmental and educational problems that they cannot be accommodated in special education programmes solely for deaf or blind children.
>
> (Section 330.7 (c) (2))

The New England Centre for Deafblind Services definition was adapted by a UK project on curriculum access for deafblind pupils (Porter, Miller and Pease, 1997, appendix 1) as follows:

1   Individuals who are both peripherally deaf or severely hearing impaired and peripherally blind or severely visually impaired according to definitions of 'legal' blindness and deafness; acuity to be measured or estimated in conjunction with a recognition of level of cognitive development supported by medical description of pathology.

2   Individuals who have sensory impairments of both vision and hearing, one of which is severe and the other moderate to severe.
    Individuals who have sensory impairments of both vision and hearing, one of which is severe, and/or language disabilities, which result in the need for special services.

3   Individuals who have sensory impairment of both vision and hearing of a relatively mild to moderate degree and additional learning and/or language disabilities, which result in need for special services or who have been diagnosed as having impairments which are progressive in nature.

4   Individuals who are severely multiply handicapped due to generalised nervous system dysfunction, who also exhibit measurable impairments of both vision and hearing.

Another area in which positivist perspectives are evident is in some forms of assessment for special children. These may be standardised on a population of children so that they show the performance of a particular child in relation to that of others of the same age. Intelligence tests, assessments of motor coordination, and many other types of assessment are developed in this way. The intention is to indicate how well a child is developing or achieving in relation to others so that if he is behind others, steps can be taken to support his learning and development. At the same time, many of these assessments show areas of weakness and strength that can inform provision. For example, an intelligence test may show relative weaknesses in short-term memory but relative strengths in verbal skills, suggesting that verbal rehearsal might be used to help with memory.

The identification and assessment of attention deficit hyperactivity disorder illustrates some of the challenges. Criteria used in identifying and assessing attention deficit hyperactivity disorder form part of wider assessment procedures bringing together information from different sources including the child, parents, teacher and other professionals on how the child functions in different circumstances and settings. Assessments may be both qualitative and quantitative. Qualitative assessments include interviews or questionnaires for the child, members of the family, peers and teachers. Quantitative assessments may involve psychological, medical and educational information. They may include standardised tests of cognitive performance; computerised tests of attention and vigilance; and a medical examination, including tests of hearing and vision (Cooper and O'Regan, 2001, p. 91).

Functional behavioural assessments for a child with attention deficit hyperactivity disorder can provide insights and can have implications for provision. The teacher, parent, school psychologist and others may observe the child in different settings and develop hypotheses about why he is behaving the way that he is. For example, what function is served by the child's work being untidy? (Perhaps it is finished quickly.) Such observations and hypotheses can suggest ways of modifying the child's environment, such as the classroom setting, to increase the behaviour that is required. This might be producing written work of an acceptable level of neatness and legibility within the child's academic capability. It might suggest new skills be taught. Various commercially produced assessments and rating scales are available from test suppliers that seek to indicate attention deficit hyperactivity disorder.

The influence of positivism is apparent in evidence-based practice. Spear-Swerling and Sternberg (2001) in 'What science offers teachers of reading' point out that science is characterised by:

- Gathering evidence through systematic observation and testing
- Claims that are open to falsification
- Evidence submitted to critical peer review by the scientific community
- Maintaining the greatest objectivity possible
- Evaluating alternative interpretations of data or phenomena
- Evaluating a cumulative body of evidence.

(Spear-Swerling and Sternberg, 2001, paraphrased)

Evidence-based practice relates to the interaction of classification and pro-vision. In the United States, the *No Child Left Behind Act 2002* enacted that all students including those with disabilities will demonstrate annual yearly progress and perform at a proficient level on state academic assessment tests.

Identifying scientific methods and evidence-based practices can contribute to these aspirations. However, identifying, implementing and evaluating prac-tices that are scientifically valid and effective pose great challenges. Neither are scientific considerations the only ones. Families and professionals have to decide on the suitability of an intervention or approach for a particular child after considering different options. Evidence-based practice can inform the way forward but other dimensions are also relevant, including professional judgement and the views of the child and family.

Simpson (2005) examines evidence-based practice and autism. His com-ments are also pertinent to other disabilities and disorders. The most secure evidence is likely to involve peer review and the validation of products and materials through research designs using random samples and control and experimental groups (ibid. p. 141–142 paraphrased). Circumstances do not always allow such rigour. Other methods such as single-subject design valida-tion or correlational methods may be used. This may be because of constraints of 'limited student samples, heterogeneous clinical education programmes, and the need for flexibility in matching research designs to specific questions and issues' (ibid. p. 142).

Parents and professionals are likely to want to know about the efficacy and expected outcomes of an approach and whether the anticipated results are in line with the child or young person's perceived needs. Also relevant is the understanding of potential risks including risks to family life and cohesion of long-term very intensive interventions. It is necessary to consider the most effective means of evaluation (ibid. p. 143 paraphrased).

Positivist research can yield replicable approaches. For example, findings can be challenged and modified in the light of future findings and evidence. Positivist research builds step by step on earlier work. It is important that where experimental evidence is used to inform more practical approaches that care is taken to ensure the strategy is followed properly and to identify who might benefit (for example children with a particular disability or disorder). A weakness of positivist research is that it may not take sufficient account of human complexity. It tends to be concerned with external observable phe-nomena, which it can be argued are not always the most important.

Evidence-based practice focuses on approaches that can be clearly described and replicated so that teachers and others can use them to aid the progress and development of children and young people. For example, pedagogy for blind children is likely to involve the use of tactile methods of reading, often Braille or Moon, which are established methods known to enable these children to achieve literacy. The curriculum for learners with profound cognitive impair-ment will have elements that are sensory-based and build on the development of infants and very young children. There is widely acknowledged evidence that such curricula enable progress and development to be made and recognised.

Organisational methods known to be effective with children with attention deficit hyperactivity disorder include shorter session times, spacing furniture to allow the pupil to move out of his seat from time to time without hindering others, and maximising the opportunities for practical activities. Therapy that works for children with anxiety and depression includes cognitive-behavioural therapy. For many examples of evidence-based practice and professional best practice regarding the curriculum, pedagogy, use of resources, school and classroom organisation, and therapy, please see Farrell (2008). For extensive therapeutic examples, please see Fonagy *et al.* (2005) and Gurman and Messer (2003).

The Commission for Scientific Medicine and Mental Health (www.csmm. org) is an organisation inaugurated in 2003 whose aim is to scientifically examine unproven alternative medicine and mental health therapies. In a statement (Commission for Scientific Medicine and Mental Health, 2005) the Commission criticised the appointment of a leading proponent of 'facilitated communication' (FC) to the appointment of Dean of the School of Education at Syracuse University. The statement indicated that facilitated communication claims to allow mute and otherwise linguistically impaired individuals with autism to communicate. However, 'numerous carefully controlled and peer-reviewed studies provide extensive and convincing evidence against FC'. The apparent success of facilitated communication is owing to 'facilitators' unintentional control over the individual's hand movements'. Several academic and professional bodies have issued policy statements advising against the use of facilitated communication for autism.

Hornby, Atkinson and Howard (1998) in their book *Controversial Issues in Special Education* set out evidence enabling readers to assess the efficacy and usefulness of various approaches in special education. Positivist-related evidence-based practice can help parents, schools and others avoid being misled by fad interventions such as facilitated communication (Hornby, Atkinson and Howard, 1998). It is difficult to see how one would proceed in circumstances such as the promotion of fad interventions if one were not to give credence to scientific evidence. If studies can demonstrate that a procedure that appears to enable children with autism to communicate is really an instance of a ouija board effect, it might not be serving children and their parents best by assuming that the foundations of science are not as secure as was once thought.

Evaluation of positivism in special education

Gould (1997) vividly notes the importance of reason and evidence and their implications for morality. He mentions two possible ways to escape from what he calls our 'dark potentialities'. The first is moral decency, the second relates to the 'rational side of our mentality'. Human reason needs to be used 'rigorously' to 'discover and acknowledge nature's factuality' and, based on this, to 'follow the logical implications for efficacious human action'. Without this, we will fall prey to 'the frightening forces of irrationality, romanticism, uncompromising "true" belief, and the apparent resulting inevitability of mob action'. For Gould, reason is 'a large part of our essence' and our 'potential salvation from the vicious and precipitous mass action that rule by emotionalism always seems to entail'. Scepticism as 'the agent of reason against organised irrationalism' is an important key to 'human social and civic decency' (ibid. p. x).

The importance of a scientific approach to social sciences and to special education is recognised by many, and sometimes other approaches are seen as wanting. Kauffman and Sasso (2006) regard science as 'nothing more than organised skepticism – skepticism with rules to live (decide) by'. It is recognised to be an imperfect tool, but is the 'best tool available for trying to reduce uncertainty about what we do as special educators' (ibid. p. 117). They contrast what they take to be self-evidently real situations with the self-indulgent speculation about the nature of reality. They maintain that 'Philosophical speculation about the nature of objectivity and reality may be personally fascinating, but it is not helpful in the face of everyday demands in dealing with what most people consider real children with real problems' (ibid.).

There are many criticisms of positivism. In part this is because it is the dominant perspective influencing special education. Also, other approaches often define themselves as setting right perceived shortcomings of positivist approaches.

One argument against positivism in the social sciences is that a scientific approach is suited to the material world but may not be applicable to the study of human individuals. There are several reasons for questioning the applicability of science to individuals. It may be considered that human 'nature' or conduct is so complicated and so susceptible to unforeseen motivations that a scientific approach is out of its depth. However, this might be deceptive. The accounts of science – for example of geology – appear so lucid and convincing that they may seem uncomplicated because the wrong turnings and confusion that led to them is hidden away in the final account. Yet the genius of the early geologists in recognising phenomena such as strata and its meaning is one of searching out systematic accounts from phenomena of enormous complexity. Such ideas were developed as opposed for example to world flood accounts of rock layers. Human behaviour and thought are of course enormously complex but it may be over-pessimistic to think a scientific approach may not lead to insights and findings of great importance. Indeed the accumulating evidence emerging from neuropsychology including brain imaging is throwing light on disorders such as reading disorder (Beaton, 2004, *passim*).

A second objection to a scientific approach to individuals is that there is a particular complication about humans that does not apply to the study of other phenomena. This is that the individual is inevitably both observer and participant in any observation. Therefore it is not possible to make objective scientific observations in the same way as one can make them about other phenomena. Observing memory is not the same as observing magnets. A variation of this argument is to point out the way individuals appear to be unavoidably immersed in their own experiences so that it is not possible to step beyond these and take up a perspective from outside, as it were. It might be argued that we are immersed in language and discourse in a similar way so that we cannot step outside this network of meaning and observe others in the same way we might be able to observe liquid evaporating in a test tube.

In response to this point, social scientists might seek to reduce the influence of their own experiences and thoughts. They might focus on the observable behaviour of others, describing and seeking to account for behaviour in a way that can be replicated. Such an approach can be criticised because it brackets out thoughts, feelings and other apparently internal features that may be important. Behaviourally orientated research might seek to address this issue by seeking to bring apparently 'internal' aspects into the observable realm, for example by eliciting accounts from participants of their feelings and thoughts and relating these to observed behaviour. To the extent that Freudian psychoanalysis might be scientific, it represents an attempt to explain observable behaviour and an individual's accounts of his thoughts and feelings in a theory embracing both.

Sokal and Bricmont (1998) summarise and expand on such concerns. They recognise the particular challenges that emerge when one is considering a scientific approach to human sciences. They see that:

> many special (and very difficult) methodological issues arise in the social sciences from the fact that the objects of enquiry are human beings (including their subjective states of mind); that these objects of inquiry have intentions (including in some cases concealment of evidence or the placement of deliberately self-serving evidence); that the evidence is expressed (usually in human language whose meaning may be ambiguous); that the meaning of conceptual categories (e.g. childhood, masculinity, femininity, family, economics, etc.) changes over time; that the goal of historical inquiry is not just facts but interpretation, etc. . . . to say that 'social reality is a social and linguistic construct' is virtually a tautology.
>
> (Sokal and Bricmont, 1998, p. 270)

There is a concern that too great a reliance on positivist approaches could lead to losing sight of the whole child who is at the heart of provision. Where positivism becomes too fixed a focus, there is a worry that a more holistic view of the child may be lost. It is therefore important that scientifically based or informed approaches are the tools for humane provision. Scientifically orientated approaches should not translate into clinically cold interaction.

A positivist view of special education is sometimes presented as comprising solely psychometric testing and behavioural interventions (e.g. Thomas and

Loxley, 2007). It is true that these are examples of positivist approaches. Psychometric assessments such as those of intelligence do inform assessments of a child's weaknesses and strengths so that provision can respond accordingly. There is a view that this of itself is only intended to show what the special child cannot do and reinforce a deficit approach. However, assessments demonstrate both what the child can do as well as what he cannot. Similarly, behavioural approaches are some of those used with special children. For example, autistic children tend to respond to structured and clear guidance to support their learning and personal and social development. But these are only a part of the overall picture of evidence-based and professionally informed provision for special children. The extensive contribution of other disciplines is very clear (Farrell, 2009, *passim*) and includes those from social perspectives, medicine, neuropsychology, psychotherapy, behavioural/observational psychology, developmental psychology, psycholinguistics and technology.

Thinking points

- Why does a positivist view continue to be the most widely held in special education?
- What are the most telling criticisms of positivism?

Key texts

Fonagy, P., Target, M., Cottrell, D., Phillips, J. and Kurtz, Z. (2005) *What Works for Whom? A Critical Review of Treatments for Children and Adolescents*, New York: Guilford Press. A review of therapeutic interventions that are demonstrated to be effective with children and adolescents.

Gallagher, D. J. (2006) 'If Not Absolute Objectivity, Then What? A Reply to Kaufman and Sasso', *Exceptionality* 14, 2, pp. 91–107. In a special edition of *Exceptionality* Kauffman and Sasso presented the case against postmodern perspectives, and Gallagher replied in this article.

Further reading

Hornby, G., Atkinson, M. and Howard, J. (1997) *Controversial Issues in Special Education*, London: David Fulton. This book brings together evidence to examine controversial areas in special education. These are diagnoses (autism, dyslexia, attention deficit hyperactivity disorder); system-wide interventions (integration, and exclusions); group interventions (conductive education, instrumental enrichment, peer/parent tutoring); and individual interventions (coloured lenses and overlays, facilitated communication, and reading recovery).

Kauffman, J. M. and Sasso, G. M. (2006) 'Toward Ending Cultural and Cognitive Relativism in Special Education', *Exceptionality* 14, 2, pp. 65–90. A criticism of postmodern perspectives from a positivist position.

Chapter 4

Being and interpretation
Phenomenology and hermeneutics

Phenomenology

Phenomenology and its early exponents

The term 'phenomenology' is derived from two Greek words, 'phainomenon' (from 'phainein' meaning 'to show') and 'logos' in the present context meaning 'study'. The composite meaning in terms of etymology is therefore, 'the study of things shown' (Macey, 2000, p. 297).

Phenomenology in the sense used in the present chapter can be traced back to the writings of the German psychologist and philosopher Franz Brentano, who for part of his career lectured at the University of Vienna. One of his pupils at that university, Edmund Husserl, was perhaps the first important phenomenologist. Other contributions include the early work of the German philosopher Martin Heidegger, and the writings of the French philosopher Maurice Merleau-Ponty.

Husserl

Husserl's phenomenology is often known as 'transcendental phenomenology'. In other words, it is concerned not with particular forms of knowledge but with something beyond knowledge. Its focus is the conditions that make any sort of knowledge possible. In *Logical Investigations* (Husserl, [1900–1901] 2001) and in *Ideas for a Pure Phenomenology* (Husserl, [1913] 1982; [1913] 1989; [1913] 1980) Husserl sets out a science of pure phenomena. The independent existence of things can be put in question. But what cannot be doubted, Husserl argued, is how things appear to us immediately in consciousness. These appearances in consciousness can be relied on whether the things themselves are real or illusory.

In order to be clear about phenomenology, it is important to make a distinction between phenomenology and 'phenomenalism'. As Kenny (2008) indicates, these are not the same. A phenomenalist holds that nothing exists except phenomena so statements about material objects have to be translated into statements about appearances. Husserl on the other hand leaves open the possibility that there is a world of non-phenomenal objects, but that they are not the 'initial concern' of the philosopher (ibid. p. 82).

In Husserl's view, knowledge is certain because it is intuitive. Objects are regarded as things that are actively construed or 'intended' by consciousness. In order to establish certainty, it is necessary to set aside anything beyond immediate experience, reducing the world solely to the contents of consciousness. It is these contents of consciousness, these phenomena, which are the bedrock of certainty. This gives rise to the term 'phenomenology' as the science of pure phenomena. Pure phenomena are a system of unchanging, universal essences. Objects are varied in the imagination until the essence, such as the greenness of green things, is grasped.

With this secure basis, phenomenology, it is believed, can offer a science of the deep structures of human consciousness. In this way, as a transcendental method of enquiry, it could explore the conditions that make any sort of knowledge possible. It opens up the structures of consciousness and the phenomena themselves, seeing the essence of things in pure perception. In Husserl's 'intentional' theory of consciousness, 'being' and 'meaning' are bound together. The human subject is the source of meaning. In *Ideas for a Pure Phenomenology*, Husserl ([1913] 1982; [1913] 1989; [1913] 1980) takes a strong idealist position that the things perceived in consciousness are things themselves not just contents.

His method was one of phenomenological reduction or 'bracketing'. Husserl asserts that the immediate knowledge one has of one's own mental states provides the sole sound basis for understanding their nature. In order to gain this knowledge it is necessary to separate out what is intrinsic to that mental state from what is extraneous. The intentionality of the mental state makes 'meaning' essential to every mental act (Scruton, [1995] 2002, p. 265). Therefore to concentrate on the essential nature of mentality is to understand the operation of 'meaning' that makes the world understandable. For Husserl, the 'I' exists as a subject of consciousness. However, it never exists as an object of consciousness. Consequently, the 'I' is transcendental.

In a later work, published posthumously, *The Crisis of European Science and Transcendental Phenomenology*, Husserl ([1954] 1970), develops a theory of the social world, as a counter to the subjective focus of phenomenology. His 'Lebenswelt' (life-world) is made up of social interaction. It has the meanings that are in our communicative acts (Scruton, [1995] 2002, p. 268).

Heidegger

As has been mentioned, Husserl's phenomenology is often known as 'transcendental phenomenology'. The phenomenology of Heidegger, a pupil of Husserl, is sometimes known as 'hermeneutic phenomenology' and his approach as a 'hermeneutic of being'. Among his many publications, perhaps

Heidegger's best-known works are *Being and Time* ([1927] 1962) and *The Basic Problems of Phenomenology* ([1975] 1982). Heidegger was initially influenced by the phenomenology of Husserl. But he had other notions of the tasks and methods of phenomenology that led him in a different direction to Husserl. In Heidegger, phenomena are not simply appearances but are things that show themselves to consciousness, making phenomenology more fundamental than the physical sciences or psychological sciences. Phenomenology studies what 'is'.

Accordingly, a central question of *Being and Time* is that of what it is to 'be'. Heidegger starts with the 'being' that individuals manifest and leads on to the wider issue of 'being' more generally. The method of enquiry to approach these questions is phenomenology, as developed by Husserl. An important issue is that human beings are conscious and self-interpreting but embodied in certain contexts: material, social and historical. Individuals are constrained by their own mortality (Mautner, 2000, p. 242). A distinction is made between 'Sein' and 'Dasein'. 'Sein' refers to 'being' and 'Dasein' concerns the being that characterises self-consciousness or that which understands being.

Heidegger enquires into the nature of existence of the entity that is a human being, which he called 'Dasein'. It is revealed in our existence and our experience. Dasein is a variety of possible ways to be. To exist authentically is to live with awareness of one's mortality in a self-determining and self-revising manner. We are 'thrown' into the world and deal with it by relating objects to our practical concerns. Our understanding of being relates to the way we are in the world and the way we relate to other entities in that world.

Scruton ([1995] 2002, pp. 271–274) presents the argument of *Being and Time* (Heidegger, [1927] 1962) as a theory of being or self-consciousness. Because being is being in the world, then the 'essence of the world as phenomena' (Scruton ([1995] 2002, p. 271) has to be explored if we are to understand being. Things in the world are to be understood as 'signs', that is, as objects to be used or ready to hand. The world first comes into consciousness as a sign, bearing meaning. Distance between ourselves and objects is abolished and this provides the phenomenon of space, which leads to a sense of spatial position. This union is broken by the appearance of the 'Other' putting one's own existence in question. This precipitates the appearance of the phenomenon of fear, which in turn leads to alienation from the world. I become inauthentic. Heidegger argues that I can become authentic only if I realise my being is in time that determines my entire outlook on the world. In Scruton's summary, the riddle of existence is answered as follows:

I am a being who is extended in time, and whose redemption lies in that freedom which time alone provides, the freedom to make of my life what I choose it to be, and thereby to change from thrown-ness to resolution.

(Scruton, [1995] 2002, pp. 273–274)

Merleau-Ponty

Merleau-Ponty held the chair of child psychology and pedagogy at the Sorbonne and was later professor of philosophy at the College de France. He drew upon the phenomenology of Husserl and the work of Heidegger. Merleau-Ponty ([1945] 1982; [1964] 1968) is concerned with the interaction of the self, action and perception in reflection and in human experience. He seeks to develop an account of knowledge based on the world of perceptual experience. Merleau-Ponty describes the world as it is experienced paying attention to the role of the body in the construction of the spatiotemporal world. He introduced the notion of the 'lived body' to phenomenological thought.

In *Phenomenology of Perception*, Merleau-Ponty ([1945] 1982) writes of philosophy as an act enabling a return to the lived world, that is a world that existed before science and metaphysics objectified it. He does not accept dualisms that imply separation of subject and object. Merleau-Ponty ([1945] 1982; [1948] 1973) regards existence as a continuum in which individuals exist with others. The body functions as a whole, and it is misleading to conceive of it as functioning as separate related units, such as behaviour or cognition.

Perception is the primary mode of consciousness and neither the phenomenon nor the act of cognition exists prior to perception. Consciousness is embodied and the body is a vehicle for being in this situation. The body inhabits space and time physically and a person perceives space and time by constructing a bodily schema from perception and memory.

Merleau-Ponty died suddenly at an early age in 1961 while working on the manuscript, *The Visible and the Invisible*. In this unfinished work, Merleau-Ponty ([1964] 1968) returns to his earlier criticisms of transcendental philosophy. The final chapter, entitled 'The Intertwining – the Chiasm' fills out his ontological position (concerning being).

Evaluation of phenomenology

Husserl's transcendental phenomenology appears at first to offer a firm foundation for the scientific examination of appearances in consciousness. Yet it soon becomes apparent that the subjectivity of the method is problematic. For Eagleton (1996) writing about literary criticism, Husserl's phenomenology is rather too contemplative and unhistorical and it 'begins and ends as a head without a world' (p. 53). It can provide a firm grounding for human knowledge, only at the huge cost of sacrificing human history. Human meanings are not, Eagleton argues, 'intuiting the universal essence of what it is to be an onion' as transcendental phenomenology would have it. Rather human meanings are more a matter of social individuals engaged in 'changing, practical transactions' (ibid.).

In Husserl's approach to phenomenology, human beings are seen as having been constituted by states of consciousness, and the subjectiveness of the method raises difficulties. An attempt to avoid its problems is apparent in

Heidegger's modification of phenomenology. For Heidegger, the primacy of one's existence, the mode of being or 'Dasein', is key. Consciousness is peripheral to Dasein. Furthermore, Dasein cannot be converted to one's consciousness of it. An individual's state of mind is an effect of existence not a determinant of existence. The emphasis is therefore on existence.

Nevertheless, for Heidegger too there are difficulties. It is suggested he strives to avoid the metaphysical aspects of Husserl's approach but creates a metaphysical entity in Dasein. He makes efforts to be historical but fails in the attempt (Eagleton, 1996, p. 57).

Scruton ([1995] 2002) draws attention to the impenetrability of Heidegger's writings. His metaphorical language is 'contorted to the point almost of incomprehensibility'. Also the reader gets the impression that 'never before have so many words been invented and tormented in the attempt to express the inexpressible' (ibid. p. 270). Scruton summarises more recent writings on phenomenology as a 'mass of phenomenological lore' (ibid. p. 280) and finds it impossible to assess the intellectual status of phenomenology. The results seem to be 'true to experience and yet irritatingly paradoxical, both in their style and in their philosophical presuppositions' (ibid.). It is difficult to distinguish what is philosophy and what is a description of Heidegger's own spiritual journey. Heidegger's conclusions are intended as universal truths and they cannot be proved or disproved by science.

Yet, Scruton argues, as an alternative, Heidegger does not provide arguments for the truth of what he says, only assertions. His important thesis is that idealism does not need to be refuted because its falsehood 'is given in Dasein's quest for self-knowledge' (ibid. p. 274). But this assertion is supported only by an appeal to Greek etymology (where 'alethia' means 'truth' and 'uncovering'). Heidegger's ideas seem like 'spectral visions in the realm of thought' (ibid.). This sort of philosophy shows, says Scruton (quoting Wittgenstein), 'the bewitchment of the intelligence by means of language' (ibid.).

Merleau-Ponty ([1945] 1982; [1948] 1973) writes of philosophy as an act enabling a return to the lived world and rejects subject–object dualism. The body functions as a whole, and perception is the primary mode of embodied consciousness. This view has proved attractive to those theorising about bodily existence, including in relation to disability.

Special education and phenomenology

Possible attractions of phenomenology

So far, the chapter has outlined three approaches:

- Husserl's transcendental phenomenology
- Heidegger's hermeneutic phenomenology, enquiring into the nature of existence and of 'Dasein'
- the innovations of aspects of Merleau-Ponty's work.

It is easy to see the attraction of these ideas to the understanding of disabilities and disorders, their nature, and the possible implications regarding views of disability and disorder and special education. Particularly fertile has been Merleau-Ponty's focus on the 'situatedness' of the body, which seems to have relevance to the experiences of individuals who have a disability, especially a physical or sensory disability.

Disability, sexuality and subjectivity

Shildrick (2009) considers disability with reference to sexuality and subjectivity. She uses analyses drawing from feminism and postmodernism and also draws on the work of Merleau-Ponty (Shildrick, 2009, pp. 25–30). Shildrick explores possible motivations for discrimination, devaluation and alienation in relation to disabled people. Furthermore, she suggests that where autonomy is a highly valued aspect of subjectivity, losses of bodily control and indications of connectivity lead to anxiety among those not disabled. This is considered especially marked with reference to sexuality and disability. There may be 'damaging consequences of the imperfectly hidden insecurity associated with able-bodiedness'. This may show itself in a need for, 'mastery over the supposed threat of disability to the normative order' (ibid. p. 21).

Criticising more conventional paradigms, Shildrick (2009) celebrates the fluidity, unpredictability and connectivity associated with disability and attempts to rethink the notion of the embodied self. She suggests the 'postconventional theories' used for analysis enable one to 'embark on the crucial ethical step of thinking differently' (ibid. p. 170). She does not argue for a model of including disabled people into socially derived norms. Rather she focuses on a view of disability as integral to human differences. The aim is to see disability not as a marginalised condition but as a mark of the possibilities of becoming and suggesting instability as a catalyst for different modes of inter-subjectivity.

Shildrick (2009) refers to the French-Algerian philosopher Derrida and his approach of deconstruction (discussed below, in Chapter 7). Deconstruction might help break down views of normality that can be harmful. She takes the view that postmodern alternatives effectively 'analyse and deconstruct the structures that maintain . . . damaging normativities' (ibid. p. 171). Such alternatives can set in motion 'new and more creatively positive ways of thinking and feeling about difference' (ibid.). This is thought to create a compelling critique of 'the exclusionary structures of modernism that have suppressed the subjectivity and sexuality of disabled people'. The only adequate response, it is suggested, is 'a call for radical transformation' (ibid.).

With reference to Merleau-Ponty and others, including the French philosopher Gilles Deleuze, Shildrick (2009) explores 'corporealities'. She argues that Merleau-Ponty's approach indicates that the phenomenological understanding is that 'the biological, social, and discursive bodies are equally unfixed and mutually constitutive' (Shildrick, 2009, p. 25). The immersion of our bodies in what Merleau-Ponty calls the 'flesh of the world' and our interweaving with other bodies, 'actualises our social and personal identities' (ibid.). Recognising some of the limitations of the application of Merleau-Ponty's ideas to disability and sexuality, Shildrick nevertheless believes aspects of his work can be developed. These are 'his insight into the non-biological aspects of sexuality, the perceptual opening of one body to another, and an affective sensibility that communicates between bodies, transforming and transposing behaviours, intentionalities and sensitivities' (ibid. pp. 29–30).

Embodiment

Iwakuma (2002) takes a different approach, and draws more directly and extensively on Merleau-Ponty's ideas, especially implications concerning the body and embodiment. The body itself, or what Merleau-Ponty later called 'the flesh', has a special position in that it can be regarded as both touching and touched, seeing and seen, hearing and heard. In this sense it can be regarded as object and subject simultaneously (Iwakuma, 2002, pp. 83–84). But the notion of the body, it is suggested, can be extended to include physical aids to bodily mobility and perception.

For individuals with some disabilities who use objects to help them, Iwakuma argues, these objects seem to become almost part of that individual's body. The cane of a blind person may become not a mere object but the person's 'tactile organ' (Iwakuma, 2002, p. 79) enabling a blind person skilled in its use to move through the environment with confidence without relying on visual information.

Interestingly, Iwakuma (2002) suggests an explanatory role for the notion of embodiment in relation to what is considered part of one's own body or at least an extension of it. This notion of embodiment might explain the attitude differences between individuals with congenital or acquired physical disabilities. A person born with a physical disability may regard a physical aid such as a wheelchair optimistically. Alternatively, someone with an acquired physical disability may reject such an aid or take a considerable time to adapt to the new type of embodiment (Iwakuma, 2002, p. 79). Iwakuma suggests that, 'As a process of embodiment, an object becomes a part of the identity of the person to whom it belongs' (ibid. p. 79).

Not being able to walk not only alters an individual's physical condition, but also 'family life, interpersonal relationships with others, self-image, the world-view and even the sense of temporality' (Iwakuma, 2002, p. 80). The notion of embodiment also helps understanding of phenomena such as a 'phantom limb'. A person who has had a recent amputation of a limb retains a body image, which still includes the limb and moves and manoeuvres accordingly until the new embodiment has been acquired (Iwakuma, 2002, p. 81).

Extending the idea of embodiment, Iwakuma (2002) considers the perceptions of individuals who are autistic and who have difficulty in interpreting the communicative intent of facial expressions or tone of voice (pp. 81–83). He argues that perception, including general limitations in perception, can also be considered a form of embodiment in that it implies a way of being in the world.

Iwakuma (2002) suggests Merleau-Ponty's work can help one understand 'disability experiences' especially in terms of the process of becoming a 'fully fledged' person with a disability. The work may also be valuable for 'the emergence of disability consciousness, the (re)habilitation of individuals with disabilities, technological evolution and people with disabilities or body politics' (ibid. p. 85).

Lived experience

As well as contributing to theoretical discussions, phenomenology can inform research as an alternative to more quantitative methods. Attempts have been made to use phenomenological approaches focusing on 'lived experience' to shed light on meanings for educational phenomena. Carrington, Papinczak and Templeton (2003) examined the social expectations and perceptions of a friendship group of teenagers with Asperger's Syndrome. The study recognised the importance of educators helping students develop social skills. However, it suggested that programme designers might take greater account of different social perspectives taken by different individuals.

Tutty and Hocking (2004) looked at the experiences of teacher aides working with students requiring high levels of support. The study raised concerns about potential negative implications of the allocation of teacher aides to students for the greater part of the day. But it also drew attention to the quality of support provided by teaching aides, the responsibilities for collaboration teaching aides assume, and the quality of the support offered by teachers.

Evaluation of phenomenology in special education

Shildrick (2009) considers disability with reference to sexuality and subjectivity drawing on various sources including Merleau-Ponty. She explores possible motivations for negativity towards disabled people. Shildrick (2009) suggests, given that autonomy is a highly valued aspect of subjectivity, losses of bodily control and indications of connectivity lead to anxiety among able-bodied individuals. This is especially so regarding sexuality and disability. She seeks to celebrate the fluidity, unpredictability and connectivity associated with disability and to rethink the notion of the embodied self. Seeing disability as integral to human differences, she presents disability as a mark of the possibilities of becoming. Instability might be a catalyst for different modes of inter-subjectivity.

This combination of psychologising possible motives and examining what seem to be central features of phenomena seems to offer a creative way of examining usual perceptions. However, Shildrick's attempt at deconstruction is rather generalised. When Derrida uses deconstruction, for example in his consideration of Rousseau's writings (Derrida ([1967] 1997, pp. 141–164), he is at his most persuasive when he points out anomalies in a particular text that may have been unrecognised by the text's author. The deconstruction works on the detailed material of the text and is either convincing or unconvincing in these terms.

Deconstruction is less convincing where it is thought to be a way of dismantling every binary opposite and breaking up structures of meaning in general, even ones that are unwelcome. Consequently, Shildrick's generalised views lack the bite that for example Derrida's close analysis of Rousseau's text can have at its most insightful. Shildrick (2009) might consider that modernism is typified by 'exclusionary structures' and that 'normativities' are damaging, but is unclear about what her 'radical transformation' would look like (ibid. p. 171). This reflects the problematic nature of deconstruction even in limited applications to texts. It is sometimes good at deconstructing but less good at constructing. (Please also see Chapter 7 Structuralism and poststructuralism, below.)

Iwakuma (2002) explores some of the implications of Merleau-Ponty's ideas of the body and embodiment. The body can be regarded as object and subject simultaneously (pp. 83–84). The notion of the body includes physical aids to bodily mobility and perception. Differences of attitude to physical aids between individuals with congenital or acquired physical disability may be related to acceptance of different embodiment (p. 79). Not being able to walk alters an individual's physical condition, relationships, self-image, worldview and sense of temporality (p. 80). Iwakuma (2002), considering the perceptions of autistic individuals (pp. 81–83), suggests perception is a form of embodiment or being in the world.

In all this, Iwakuma (2002) makes the case that Merleau-Ponty's work can assist understanding of experiences of some forms of disability with regard to developing full potential, disability consciousness, rehabilitation and habilitation, technological evolution and body politics (ibid. p. 85).

In research, attempts have been made to use phenomenological approaches focusing on 'lived experience' to shed light on meanings for educational phenomena (Carrington, Papinczak and Templeton, 2003; Tutty and Hocking, 2004). It has been stated that 'Phenomenological enquiry gives a researcher a specific vantage point for exploring participants' conscious experience' (Smith and Fowler, 2009, p. 163). Also, 'Researchers who are interested in exploring participants' conscious experience and are interested in discovering what factors are central to its core will find phenomenological enquiry particularly useful' (ibid. pp. 163–164). This insight is considered to relate to grasping the 'major' principles of phenomenology: the nature of conscious experience, intentionality of directed action, the person in context, and situated human experience (ibid. pp. 165–169). Using phenomenology as a research method attempts to draw on conscious experience through, for example, carrying out interviews and analysing them.

Among the strengths of phenomenological research are that it can involve complex and subjective phenomena. It focuses on what for some are the most important aspects of human experience, how the world is experienced by particular individuals. However, it is recognised that numerous assumptions are made in believing that such approaches give access to another person's consciousness. There is considerable difficulty in trying to interpret 'the enormous complexity in the human experience' (Smith and Fowler, 2009, p. 169). A search for 'the essence of the phenomenon' is a distinguishing feature of 'phenomenological enquiry' (ibid. p. 169). This in itself is fraught with difficulty. Also, phenomenological research may not be replicable and can be so subjective as to be little more than anecdote.

The complexities of human motivation, perception, thought and other factors present an enormous obstacle to any kind of interpretation. The notion that interviews and their analysis, even though carefully structured, can provide an insight into the process of consciousness seems rather optimistic. This is not to suggest that efforts might not be made, but that the methods and any supposed findings are problematic.

For the philosophical method of phenomenology a problem is the subjectivity of the approach and its tendency towards transcendence. In its theoretical applications to disabilities and disorders, phenomenology offers interesting insights especially concerning the centrality of embodiment through the work of Merleau-Ponty. In research, the potential strengths of phenomenological research in providing nuanced understanding of perspectives is balanced by the limitations of not knowing the extent to which subjective insights are transferable to other situations.

Implications for thinking and practice of phenomenology in special education

Someone influenced by phenomenology might regard bodies – including disabled bodies – in a particular way. She might understand bodies in the very wide sense of referring to the biological body, social 'bodies' and 'bodies' that emerge from the way people communicate. Apparently individual bodies may be seen as immersed in the world in such a way that they interweave with other bodies to bring into reality personal and social identity. Consequently, bodies can be open to one another not just physically but also perceptually and emotionally. This might influence the behaviour, intentions and sensitivities of anyone taking a phenomenological perspective.

Perception, including general limitations in perception such as those associated with autism, can also be considered a form of 'embodiment' in that it implies a way of being in the world. 'Disability experiences' may be understood in terms of the process of becoming a 'fully fledged' person with a disability. She may recognise that not being able to walk, for example, influences not only an individual's physical condition, but also relationships, self-image, their worldview and sense of time. This may inform a view of the curriculum as contributing to self-image and relationships, perhaps suggesting full use of personal, social and health education and the importance of social and friendship groups – for example, in school clubs and leisure time.

In pedagogy too, social and personal development may be considered particularly important. The teacher and others might be especially aware of the social expectations and perceptions and different perspectives of, for example, friendship groups of individuals with particular disabilities or disorders. This might show itself in using such insights when seeking to help students develop social skills. Such skills might be seen, not so much as skills within a person or demonstrated by a person, but as a shared way of interrelating with others, in which others form a crucial part of the social skills interaction.

She may regard the body as having a special position in the world, in that it can touch and be touched, for example, so it is at the same time an object and a subject. The notion of the body may be extended to include physical aids to bodily mobility and perception. For individuals with some disabilities who use objects to help them (for example a cane used by a blind person) these objects seem to become almost part of that individual's body. Technology may be seen as playing an important part not just in helping communication or mobility, important as these are, but as helping expand an individual's horizons and self-image.

If the body is seen in a wide sense, including in terms of social 'bodies' and 'bodies' that emerge from the way people communicate, then organisation is likely to be seen as very important. If individual bodies are immersed in the world so they interweave with other bodies to bring into reality personal and social identity, then social groupings, friendship groups, and groupings for learning are all likely to influence deeply the way the individual body and self is seen.

Psychotherapy might sit quite comfortably in a range of provision for special children for someone taking a phenomenological view. The openness of 'bodies' to one another – perceptually and emotionally – can be seen as one of the foundations of therapy. It is necessary now to turn to a consideration of hermeneutics.

Hermeneutics

The meaning of hermeneutics

The term 'hermeneutic' is thought to allude to Hermes, the messenger of the gods who, in communicating between gods and humans, was also associated with interpretation. Accordingly, hermeneutics concerns the study and application of interpretation. There is a long tradition of hermeneutics regarding scriptural, legal and ancient classical texts. Contemporary hermeneutics extends to the interpretation of all vehicles of meaning, not only to written forms but also to human actions and aspects of society and culture.

Hermeneutics presents a radically different view of knowledge and understanding to that of science. Three widely accepted central aspects of positivism are: that in principle scientific methods must be applied in all fields of inquiry to gain knowledge; that the method of the physical sciences offers the ideal paradigm; and that facts are to be explained causally, such explanations consisting in subsuming particular cases under general laws (Mautner, 2000, p. 248). Hermeneutics as the study of the principles by which kinds of knowledge can be gained claims that interpretation provides knowledge, a position incompatible with the tenets of positivism.

Among early foundational work in hermeneutics is that of Schleiermacher and Dilthey. One of the best known contributors to modern hermeneutics is Gadamer.

Schleiermacher and Dilthey

Schleiermacher's publication, *Hermeneutics and Criticism* (Schleiermacher, [1808] 1998) focusing on the interpretation and textual criticism of the New Testament is considered to be a foundational contribution to hermeneutics. Previously, hermeneutics had been concerned mainly with religious and legal documents. But Schleiermacher uses grammar, philology and textual analysis to develop a general method for interpreting a text and seeking to eradicate misunderstanding. He gives consideration to aspects of language and to the individual subject in constituting meaning.

Dilthey was influenced by Schleiermacher's view of hermeneutics. Dilthey ([1883] 1991), drew distinctions between knowledge gained by scientific method in the natural sciences, and knowledge of social, cultural and historical facts in the human sciences. He argues that the natural sciences seek causes and explanations whereas the human sciences search for understanding through interpretation.

Linge (1976, editor's introduction p. xx) depicts the hermeneutics of Schleiermacher and Dilthey as 'reconstructive'. They take the language of the text as a 'cipher' for something lying behind it, such as the worldview of the author. In this respect, he contrasts Schleiermacher and Dilthey with Gadamer.

Gadamer

In looking at Gadamer's 'philosophical hermeneutics', this section seeks first to give an indication of the nature of Gadamer's approach. I say something about his magnum opus *Truth and Method* (Gadamer, [1960 and later editions] 2004) with a brief mention of his essay 'The Universality of the Hermeneutic Problem' (Gadamer, [1966] 1976). I then outline some main points from Gadamer's essay 'Hermeneutics as a Practical Philosophy' (Gadamer ([1976] 1981).

The nature of philosophical hermeneutics

Gadamer's philosophical hermeneutics is said to seek 'a general theory of understanding and interpretation which shows that these are by no means rule-governed procedures or methods for ensuring the objectivity of the "human" . . . sciences' (Christensen, 2000, p. 215).

Linge (1976, editor's introduction, p. xi) sees the task of philosophical hermeneutics as to throw a light on 'the fundamental conditions that underlie the phenomena of understanding in all its modes, scientific and non-scientific alike'. These fundamental conditions 'constitute understanding as an event over which the interpreting subject does not ultimately preside' (ibid.). The hermeneutical phenomenon embraces 'both the alien that we strive to understand and the familiar world that we already understand' (ibid. p. xii).

'Truth and Method'

The publication, *Truth and Method* (Gadamer, [1960 and later editions] 2004) is widely considered Gadamer's major contribution to modern hermeneutics. It discusses the question of truth as it emerges in the experience of art and its extension to understanding in the human sciences. Gadamer is focused on the problem of hermeneutics, asking how understanding is possible. He criticises Dilthey's approach, regarding it as being insufficiently concerned with the place of the interpreter and his interpretations, which for Gadamer are not outside tradition but occupy a place within it.

Physical sciences do not provide comprehensive knowledge but offer a continuing process of investigation in which hypotheses are hermeneutic operations. They yield not understanding but explanations. The methods of physical sciences are not appropriate to social sciences because 'The theme and object of research are actually constituted by the motivation of the inquiry' (ibid. p. 285). For Gadamer, understanding is mediated by language. The final chapter of *Truth and Method* concerns 'Language and Hermeneutics' and begins by exploring language as the medium of hermeneutic experience (Gadamer, [1960 and later editions] 2004, pp. 385–406).

Gadamer uses the term 'prejudice' not to necessarily imply 'false judgement' (Gadamer, [1960 and later editions] 2004, p. 273) but to convey a prejudgement that helps lead to understanding. Indeed, in the essay 'The Universality of the Hermeneutic Problem' Gadamer (1966) elaborates on this view of prejudices. These are not necessarily 'unjustified and erroneous' so that they distort truth. On the contrary, prejudices 'constitute the initial directedness of our whole ability to experience' (ibid. p. 9). Language is the form in which understanding is reached, that is, understanding is 'language bound' (ibid. p. 15).

'Hermeneutics as a Practical Philosophy'

The book, *Reason in the Age of Science* (Gadamer, [1976, 1978, 1979] 1981) includes a chapter originally published as an essay, 'Hermeneutics as a Practical Philosophy'. In this essay, Gadamer ([1976] 1981) distinguishes between traditional and philosophical hermeneutics. In contrast to traditional hermeneutics, philosophical hermeneutics is 'more interested in the questions than the answers' (ibid. p. 106). More precisely, it 'interprets statements as answers to questions that it is its role to understand' (ibid.). A certain anticipation of meaning contributes to considering questions. Gadamer recognises the importance of 'an inner tension between our anticipations of meaning and the all-pervasive opinions'. He also sees the centrality of 'a critical interest in the generally prevailing opinions'. Without these, he believes, 'there would be no questions at all' (ibid. p. 107).

The role of language in meaning is central and Gadamer speaks of the 'intrinsically linguistic condition of all our understanding' ([1976] 1981, p. 110). He suggests there are 'vague representations of meaning that bear us along'. These are brought 'word by word to articulation and so become communicable' (ibid.). The 'communality' of all understanding founded in its intrinsically linguistic quality is an 'essential point' of the hermeneutic experience (ibid.).

Philosophical hermeneutics is not a new procedure of interpretation but only describes what happens when an interpretation is 'convincing and successful' (ibid. p. 111). Hermeneutics is the core of philosophy in Gadamer's terms. It concerns a 'theoretical attitude toward the practice of interpretation, the interpretation of texts, but also in relation to the experiences interpreted in them and in our communicatively unfolded orientations in the world' (ibid. p. 112).

For Gadamer, understanding is not achieved by finding an inner source of subjective meaning. Understanding is an ongoing process so that there is no end point where it is possible to say understanding is complete. Consequently there is no method for arriving at some ultimate truth. There is no methodology that is up to the task of understanding the human and historical realm or even the natural world. The continual process of developing understanding is antipathetic to such ideas that knowledge can be in a completed state. Understanding cannot be reduced to method, including scientific method.

Evaluation of hermeneutics

Adherents regard hermeneutics as a subtle alternative to the belief that truth is somehow out there to be grasped and that language is a tool to enable this. Its view that truth cannot be reached by an explicit method is appealing for those preferring a view of understanding being continuingly built through successive interpretation. Philosophical hermeneutics places value on tradition and on successive interpretations of texts and actions. It also sits well with contemporary interests in the role of language and its permeating influence.

One criticism of philosophical hermeneutics focuses on Gadamer's view that individuals have a prior hermeneutic involvement in experiences. It may be argued that any such involvement must be subjective. This is because our involvement is shaped by individual dispositions to experience things in a certain way rather than in another way. Involvement in this view is based on subjective prejudice.

In fact, Gadamer rejects such a view of subjectivity. Also his view of prejudice, as has already been indicated, is not one of negative closing off other experiences, as the word has come to mean in everyday parlance. It is that prejudice is more like a prejudgement that is necessary for any understanding. For Gadamer, prejudice is a pre-structuring of understanding without which no understanding can take place. Through this process, that which is to be interpreted can be grasped in a preliminary way. Understanding therefore always involves the anticipation of completeness. This is a presumption that what it is that is being understood is indeed something that is understandable in terms of being a meaningful whole.

It is not clear how an individual can distinguish among the prejudgements that he brings to understanding. Some of these may be prejudices in the commonly used sense, that is, ways of understanding that are to others demonstrably warped and at odds with common agreements. Yet an individual may not be able to distinguish these real prejudices from prejudgements. It may be that, through conversation with others, such distinctions may come to be revealed, but it is not clear how this can be assured.

Others have criticised Gadamer's conception of 'understanding'. Derrida, for example, whose development of deconstruction lies uneasily with hermeneutics, takes a different view of 'understanding'. For Derrida, understanding would involve a form of appropriation of the other and its otherness, as is apparent in a debate between Derrida and Gadamer in 1981. Derrida questions Gadamer's assumption that understanding suggests the goodwill to understand the other.

That 'will', suggests Derrida, is linked to a will to dominate that is emblematic of the metaphysical tradition and the tradition of Western philosophy. In consequence, Derrida is sceptical about the hermeneutic drive to understand the other. He also mistrusts the hermeneutic claim to universality. Derrida disputes Gadamer's view that understanding is primary and denies agreement is possible, one of the claims of hermeneutics (Michelfelder and Palmer, 1989).

Hermeneutics and special education

Two writers in special education taking a hermeneutic view are Richard Iano and Deborah Gallagher. Iano (2004) focuses on the perceived incompatibility of scientific method to the social sciences, while Gallagher (2004a) draws explicitly on Gadamer's philosophical hermeneutics.

Limitations of scientific method in the social sciences

Iano (2004) uses a hermeneutic perspective to inform his position towards special education that scientific method is out of place in social sciences. In hermeneutic vein, he criticises the 'idealised image' of science. In this image researchers 'try to treat the subject matter of the social sciences similar to the way physical scientists treat their subject matter – as naturally occurring phenomena having objective existence independent of our language, constructs and interpretations' (Iano, 2004, p. 72). Hermeneutics, it is maintained, recognises that, unlike physical reality, 'the subject matter of the social sciences is entirely a human creation' (ibid.).

Quoting Ericson and Ellett (1982), Iano puts the case that social reality and practices are interpretative in two respects. Like the physical scientist, it is suggested, the social scientist 'applies interpretative constructs and theory to subject matter' (Iano, 2004, p. 72). But additionally the social scientist's subject matter is 'itself constituted by interpretation' (ibid.). Consequently, it is argued, for social scientists to know what they are studying and the meaning of the social practices they are researching, they first must know 'how the participants themselves interpret their practices and actions' (ibid.). Social scientists must have a subject 'to elucidate, explain and describe', and the subject matter is itself 'constituted by the interpretations of the individuals being studied' (ibid.).

Teaching and learning is not regarded as an objective practice outside which an observer can stand. Rather, it is seen as constituted by teachers' and students' 'intersubjective interpretations'. Educational researchers would therefore need to observe a teaching and learning occurrence unfolding. They would have to communicate with students and the teacher to establish their 'interpretations and understandings of the occurrence' (Iano, 2004, p. 72). The researcher would also need to know something of the context that helped produce the occurrence.

Iano, from this standpoint, is clearly at odds with positivist research in education, which he calls a 'natural science-technical model' (Iano, 2004, p. 73). He criticises experimental and control group studies looking at particular teaching methods because, 'participants in different settings might not see as the same a set of activities and actions that are designated as the "same" across settings according to fixed operational criteria' (ibid.). The alternative is 'a more naturalistic or ethnographic type of research'. In such research, settings of teaching and learning are 'studied in their full and ongoing contexts' (ibid. p. 84).

Interpretation

Gallagher characterises her position as 'philosophical hermeneutics' (personal communication, 2009), as illustrated in the publication, *Challenging Orthodoxy in Special Education: Dissenting Voices* (Gallagher *et al.*, 2004). Rejecting a 'correspondence theory' of truth whereby statements are taken to be true if they correspond to or represent reality, Gallagher instead emphasises the importance of interpretation. If observation is subject to the beliefs and experiences of the observer, what is produced is 'not simply an objective statement or description of the facts' but 'an *interpretation* of the sense data or what was "seen"' (Gallagher, 2004a, p. 7, italics in original). Also, observations cannot be made 'free of our own pre-existing theories or unmediated by our own interpretations' (ibid.).

Gallagher suggests behavioural approaches are limited because behavioural indices such as 'on task' are confined to what is observable and cannot take into account what the student might be thinking. It is stated, 'Because the student's frame of mind is entirely subject to interpretation and obviously not directly observable, visible indicators are made to stand for the actual topic of interest' (Gallagher, 2004a, p. 19). Speaking of decontextualisation, Gallagher affirms that 'We all know that the same action in a different context results in different interpretations of its meaning' (ibid.).

Discussing Down syndrome, she argues 'disability is not merely a matter of difference; it is a matter of how we interpret and interact with perceived difference' (Gallagher, 2004a, p. 14). Although we do not 'create the chromosomal difference associated with Down syndrome', we do 'decide through the act of interpretation what that difference means' (ibid.).

In a later article, Gallagher (2006) responds to broad criticisms of 'postmodernism' by Kauffman and Sasso in which they include hermeneutics (Gallagher, 2006, pp. 65–90). Gallagher states, 'Because researchers cannot achieve theory-free observation, it is therefore impossible to attain absolute objectivity' (ibid. p. 91). This raises questions about 'the nature of knowledge, truth, reality, and relativism' (ibid.).

Gallagher suggests a dialogue to try to 'more closely achieve what Habermas (1981) described as the ideal speech situation (community)' (Gallagher, 2006, pp. 91–92). This is one in which 'discussion and debate takes place in a free, open and non-coercive manner'. Also, in an ideal speech community, individuals taking opposing perspectives 'try as much as possible to understand others' points of view' (ibid.). Referring broadly to Gadamer's *Philosophical Hermeneutics*, Gallagher states, 'One must be willing as Gadamer (1976) phrases it, to . . . risk his or her prejudices' (Gallagher, 2006, p. 93).

In applying hermeneutics to special education, apparent external facts are not always taken to be what they seem. The nature of human beings and physical reality are quite different. Interpretation, which is integral to understanding, implies that individuals are dependent on their prejudgements to make the most correct interpretations of experiences. These prejudgements form the basis from which understanding takes place and are not a hindrance to that understanding. To assume there are no such prejudgements or prejudices is to fail to recognise the impossibility of purely objective observation. In special education, as it is deeply concerned with responses to others, such a position limits the perception of human experience.

Evaluation of hermeneutics in special education

Two kinds of evaluation may be made of hermeneutics in special education. The first is to do with the validity or coherence of its criticisms of other perspectives, particularly positivism. The second concerns the positive contribution that hermeneutics can make to special education.

The first type of evaluation of hermeneutics in special education relates to its criticisms of other perspectives, such as positivism. Gallagher has argued from a hermeneutic point of view for challenging an uncritical acceptance of positivist scientific approaches to special education (Gallagher, 2006, pp. 91–107). One of Gallagher's criticisms of science is related to a correspondence theory of truth. This is that something is true if it corresponds with something else or, in logical notation, '"p" is true if and only p'. Among criticisms of this theory of truth is that it may not be clear what it is that is said to be true – for example, whether it is a statement or a belief. Similarly it may not be apparent what the correspondence is with – for example, reality or a fact. Also, it may not be clear what the relationship 'correspondence' is.

It is not always clear whether attempts to apply hermeneutics in line with Gadamer's work are consistent with it. As already mentioned, Gallagher states, 'One must be willing as Gadamer (1976) phrases it, to . . . risk his or her prejudices' (Gallagher, 2006, p. 93). Because of the lack of page referencing or a direct quote, it is not clear here whether what Gallagher is referring to is Gadamer's technical use of the expression 'prejudice' as used in *Truth and Method* (Gadamer, [1960 and later editions] 2004). Here, Gadamer uses 'prejudice' not necessarily in the sense of 'false judgement' but instead, referring to prejudgement, which forms the basis of questioning of the world leading to fuller understanding (ibid. pp. 278–279). It is difficult to know whether Gallagher's position refers to getting rid of prejudices in the sense of false judgements or whether she is rejecting the hermeneutic approach at this point.

Hermeneutics points to a particular view of disabilities and disorders. Disability is seen as a 'culturally and historically conditioned interpretation of certain differences' (Gallagher, 2004b, p. 367). This suggests taking 'moral ownership of the meaning we bring to human differences'. Disability labelling is seen as 'imposing invidious social comparisons that inevitably create injustices' (ibid.). This perspective can raise awareness of the potential or actual creating of exclusion that can be associated with negative labelling.

To the extent that disability labelling is interpretative and interpretations can be modified, such a view can help avoid divisiveness. However, a view of labelling disability as entirely and inevitably negative does not paint the whole picture. It fails to take account of the views of special children and young people and their parents who welcome such labels. Parents may find that labels for conditions help explain much that has bewildered them and that labels help put them in touch with parent support groups (Farrell, 2006, p. 36).

Research may also be informed by hermeneutics. Gallagher (2006) refers to 'interpretive inquirers' and 'interpretive researchers' (p. 369). Such researchers, it is stated, are aware that they bring assumptions about the nature of disability to their research and that they affect and are affected by the research participants. They understand research has moral consequences for which they are responsible (ibid.). Interpretivist inquiry is not intended to lead to 'generalizable techniques in a positivist sense' but aims for greater understanding of 'who we are as people, as learners, and as educators' (ibid. p. 370).

But it is unclear how any such understanding can be useful if it cannot be generalised to other situations or people. How is it helpful to know who you are 'as a learner' if this does not relate in any way to how others are 'as learners'? What is the point of knowing who you are as an educator, if this cannot be related to what others are as educators? The rejection of what can be generalised can too easily become narcissistic.

Hermeneutics suggests support for a more ethnographic type of research. If the arguments about the limitations of a 'natural science-technical model' (Iano, 2004, p. 73) have credibility, then ethnographic research itself comes across similar difficulties. If participants in different settings might interpret situations differently, making it difficult to ensure that like is being compared with like, similar constraints apply to gathering participants' accounts.

If educational researchers need to observe a teaching and learning occurrence 'unfolding', how can the researcher's interpretation of this be known to be secure? If the researcher has to communicate with students and the teacher to establish their 'interpretations and understandings of the occurrence' (Iano, 2004, p. 73), how can it be known whether the participants are providing an accurate or even a credible account? How does one proceed where children cannot understand situations very well or have severe communication difficulties?

Of course, attempts to address such issues can be pursued. However, it is difficult to accept that a hermeneutic approach avoids difficulties of attempting to observe and make sense of the human condition and human behaviour any more than do positivist approaches. Attempts to mitigate the difficulties may be different – but the challenges remain.

Implications for thinking and practice of hermeneutics in special education

In special education, as hermeneutics is deeply concerned with responses to others, someone taking such a view may consider apparent external facts are not always what they seem. She may regard the nature of human beings and physical reality as quite different. Interpretation may be seen as integral to understanding, implying that individuals are dependent on their prejudgements to make the most correct interpretations of experiences. These prejudgements form the basis from which understanding takes place. Accordingly, an advocate of hermeneutics might regard disability as not just concerning difference but how others interpret and interact with perceived difference.

A supporter of hermeneutics may value particularly naturalistic or ethnographic research where settings of teaching and learning are studied in the round, including their developing contexts. She may consider that researchers cannot achieve theory-free observation, and that it is impossible to attain absolute objectivity.

For someone who regards disability as not just concerning difference but how others interpret and interact with perceived difference, such a view might influence areas of the curriculum. In discussions, students may be given opportunities to examine the extent to which interpretation influences views of difference. This could be discussed in a wide range of contexts. Part of the study and understanding of history for example, involves exploring how different interpretations of events might be justified and weighing evidence to come to a judgement on this. With regard to personal and social development, hermeneutics might contribute to understanding cultures different to one's own as well as interpretations of others different to oneself in terms of gender, race or disability.

Someone taking a hermeneutic view might be suspicious of the influence of scientific thinking and application in special education (and the social sciences), seeing the subject matter of the social sciences as an entirely human creation. Consequently, the findings of evidence-based practice may not be considered of particular importance. For example, she might consider behavioural approaches limited because behavioural indices such as 'on task' are confined to the observable and cannot take into account what the student might be thinking.

In day-to-day teaching or working she will be interested in how the participants themselves *interpret* their practices and actions. She will encourage pupils to explain and describe their understandings in order to try and see how they interpret their world. She might regard teaching and learning as constituted by teachers' and students' intersubjective interpretations. In teaching and learning, the possibly different interpretations and understandings will be important as well as the context, and these will be explored.

With pupils and with colleagues, someone holding a hermeneutic perspective is likely to value opportunities for discussion and debate in a free, open and non-coercive manner, where individuals taking opposing perspectives try to understand others' points of view.

From a hermeneutic view, resources may be seen as materials that contribute to understanding. Resources provided for the student to examine and interpret can be a powerful way of learning. This applies more obviously to some disciplines than others – and history, literature and arts seem on the face of it to be more amenable to hermeneutic approaches than sciences. In sciences too, however, resources can be presented in way that initially at least encourages prejudgement and interpretation, so that a student's initial understanding can be compared with the findings of others. Similar issues arise as those surrounding discovery learning. It is not suggested that students go unaided into learning, but that time to explore and see various alternatives can be productive. In educating special children, such an approach is likely to be similar to that with any student.

The general views of hermeneutics as deeply concerned with responses to others, and as seeing interpretation as integral to understanding, does not seem incompatible with psychotherapy. In cognitive psychotherapy for example, interpretations are examined and sometimes challenged with an underlying implication that perception can be as influential as possible reality. Different ways of thinking may be encouraged where present patterns appear dysfunctional.

Thinking points

- Why might Merleau-Ponty's view that the body functions as a whole and that perception is the primary mode of embodied consciousness be attractive to those theorising about bodily existence in relation to disability?
- In your view, is the position of hermeneutics stronger in its criticisms of other perspectives, particularly positivism, or in the contribution that it can make to special education such as interpretative research?

Key texts

Phenomenology

Merleau-Ponty, M. ([1945] 1982) *Phenomenology of Perception* (translated from the French by Colin Smith), New York: Routledge.
Iwakuma, S. (2002) 'The Body as Embodiment: An Investigation of the Body by Merleau-Ponty' in Corker, M. and Shakespeare, T. (2002a) (Eds.) *Disability/Postmodernity: Embodying Disability Theory*, London and New York: Continuum.

Hermeneutics

Gadamer, H-G. ([various dates from 1960 to 1972] 1976) *Philosophical Hermeneutics* (translated from the German and edited by David E. Linge), Berkeley: University of California Press. This series of essays forms a good introduction to some of Gadamer's concerns.

Gallagher, D. J. (2006) 'If Not Absolute Objectivity, Then What? A Reply to Kaufman and Sasso', *Exceptionality* 14, 2, pp. 91–107. This forms part of a series of papers in which hermeneutics and positivism are represented in a special issue of *Exceptionality*.

Further reading

Gadamer, H-G. ([1960 and later editions] 2004) *Truth and Method* (revised translation from the German by Joel Weinsheimer and Donald G. Marshall), New York: Continuum. This book brings together the major themes of Gadamer's work and is widely considered his *magnum opus*.

Chapter 5

Economic forces and suspicion
Historical materialism and critical theory

Historical materialism and related ideas

Marxism is a body of thought arising from the writings of the economist and philosopher Karl Marx and his collaborator Friedrich Engels. It presents a materialist philosophy of history and of nature, a theory of politics, and a system of political economy. Marx was considerably influenced by the philosophy of the German philosopher Georg Wilhelm Friedrich Hegel. Particularly influential were Hegel's notions of the dialectic and alienation. Among key concepts of Marxism are 'alienation', 'ideology' and 'commodity fetishism'.

Alienation refers to the estrangement of workers from their own labour. Because in a capitalist system a worker does not own the products of his own labour, his labour assumes an alien existence of its own. The process of labour therefore loses its reality. Only when private ownership of the means of production and the commodity system are ended, it is believed, will alienation be eradicated, leading to a better society.

Ideology concerns the various ideological forms such as political and religious ones. It is through these that people become conscious of the conflict between the material productive forces of society and the existing relations of production.

Marx explains commodity fetishism in *Capital, Volume 1* (Marx, [1867] 1992) in a chapter entitled 'The Fetishism of the Commodity and its Secret'. It refers to a type of alienation brought about in a capitalist society by the structures of commodity exchange. The exchange does not take into account the quality of the labour going into making the item. The labour exchanged for a wage produces value in the form of the item, but is treated as an abstract commodity. Social characteristics of labour come to seem like objects existing independently of social relations. Products of labour appear to have no relationship to the labour producing them, and the characteristics of labour appear to be the natural properties of objects. Commodities exchanged in a capitalist society become fetishes in being awarded 'magical' powers and illusory autonomy. Staley (1991) suggests the essence of exchange for Marx is found in human labour, which is common to all commodities. To exchange commodities is to engage in the social relationship of exchanging labour, and ignoring this is what is meant by 'commodity fetishism' (p. 123).

Historical materialism which, along with dialectical materialism, is a philosophical theme of Marxism, maintains that human life is determined by the material and social conditions of existence. Human history is produced by two phenomena: a struggle between social classes; and a dialectic between forces of production and relations of production. 'Forces of production' are forms of ownership and control of industry and commerce. 'Relations of production' are the forms (social, legal and ideological) determining how classes with opposed interests get on together in a society.

Social development is determined by the growth of productive forces, such as large-scale industry. The growth of industry breaks down the social relations that typified feudal society, replacing them with social relations based on exchanging labour power for a wage. Social revolution is precipitated when a society's productive forces conflict with existing relations of production or with property relations.

Historical development is typified by the emergence of a sequence of modes of production – feudal and capitalist, for example. Each has a form of social organisation relating to ownership and the way surplus is extracted. In a capitalist society, a labourer working for a wage covers the cost of his wages then produces a surplus taken by the capitalist. Different modes of production succeed one another. However, with the development of socialism and communism, it is theorised, the sequence will come to an end as private property is abolished and antagonistic classes no longer exist.

In the preface to *A Contribution to the Critique of Political Economy* Marx ([1859] 1981) summarises his position regarding the relationship between economic conditions of production and 'ideological forms' (p. 21). Hegelian views maintained history is the product of consciousness and ideas. However, Marx states, 'The mode of production of material life conditions the general process of social, political and intellectual life'. Social existence determines men's conscience. At a certain stage of development, the 'material productive forces of society' clash with 'the existing relations of production' or with 'property relations' in the framework of which they previously operated. These relations that had once been 'forms of development of the productive forces' become 'their fetters' (p. 21, preface). This marks the beginning of social revolution and 'changes of the economic foundation lead to the transformation of the super structure' (ibid.).

In studying such transformations, Marx considers legal, political, religious, philosophical and artistic ideological forms. He distinguishes between 'the material transformation of the economic conditions of production' and the 'ideological forms in which men become conscious of this conflict and fight it out' (ibid.). The capitalist ('bourgeois') mode of production for Marx is 'the last antagonistic form of the social process of production' in the sense of antagonism emerging from individuals' 'social conditions of existence'. However, the productive forces developing within capitalist society create the material conditions that form the solution to the antagonism (ibid. pp. 21–22).

Evaluation of historical materialism

As an aspect of Marxism, historical materialism is part of a grand and comprehensive attempt to explain how society has developed and to indicate trends for the future. In *A Contribution to the Critique of Political Economy* (Marx ([1859] 1981), the three volumes of *Capital* (Marx, [1867] 1992; [1885] 1993; [1894] 1993), and elsewhere, Marx developed a critical appraisal of capitalist economy. Complementing this, he drew on the ideas of the German philosopher Hegel in setting out a philosophy of history – historical materialism. In the *Communist Manifesto*, for example, Marx and Engels ([1848] 1996) argued that the momentum of history is created by social class conflict in a 'dialectic'.

One difficulty with a Marxist historical materialist position is that Marx argues that the laws of liberal economics represent the institution of property as permanent. Consequently, these laws 'discourage an examination of other arrangements in which property, and the alienation that stems from it, might disappear' (Scruton, 2002, p. 224).

In such circumstances, 'the rewards and fulfilments of human nature will also change' and if alienation were overcome the change would be positive. The nature of man is represented as self-created yet there is a state of man in which he is restored to himself which has a sort of 'supreme and distinctive value'. In this respect, Marx seems to both accept and reject the notion of a 'permanent human essence' (Scruton, 2002, p. 224).

Marx's claim that alienation is directly connected with the institution of property is contentious and at no point convincingly established (Scruton, 2002, p. 227). Marx's philosophy 'recognised as the basis of all political thought the intuition that man is both object and subject for himself' (ibid. p. 232). This leads to the notion of 'praxis', uniting theory and practice. Only the theory that can be 'incorporated into the practical reasoning of the agent' will remove the mystery from human things (ibid.).

However, Scruton (2002) argues, this philosophy, in assuming the credentials of science, renounces 'the viewpoint which makes it intelligible' setting up an impassable barrier between theory and practice (p. 232). Seeking to show the social reality behind human illusion 'demystifies' consciousness but 'ends by removing the values which are the sole stimulus to social action, and so generates a new mystery of its own' (pp. 232–233).

Historical materialism in special education

Disability as a social restriction

Oliver (1990) develops a historical-materialist account of disablement, suggesting that disabled people 'experience disability as social restriction' (p. xiv). These restrictions may occur as a consequence of different factors, including 'inaccessible built environments, questionable notions of intelligence and social competence, the inability of the general population to use sign language, the lack of reading material in Braille or hostile public attitudes to people with non-visible disabilities' (ibid.).

Differences in the treatment of disabled people, including discriminatory ones, are said to be produced culturally via the relationship between 'the mode of production and the central values of the society concerned' (ibid. p. 23). Oliver cites Marx's view (Marx, [1859] 1981, pp. 20–21, preface) that social existence determines men's consciousness. Disabled individuals are seen as 'an ideological construction related to the core ideology of individualism' as well as the ideologies of medicalisation and normality. The individual's experience of disability is structured by the 'discursive practices' emerging from these ideologies (Oliver, 1990, p. 58).

Oliver's (1996) definition of disabled people contains three elements: 'the presence of an impairment', the 'experience of externally imposed restrictions', and 'self identification as a disabled person' (p. 5). It is argued that political economy suggests that all phenomena, including social categories, are produced 'by the economic and social forces of capitalism itself'. Also, the forms in which they are produced are 'ultimately dependent upon their relationship to the economy' (ibid. p. 131). The category of disability is 'produced' in the particular form it appears by such economic and social forces (ibid.).

Accordingly, Oliver (1999) regards the production of disability as no different to the production of 'cars or hamburgers' (p. 83 – page numbers for Oliver's 1999 paper refer to its reproduction in Mitchell, 2004). The category of 'disability' is produced as an economic problem, owing to changes in what constitutes work and 'the needs of the labour market within capitalism' (ibid. p. 84). With the rise of capitalism, it is suggested, disabled people 'suffered economic and social exclusion' (ibid. p. 86). Owing to this exclusion, disability was 'produced' as an individual problem needing medical treatment and the institution was central to this exclusion (ibid.).

The rising cost of institutional care is said to have strongly influenced the move to community-based care (ibid. p. 87, paraphrased). The latter's continuation in the period of late capitalism is interpreted as 'an extension of the process of control within the capitalist state' (ibid.). The power relationships between disabled people and professionals is unchanged. The social structures of late capitalist societies are characterised by 'difference' based on gender, ethnic background, abilities, and so on (ibid. p. 88).

Barnes (1998) explains the social model of disability as 'a focus on the environmental and social barriers which exclude people with perceived impairments from mainstream society'. It distinguishes between impairment as 'biological characteristics of the body and mind' and disability as 'society's failure to address the needs of disabled people'. While not intended to deny the importance of impairment (despite the implication that they are only 'perceived' rather than real), the model offers a 'framework' within which policies can be formed, focusing on 'aspects of disabled people's lives which can and should be changed' (ibid. p. 78). The nature of disability is considered to change according to the social and economic structure of a society and its culture, locating the model within a neo-Marxist framework (Oliver and Barnes, 1998). The knowledge and practice of the social model concerns the 'political project of emancipation' and in some versions, developing an 'oppositional politics of identity' (Corker and Shakespeare, 2002b, p. 3).

Similarly, Thomas's understanding of the nature of social and cultural systems 'draws on historical materialist premises' (Thomas and Corker, 2002, p. 19). She tends to think disability and disablism in contemporary society is bound up with two aspects of society. The first is society's economic foundations of 'capitalist and social relations of production'. The second aspect is 'the cultural forms and ideological phenomena'. These forms and phenomena are considered to be 'shaped by, and impact back upon' the economic foundations (ibid.).

Thomas does not view historical materialist theory as 'crudely economic determinist'. To do so would insufficiently acknowledging the relevance of cultural and psychological processes in shaping social phenomena. The material perspective, in Thomas's view, can 'engage richly with the cultural, ideological and psychosocial (for example identity)' (ibid. p. 20). It is suggested (Corker and Shakespeare, 2002b) that a social model of disability, rooted in historical materialism, is an example of a challenge to modernism in the form of socialist counterculture (p. 3).

Historical-geographical relationships

Gleeson (1999) aims to theorise historical-geographical relationships 'that have conditioned the social experience of disabled people in Western societies'. He seeks to describe and explain 'the social experiences of disabled people in specific historical-geographical settings' (p. 3). His focus is primarily on physical disabilities (p. 6). Historical and geographical organisation of cultural-material life, it is argued, 'shapes all social experiences, including disability' (p. 8). The theoretical framework can be described as 'embodied materialism' (p. 195).

While social views of disability might support 'transformative ideals', it first has to be shown that fundamental change can be brought about (Gleeson, 1999, p. 31). One strategy is to indicate that change has already happened, showing that disability is 'a socio-historical construct' and an 'oppressive structure' erected at a certain time 'over the lives of impaired people'. Consequently, the structure can be dismantled and replaced by 'inclusive social relations' (ibid.). The historical-materialist perspective offers the possibility of 'an emancipatory politics' aiming to overcome 'the oppression of disability' (ibid. p. 26).

Presenting a historical-geographical account of 'embodiment', Gleeson (1999) seeks to derive a framework by which disability in particular societies can be analysed (p. 55). He regards embodiment as central to 'the material processes through which human beings transform received nature'. In doing so they 'create unique social spaces'. Social embodiment is (like the material processes that produced it) 'sourced' in 'specific historical-geographical contexts'. Therefore material analyses of embodiment must specify social spaces and social groups within their empirical frames (ibid.).

Gleeson (1999) suggests disability as social oppression was weakly developed within feudalism. However, the rise of capitalism delimited the 'capacity for self-determination by bringing new, compulsive socialisations to bear on the body' (p. 98). The growth of markets eroded away the socio-cultural contexts that, in the feudal era, had 'valorised the labour and social contributions of disabled people' (ibid. p. 101). In contemporary capitalist cities, Gleeson (1999) suggests, disablement is 'a distinct form of social oppression' emerging from the 'broad socio-cultural arrangement of capitalist societies' (p. 151). Disability oppression involves both political economic hardship and 'cultural misrecognition'. Dimensions of disability oppression include 'labour market exclusion, poverty, socio-cultural devaluation, and socio-spatial marginalisation' (ibid.).

Disability, inclusion and exclusion

Links have long been made between disability and limitations on integration and participation, or exclusion. Where the material conditions of disabled people are poor, it is suggested this is owing to 'the presence of physical and social barriers' preventing 'the *integration and full participation*' of disabled people in the community (Despouy, 1991, p. 1, italics added). Accordingly, numerous disabled people 'are *segregated* and deprived of virtually all their rights, and lead a wretched, marginal life' (ibid., italics added)

Capitalist society is linked with disabled people experiencing 'economic and social *exclusion*' (Oliver, 1996, p. 127, italics added). It has been associated with 'the production of disability as an individual medical problem' (ibid.). With the development of late capitalism, this view has been challenged and there have been attempts to 'produce disability in a different, social form commensurate with *inclusion*' (ibid., italics added). Here disability is associated with oppression and exclusion, and the emancipatory response is to lift oppression and to include.

In a similar vein, Oliver (1996, ch. 6) maintains the special education system, 'has functioned to *exclude* disabled people not just from the education process but from mainstream social life' (p. 79, italics added). Oliver speaks of a 'segregated' special education system (p. 80). He states that 'by the 1960s it was becoming obvious that it was failing the vast majority of disabled children, both in educational terms and in terms of personal and social development' (ibid.). Also, 'most disabled children are still being educated in special schools and still receive an education inferior to other children' (ibid.). This statement refers to reports by school inspectors of 36 special schools in the United Kingdom cited in Barnes (1991, pp. 43–46). Disability is seen as a 'human rights issue' (Oliver, 1996, p. 82). Current 'segregative practices' are 'the denial of rights to disabled people' (ibid.). They are compared with South African apartheid and the exclusion of the poor from major parts of cities (ibid. p. 83, paraphrased).

Oliver (1996) suggests, 'There is almost universal agreement that integration is a good thing' although he recognises this would depend on such factors as the right level of resources and suitable training of teachers (p. 85). Accordingly, he argues that mainstreaming should be increased through: changes in school ethos (pp. 86–87); teachers becoming committed to integration (p. 87); the removal of 'disablist' curriculum materials (p. 88); and the celebration of difference (pp. 88–89). Inclusion is preferred to integration. It is maintained, 'the special education system has failed to provide disabled children with the knowledge and skills to take their rightful place in the world' (p. 93). In the 'struggle' for inclusion, 'special, segregated education has no role to play' (ibid. pp. 93–94).

Evaluation of historical materialism in special education

Oppression and barrier removal

The social model refers to structural effects of society, and concerns social procedures considered oppressive. In locating disability in a historical materialist context, the model opens up the prospect of negative consequences of disability changing under different historical and material circumstances.

Its implications for action are that individuals must transform themselves through collective action (Oliver, 1999, p. 94). Empowerment is seen as a process by which those having little power seek to resist oppression 'as part of their demands to be included, and/or to articulate their own views of the world' (ibid.). Materialist social theory can offer disabled individuals, a chance to 'transform their own lives'. By doing so it is suggested the theory can change their society into one valuing all roles (ibid. p. 97).

Reflecting a social view, provision for special children may be depicted as removing perceived barriers (Bowe, 1978). This implies that society – through its built environment, social organisation, relationships and practices, and people's attitudes – has obstructed a special child. Therefore society can remove such barriers by: changing the physical environment, modifying the way things are done and the associated social relationships, and changing attitudes (Farrell, 2009, pp. 65–67).

A social approach applies more convincingly to some types of disabilities and disorders than others (MacKay *et al.*, 2002). For a pupil with orthopaedic impairment, motor impairment, some health impairments, and sensory impairments, the arrangement of the environment and the mitigation of barriers might be a useful way of approaching provision, although not without its difficulties. For cognitive impairment the social basis of intervention is less clear.

Whereas the social model assumes the notion of 'impairment' is outside the social context, it can be argued that impairment as well as disability is part of the social context. It is difficult in practice to separate mental distress caused by biological impairment and 'socially engendered psycho-emotional problems' because illness and impairment 'undermine psycho-emotional well-being' (Shakespeare, 2006, p. 36). Disability is a complex interaction of factors, 'biological, psychological, cultural and socio-political' that can only be imprecisely extricated (ibid. p. 38).

Injustices to disabled people cannot be understood as generated solely by cultural, or socio-economic, or biological mechanisms. Disability as a phenomenon can only be analytically approached, by 'taking different levels, mechanisms and contexts into account' (Danermark and Gellerstedt, 2004, p. 350). Tremain (2002) also criticises the social model for unjustifiably separating impairment and disability. For Tremain, following Foucault, this separation fails to theorise the nature of impairment and biomedical practices.

A capability approach and the social model

An interesting perspective relating to the social model and more individual understandings of disabilities and disorders can be derived from the 'capability approach' (Sen, 1992). The capability approach is a normative framework. It is used to assess inequality, poverty and the design of social settings. In a capability approach, equality and social arrangements are evaluated with regard to the theoretical 'space' of capabilities. This 'space' is that of the freedoms that individuals have in order to achieve the valued functioning that goes to make up their well-being. A valued functioning might be reading or walking or having an education. Capabilities are the opportunities and freedoms individuals have to achieve such functionings. Sen (1992) refers to functionings in terms of 'beings and doings' (p. 40). Similarly, Nussbaum (2000) speaks of what people are really 'able to be and do' (p. 40). Human diversity is seen as 'a fundamental aspect of our interest in equality' (Sen, 1992, p. xi). Diversity involves:

* individual personal characteristics, such as gender or physical abilities
* different external circumstances, such as wealth
* the ability to convert resources into valued functionings.

Variations in these three differences inform the capability metric and are accounted for when considering the demands of equality.

Terzi (2005) relates these considerations to impairment and disability. Disability is presented as relational with respect to impairment and to social institutions. The centrality of human diversity in evaluating individuals' relative advantages and disadvantages involves the evaluation of disability with regard to distributive patterns of relevant freedoms. Ultimately this relates to justice. Terzi (2005) sees these insights as offering an opportunity to overcome the 'duality between individual and social models' (p. 451).

Limited application

Other criticisms of the social model concern its limited application. Oliver (1999) defines disabled people to whom the social model might apply as having an impairment, experiencing oppression as a result, and identifying themselves as disabled persons (p. 83). This is problematic for children with profound cognitive impairment who may have little understanding of themselves and none of such an abstract concept as 'disabled person'. The idea that 'disability as social restriction' experienced by disabled people is similar for all restrictions – however they arise – fails to address this difficulty.

It is hard to equate restrictions occurring owing to 'inaccessible built environments' and restrictions arising from 'questionable notions of intelligence and social competence' (Oliver, 1990, p. xiv). Indeed it is hard to grasp what Oliver means by 'questionable notions of intelligence and social competence' in relation to children who require lifelong support and care because of profound cognitive impairment related to brain damage, and severe functional limitations. When these notions are 'questioned', what is the outcome for these children in terms of the social model?

Goodley (2001, p. 211) maintains that 'social structures practices and relationships continue to naturalise the subjectivities of people with "learning difficulties", conceptualising them in terms of some a-priori notion of "mentally impaired"'. This may have relevance to some children with mild cognitive impairment (Farrell, 2008, ch. 4). However, a teacher and others may be working with a child with profound cognitive impairment who experienced brain damage at birth and who at the age of sixteen is functioning largely at a level of a child under the age of one year.

It is difficult to know what the teacher would make of the apparent criticism that she is conceptualising the child in terms of an 'a-priori notion'. Also, it is not apparent what barriers of 'social structures, practices and relationships' society (and the teacher and parents as representatives of it) has put in the way of the child that they should now remove. Similarly, for a child with autism, it is difficult to see what the removal of barriers might mean in daily living (Singer, 1999) or how the community could be changed to enable him to be accommodated with other people.

Also, both the social model and the individual (or medical) model, it is suggested, 'seek to explain disability universally, and end up creating totalising meta-historical narratives that exclude important dimensions of disabled people's lives and of their knowledge' (Corker and Shakespeare (2002b, p. 15). It is argued that work on the social model (because it has given insufficient attention to experiential perspectives) tends to privilege the 'restrictions on doing' dimensions of disability over the 'restrictions on being' dimensions (Thomas and Corker, 2002, p. 19).

Negative practical consequences

The social model can lead to negative practical consequences for special children. Social model arguments for mainstreaming special children can lead to the unhappy placement of children in the mainstream on grounds lacking empirical justification. 'Oppression' and the quest for greater 'equity' may be cited as the reason why special children should be mainstreamed. But these can become accepted positions from which analysis begins, relegating empirical enquiry to a merely illustrative role (Clarke, Dyson and Millward, 1998). Attempts have been made to relate a socially constructed view of 'learning difficulty' to the supposed oppression of those so labelled and link this to emancipatory resistance, drawing on experiences of special schooling decades previously (Armstrong, 2003). However, it has been pointed out (Warnock, 2005) that special children in mainstream schools can be isolated, unhappy, marginalised and disaffected.

The social model is considered 'incompatible with an impairment-specific approach to disabled people' (Oliver, 2004, p. 30). On the other hand, 'people with different impairments experience specific issues and problems' (Shakespeare, 2006, p. 32). Also, evidence-based practice suggests that for different types of disabilities and disorders, different types of provision are effective in encouraging educational progress and psychosocial development (Farrell, 2008, *passim*). A social perspective sees 'difference' as being at the level of the individual. It criticises the construction of categories of pupils because these may ignore individual complexity and lead to arbitrary or oppressive responses.

Responses to individual pupils are therefore ad hoc, hindering the development of an explanatory theory of difference and any formalisation of pedagogy. Socially informed attempts at developing pedagogy concentrate on problem solving and adhocracy, from which it is expected structures and practices that will deliver inclusion and equity will emerge. But this overlooks that once a curriculum is determined, some pupils will always learn within it better than others, perpetuating pupil differences whether categories are constructed or not (Clarke, Dyson and Millward, 1998, p. 166).

Implications for thinking and practice of historical materialism in special education

Someone taking a historical materialist view in special education may not use expressions such as 'disabilities and disorders'. She would be more likely to view the term 'disability' as overarching, although this may refer more to physical disabilities. She may regard disability as experienced by disabled people as a social restriction and see medicalisation and 'normality' as ideologies. Therefore she might question the identification of disabilities and disorders, and challenge some of the assumptions around medicalisation and normality. She may be aware of cultural and psychological processes that shape social phenomena.

In the longer term, she might consider that teacher training could be changed to help the inclusion of disabled students through raising the awareness and knowledge of student teachers about inclusion. A similar agenda might be considered relevant for the continuing professional development of teachers and others.

Regarding attitudes, she may be aware that potentially negative attitudes – her own and those of school staff and others – can hinder greater inclusion. For example, negative attitudes about the capabilities of special pupils could reduce expectations of their progress and development. She is likely to be aware of the influence of negative attitudes to children with non-visible disabilities and might be careful in the use of notions of intelligence and social competence. She may be sensitive to the importance of the school ethos being welcoming to all, teachers becoming committed to inclusion, and celebrating difference. She might seek to enable inclusive social relations.

The curriculum would be examined to see if materials were as accessible as possible for special pupils. More widely, she would consider whether the curriculum conveyed negative expressions of disability and would seek to change these as necessary. This accessibility would be extended to forms of assessment so that these would be accessible and show what students could do rather than focusing too much on what they could not.

She may be aware of the possibility for disabled people of being excluded from the labour market, and of poverty. Consequently, in a practical sense, she may seek to help ensure that disabled students are not economically or socially excluded – when they seek work, for example. This would suggest sufficient emphasis on: work-related skills in the curriculum; team work; developing good literacy, numeracy and computer skills; and offering work experiences and opportunities to get to know the world of work.

In a historical materialist view of special education, less tends to be said about pedagogy than about other aspects of provision, but implications can be derived. Pedagogy is likely to focus on removing barriers so that the concentration is on the teacher and the pedagogy rather than the things the student might find difficult. If a student finds an activity difficult, the task might be modified so that it is achievable and leads to the same learning outcome. For example, aspects of inclusive physical education might be used.

Disabled people might be considered to be devalued socially and culturally and marginalised in society and in different environmental spaces. Integration and full participation in the community for disabled people is likely to be an aim. The special education system, and special schooling, may be regarded as a segregated system that has the effect of excluding disabled people from the education process and from mainstream social life. Special schools may be considered to be failing pupils with regard to personal and social development and offering an inferior education. In a mainstream school context she would be likely to seek to minimise physical barriers in and around the building and grounds, and with regard to classroom furnishings.

Resources would be seen as part of the efforts to improve accessibility and remove barriers. For example she would ensure a wide range of Braille reading material was available as necessary for blind students. Where students communicated through sign languages she would recognise the importance of members of the school community (including herself) learning sign language. Much of this might be seen as partly or mainly a resources issue, so that if resources were found, segregation could be reduced.

Removing barriers might be seen as a key function of physical therapy, which may be seen as enabling movement and en-skilling with a functional purpose. Psychotherapy tends to be little mentioned in a historical materialist perspective, as might be expected in a view that emphasises social factors rather than possible psychological ones.

Critical theory

Adorno, Horkheimer and Marcuse

The term critical theory may refer to any sustained theoretical criticism of traditional views and practices. It may delineate theories taking 'a critical view of society and the human sciences' or seeking to 'explain their objects of knowledge' (Macey, 2000, p. 74). In the second sense, critical theory includes theory aiming to be emancipatory, and is politically left of centre. It may be informed by Marxism and so-called 'Continental philosophy' and embraces aspects of psychoanalysis and psychiatry, politics, economics, history, linguistics and rhetoric. It may be applied to issues of gender, social class and ethnicity. Critical theory informs drama, literature, the visual arts, cinema and film, and architecture (Macey, 2000, *passim*). Various disciplines preceded by the word 'critical' may be underpinned by critical theory: such as 'critical psychology', 'critical psychiatry' and 'critical sociology'.

More specifically, critical theory relates to the work of the Frankfurt School and especially the work of Adorno, Horkheimer, Marcuse and, more recently, Habermas. The Frankfurt School was so named because its ideas were associated with the Institute for Social Research at the University of Frankfurt am Main, Germany. It drew on a range of influences, including Marxism and aspects of Freudian theory.

Adorno (1931) sees critical theory as a study of society recognising tensions between two factors. The first of these is socially foundational work process relationships. The second factor is individual spontaneity. Critical theory aims to rise above these tensions, seeking to give individuals in society a critical understanding of what often goes unquestioned. By getting rid of the illusions of ideology, critical theory aims to encourage a free and self-determining society.

Horkheimer ([1937] 2002, pp. 188–243) delineates the differences between what he calls 'traditional theory' which is essentially scientific theory, and 'critical theory'. So-called 'empirical sociologists' follow traditional theory (p. 191). Horkheimer emphasises the importance of an interdisciplinary mode of thought with sources including philosophy, economics, sociology and history, to examine the dialectical relationship between the individual and society (ibid. pp. 188–243).

Marcuse ([1937] 1972) argues that bourgeois society may liberate individuals from past constraints but does so only if they exert control over themselves. Their apparent (although in fact illusory) freedom is paid for by the prohibition of pleasure. Culture and the arts serve the purpose of calming rebellious desire and embed in individuals an acceptance of the lack of freedom, which is integral to social existence.

An influential concept is that of hegemony. This refers to notions of dominance and control. The Italian Marxist Antonio Gramsci used the term in a way that is now widely taken to be the core meaning. In this sense, hegemony refers to the way the political and social domination of the property-owning class in capitalist society is extensively expressed. This domination in Gramsci's view is not only expressed in ideologies but in all realms of culture and social organisation. In social life, the comprehensive and unquestioned expression of the values of a class-divided society enables such a society to appear natural and inevitable. This removes it from examination, criticism and challenge. It is this aspect of hegemony that distinguishes it from ideology in that hegemony involves the illusion of normal reality by those who are subordinated by the ruling classes. The control of culture is an important element of domination.

Habermas

Habermas is also associated with the Frankfurt School. In his writings informed by critical theory, Habermas draws on Marxist criticisms of ideology. In this context, ideology refers to a distortion of the perception of social relationships. For example, such relationships may be seen through a religious or metaphysical perspective. The alienation associated with a capitalist society gives these distortions the appearance of reality as if they were external features of the world rather than contingent interpretations. The existence of an ideology is explained with reference to material reality. In Marxism, this is the totality of capital, productive forces, and social forms of existence.

Insights into ideology provide insights into power relations and point to routes to emancipation. In advanced capitalist societies, the force of oppression is not at the economic level through the labour market, but through the social and psychological forces of the leisure market (Habermas, 1971). Critical theory for Habermas is informed by the desire to bring about a rational society in which individuals shape their history with fuller awareness and intention (Habermas, 1973).

Critical theory provides a guide for human action, and is emancipatory, self-conscious and self-critical. It differs from positivism with regard to objects of knowledge. Scientific theory and a positivist approach may be seen as making objects of knowledge so as to arrange the external world using objective reason. However, critical theory does not make objects of knowledge in this sense and is said to be non-objectifying (Geuss, 1981). It does not externalise objects of knowledge but remains always critical of the circumstances in which the theory is developing. It tries to explain why social agents accept 'systems of collective representations' (Macey, 2000, p. 75) that do not serve their interests but merely support the current power structure of a society. Critical theory tries to show the falsity of beliefs such as value judgements put forward not as particular conceptions but as unchallenged cognitive structures. It aims to identify false perceptions and analyse how they come to emerge in particular circumstances.

Critical theory hopes to avoid a situation where the objective reason of scientific theory is distorted into a subjective reason in which rationality is regarded only in terms of consumer needs. Such consumer needs are seen as false needs defined by the functioning of a consumer society. The consumer society is regarded as malign in resting on the interests of manufacturers and traders whose motive is profit and who are as interested in creating demand as in fulfilling genuine needs. In such a scenario, society would have ideological control over the desires and feelings of subjects.

Yet these subjects would remain quite unaware of their unhappiness and exploitation. To avoid this, critical theory seeks to show that current society is unsatisfactory and should be changed, and that change to a better and freer society is possible. The critical theorist must show how and where society as presently configured falls short of what is possible and is unsatisfactory. This leads to the second step in which change can be suggested that would lead to a better situation.

Evaluation of critical theory

The broad way in which the expression 'critical theory' is sometimes used has been acknowledged. But its use in the sense developed by the Frankfurt School is comparatively clear. Critical theory offers the prospect of a position from which otherwise unquestioned assumptions and practices can be viewed. The apparent insights it generates may range from unjustified suspicions to the recognition of substantial injustices.

This approach to theory remains constantly critical of the circumstances in which the theory is developing. Critical theory tries to explain why social agents accept systems of collective representations that do not serve their interests but that only support society's current power structure. It seeks to show the falsity of beliefs such as value judgements put forward as cognitive structures. Critical theory aims to identify false perceptions and analyse how they come to emerge in particular circumstances.

However, the basis from which the critical aspect of critical theory takes place is not without difficulties. The suggestion is that most of society accepts ideology because it is by its nature invisible. It is a concomitant of an essentially malign capitalist system. Yet how anyone is able to step outside ideology and recognise it for what it is, an apparently oppressive way of keeping members of society in the dark while they are exploited, is not always clear. Critical theory attempts to address this by pointing to the reflective and self-aware nature of critical theory, but if ideology is so permeating and evasive, even this is not always convincing.

A particular difficulty arises with Adorno and Horkheimer's *Dialectic of Enlightenment* (Adorno and Horkheimer, [1947] 2002). They argue that individuals shape their world through mental and physical activity. The Enlightenment placed scientific and technologically useful knowledge above other forms. Science is seen as an instrument assisting man's need to master the environment. Not just science and technology but rationality itself is seen as implicated in the desire to dominate the environment and other people. The Enlightenment, which was meant to liberate people from nature, has the opposite effect. Capitalism and industrialisation increasingly ensnared individuals and reduced freedom.

Habermas rejects this pessimistic view. If it is held, then it would seem that the destructive effect of the Enlightenment could apply to critical theory itself. It aims at liberation but is bound up with Enlightenment reason, which carries the threat of denying freedom. In *Structural Transformation of the Public Sphere*, Habermas ([1962] 1989) tries to avoid the pessimistic implications of responses to the Enlightenment. The ideals of the historical Enlightenment are seen as expressed in the public sphere. He emphasises the importance of free rational discussion between individuals treated as equals. This has not been achieved but is worth pursuing. In this way, Habermas attempts to avoid the impasse in which earlier developments of critical theory find themselves.

Critical theory in special education

Institutional and professional interests

An early advocate of critical theory in a broad sense was Tomlinson (1987). She argued that reasons why children fail might be found not only in factors intrinsic to the child but equally 'in the social, economic and political structures of a society' (p. 34). It was important to examine the social processes by which achievement was defined. Tomlinson asked who decides what achievement is, in a society where the highest achievers tend to be very predominantly 'white, upper- or middle-class males' (ibid.). She also questioned institutional and professional interests in special education.

Tomlinson used critical theory to interrogate the role professionals might play in 'the social and cultural reproduction of a particular class in our society' (ibid. p. 39). Critical theorists, states Tomlinson, have drawn attention to the way education frequently helps 'reproduce the children of blacks, minorities, working class – the handicapped – into inferior, powerless, social positions' (ibid. p. 34). Cultural capital (Bourdieu, 1984) is sometimes cited as contributing to the process of replicating power and privilege.

Hidden ideology, hegemony and unrecognised forces

In her book, *Who Benefits From Special Education? Remediating (Fixing) Other People's Children*, Brantlinger (2006) develops a critical theory perspective of special education. In examining textbooks on special education, Brantlinger (2006a) refers to critical theorists as highlighting 'the oppressively negative identity constructions for subordinate groups'. Such theorists claim that this is not 'an unintentional by-product of useful practice'. It is an intentional way of keeping 'social hierarchies that benefit dominant groups' (ibid. p. 55). Critical theorists take an 'openly value-orientated or political stand' in examining differences in power so they can be eliminated in contemporary education practices (ibid. p. 56). In a later chapter, Brantlinger (2006b) writes more generally of critical theorising. She refers to Gramsci who sought a new Marxist theory applying to the conditions of advanced capitalism. His view, reflected by Brantlinger, was that intellectuals are 'consciously reflective social analysts' who question their 'own tacit knowledge and class-embedded ideologies' (Brantlinger, 2006b, p. 223).

The hidden nature of ideology is suggested with reference to Foucault's work and also to Apple's (1995) *Education and Power*. Brantlinger summarises Apple's position as asserting that the world is 'discursively constructed by text and that textual discourses – and the ideologies infused in these discourses – hide the particular interests they serve and the uneven power relationships they maintain' (Brantlinger, 2006a, p. 67). She refers to Apple's work (Apple, 1989; Apple and Christian-Smith, 1991) in relation to 'the process by which the curriculum gets to teachers' (Brantlinger, 2006a, pp. 67–68). This process includes 'the politics of textbook production and sales, the ideological and economic reasons behind textbook decisions, and how culture, economy, and governments interact to produce official knowledge' (ibid.).

Brantlinger (2006b) argues that through circulating 'liberal and neoliberal' ideologies supporting the legitimacy of social hierarchies and high stakes testing, dominant groups 'justify their negotiations for advantage' (ibid. p. 201).

Consensus is gained from subordinated groups by the dominant group circulating ideologies 'that obfuscate power imbalances' (ibid.). Ideologies avoid the resistance of subordinated groups. When these groups begin to recognise their lower status or material wealth, further apparent evidence is created by ideology to bolster interpretations favourable to the dominant group (ibid. p. 202).

It is also suggested (Brantlinger, 2006c) that labelling – identifying a child as having a particular disability or disorder, for example – can have negative effects. It takes place within the unexamined ideology of an individualistic view of disability (for example, a 'medical model') (ibid. p. 234, paraphrased). Brantlinger cites Collins's (2003) example of the labelling of a fifth grade Afro-American boy. The boy is angry about being classified as having a learning disability and being placed outside the general classroom and struggles to be seen as competent after being so labelled (Brantlinger, 2006c, p. 234).

The theme of hidden ideology, hegemony and unrecognised forces shaping events to their own ends while appearing to provide benefits to others is pervasive in Brantlinger's (2006) book, *Who Benefits From Special Education? Remediating (Fixing) Other People's Children*. Brantlinger is essentially expressing a critical theory view. The question posed by the book's title, 'who benefits from special education?' explores possible ways in which the immediately obvious response – that the individuals who benefit are the special children – may not be the whole picture.

Benefits to others

Others benefiting include test producers, from income generated by the sale of assessments (Brantlinger, 2006b, pp. 209–210). Transglobal capitalists gain when 'capitalist controlled mass communication' creates themes that 'resonate with the ideologies of neoliberals, neoconservatives' and others (ibid. pp. 210–212).

Media 'moguls' benefit from special education by supporting views leading to standards and accountability (Brantlinger, 2006b, pp. 212–213). As media ownership became more centralised, concern about the decline of society and perceived declining pupil standards became heightened (p. 212). Working–class Americans were 'persuaded to associate with free market capitalism' (p. 212). The 'mostly undocumented sound bites' coalesced into a 'discourse' of school and social decline convincing the public of the need to 'raise standards and hold public schools accountable for improvements in educational – and economic – outcomes' (pp. 212–213). This sort of coverage 'gains and retains audiences' (p. 213).

Other countries are said to have similar 'Hyperbolic concerns' about literacy that are linked to 'fears of workforce collapse and national vulnerability' (Brantlinger, 2006b, p. 213). However there are reports contrary to the view of decline, and student achievement is considered by some to have 'consistently improved' (p. 213). It appears Brantlinger's concerns here is that special education may be identifying pupils in an atmosphere of concern bordering on hysteria that standards are declining. Also, such concerns may not be well founded. Consequently, pupils with disabilities and disorders such as reading disorder may be over-identified or incorrectly identified.

It is also suggested that there are benefits to politicians and 'political pundits' (Brantlinger, 2006b, pp. 213–214). Politicians, it is said, have little to lose and much to gain from pursuing 'improve education' agendas (p. 214). Mandates for high stakes tests and accountability sanction hierarchical relations by 'avoiding the equity or redistributive reform that would undermine their privilege' (ibid.).

Benefits may also be identified for advocates of school privatisation (Brantlinger, 2006b, pp. 215–216). Evidence of public school failure 'provides an incentive for privatisation' (p. 215). Society forsakes the 'pluralist, democratic dream of diverse children coming together in comprehensive public schools' (p. 216). 'Enterprising' school superintendents may manipulate the test pool to make it appear their district is performing better than it is. Students may be classified as disabled to remove them from the test pool and therefore improve school or district test scores. This may, however, have 'negative consequences for retained and classified students' (ibid.).

Professionals and the professions may benefit from school competition and hierarchies (Brantlinger, 2006b, pp. 216–217). As greater numbers of children and youth are found to require special education, the numbers of professionals to help and support them increases. It is stated, special education gives evidence of 'proliferating disability categories and swelling ranks within them' (ibid. p. 216). It is argued the proliferation of 'high incidence disabilities' such as learning disability, attention deficit hyperactivity disorder, and emotional disturbance may relate more to the nature of schools than that of children. Some psychologists present difference as 'deviance'.

There are also benefits for members of the 'educated middle class' (Brantlinger, 2006b, pp. 218–219). High stakes testing offers evidence to the middle class of their worth to provide a 'grounding for privilege' (p. 219). Dominant classes are said to depend on ideologies for the failure of 'Others' rather than admit unfair conditions (ibid.).

Brantlinger (2006b, pp. 222–224) concludes that society should become more egalitarian and there should be more emphasis on redistributive justice. Readers of Brantlinger's book are invited to join a 'countermovement' to resist 'stratifying measures' and strive to 'overcome hierarchical and excluding relationships in school and society' (p. 224).

Evaluation of critical theory in special education

The writings of Brantlinger (2006a, 2006b) offer a good example of critical theory applied to special education. Her views are close to standard critical theory positions in which the influence of the Frankfurt School is apparent. Notions in line with critical theory include hidden ideology and hegemony shaping events to benefit the few while appearing to benefit others.

An important step in Brantlinger's arguments is that the obvious beneficiaries of special education – special children – are not the only ones. They
also include test producers, transglobal capitalists, media moguls, politicians and
political pundits, advocates of school privatisation, school superintendents and
the educated middle class.

The consideration of beneficiaries in special education other than special
children is of course not new. Neither does it necessarily imply that it is
improper for others to be beneficiaries of provision. In a sense, a fire officer
'benefits' from people's houses catching fire but this does not necessarily lead
others to suspect malign motives. Critical theory goes further than this
however in maintaining that those making profits from provision may be
manipulating circumstances to gain greater benefits. One way of suggesting
this is to point to power imbalances.

Power imbalances are seen as influencing the way the school curriculum is
conveyed to teachers and political aspects of textbook production and sales
(Brantlinger, 2006a, pp. 67–68). Dominant groups circulate 'liberal and neoliberal' ideologies supporting the legitimacy of social hierarchies and high stakes
testing. In doing so these groups 'justify their negotiations for advantage', avoid
the resistance of oppressed groups and provide apparent supportive evidence
only in terms of the existing ideology (ibid. pp. 201–202). A related worry is
that special education may be identifying pupils in a manipulated atmosphere
of possibly ill-founded concern that standards are declining. Consequently, special pupils including those considered to have reading disorder may be being
over-identified or incorrectly identified (Brantlinger, 2006b, p. 213). There may
be nothing wrong with people and companies taking profits where they
benefit others, but to manipulate the situation in order to do so is improper.

This may be a particular concern if labelling, including identifying a child as
having a particular disability or disorder, can have negative effects. It may raise
further concern if labelling takes place within the unexamined ideology of an
individualistic model of disability (ibid. p. 234, paraphrased). However, such a
view does not take into account the benefits of labelling where the identification and the label are not manipulated for profit-making or other disputable
ends. There are many examples of the parents of special children welcoming
identification and a label as a boon. Similarly, there are examples where children and young people find identification of a disability or disorder beneficial
where it leads to good provision being made (Farrell, 2006, *passim*).

A further important point is that professionals and the professions may
benefit from school competition and hierarchies (Brantlinger, 2006b, pp. 216–
217). As greater numbers of children and young people are found requiring
special education, the numbers of professionals to help and support them
increase. Special education is said to give evidence of 'proliferating disability
categories and swelling ranks within them' (ibid. p. 216). It is argued that the
proliferation of 'high incidence disabilities' may relate more to the nature of
schools than the nature of children.

This point may be justified in some instances. It is not hard to find schools in which there is a concern that the identification of supposed emotional and behavioural disorders says more about the behaviour management strategies of teachers than it does about the apparent 'within child' disabilities or disorders. However, the response does not have to be that 'therefore all labelling is malign'. An equally justified response is to take care in identifying learners as having particular disabilities and disorders, especially where these are contentious and difficult to assess.

Therefore, Brantlinger's call that society should become more egalitarian with greater emphasis on redistributive justice is not the only response to the situation she depicts. One view might be to hope for a 'countermovement to oppose stratifying measures and work to overcome hierarchical and excluding relationships in school and society' (Brantlinger, 2006b, p. 224). Another might be to be aware of the benefits to others of special educational provision and to examine the possible distortions of identification and provision in special education that may result.

Implications for thinking and practice of critical theory in special education

Someone taking a critical theory view in special education is generally likely to emphasise the influence of hidden ideology, hegemony and unrecognised forces selfishly shaping events while appearing to provide benefits to others. Accordingly, she may point to a range of people that benefit from special education other than special students.

Professionals who support special pupils may attract suspicion. This is because they benefit from increased numbers of pupils being identified and of categories of supposed disabilities being expanded. A critical theorist may look to schools for the explanation of such expansion rather than assume there is a 'real' increase in disorders in the population.

If among those benefiting from special education are test producers, a critical theorist might be critical of the motivation for testing and seek to ensure that where assessments are made there are benefits to students. She may be critical of high stakes testing such as that which determines places in schools and progress within schools.

In pedagogy, there may be a tendency to avoid assuming that any difficulties in learning or development are predominantly with the student rather than the school. It may not be immediately assumed a student has behaviour problems. A school's inability to manage behaviour well or build good relationships might be considered an alternative explanation. There may be caution labelling a student as having a disability or disorder because of its potentially negative effects. An individual/medical view of disabilities and disorders may be regarded as an unexamined ideology.

A critical theorist might question political and economic reasons influencing the production and sale of textbooks, and the way official knowledge is produced by the pervading culture, the economy and governments. She might see in textbooks on special education evidence of oppressive negative constructions of special pupils. This might be interpreted as a deliberate way of retaining social hierarchies that benefit dominant groups.

She may see reasons for student failure in the social, economic and political structures of a society and may question institutional and professional interests in special education. Differences in power may be critically examined so that they can be reduced or eliminated in educational practice. This might suggest a school organisation in which students have a greater say than is typical and where staff organisational structures are flatter than usual.

A critical theorist may be suspicious of those providing therapy as they are beneficiaries of special education. Apparently rising numbers of certain conditions supposedly requiring therapy may be treated with caution and challenged.

Thinking points

- How valid are criticisms of the social model, and does a 'capability approach' offer a viable way of taking into account social and individual models?
- Considering various beneficiaries of special education other than special children, can you develop a list of their possible malign and possible benign motives and outcomes?

Key texts

Historical materialism and social perspectives

Marx, K. ([1859] 1981) *A Contribution to the Critique of Political Economy* (translated from the German by S. W. Ryazanskaya), Moscow: Progress Publishers and London: Lawrence & Wishart. This short book sets out the theoretical prelude to much of Marx's work.

Barton, L. (ed.) (2006) *Overcoming Disabling Barriers: 18 Years of Disability and Society*, New York and London: Routledge. This comprises articles from the journal *Disability and Society*. The first section, on disability studies, includes articles on the social model of disability.

Critical theory

Brantlinger, A. E. (ed.) *Who Benefits From Special Education? Remediating (Fixing) Other People's Children*, Mahwah, NJ: Lawrence Erlbaum Associates. This volume contains several contributions taking a critical theory perspective and a strong penultimate chapter by the editor.

Wiggerhaus, R. ([1986] 1995) *The Frankfurt School: Its History, Theories and Political*

Significance (translated from the German by Michael Robertson), Cambridge, MA: Massachusetts Institute of Technology. The first chapter includes sections on Horkheimer and Adorno. Chapters 7 and 8 refer to the work of Habermas.

Further reading

Marx, K. ([1867] 1992) *Capital: A Critique of Political Economy, Volume 1* (translated from the German by Ben Fowkes), London and New York: Penguin. This well-known text sets out Marx's vision of the nature of political economy.

Oliver, M. (1990) *The Politics of Disablement*, Basingstoke: Macmillan. This book, which is in the 'Critical Texts in Social Work and the Welfare State' series, presents the view of a social model of disability.

Staley, C. E. (1991) *A History of Economic Thought: From Aristotle to Arrow*, Cambridge, MA and Oxford: Blackwell. This places the economic ideas of Marx and Engels (Chapter 11) in the development of economic thought.

Thomas, C. (2007) *Sociologies of Disability and Illness: Contested Ideas in Disability Studies and Medical Sociology*, New York and London: PalgraveMacmillan. The book sets out in historical context some of the areas of overlap and differences between medical and other views.

Chapter 6

Seeing the big picture and making knowledge

Holism and constructivism

Holism

Hegel

The writing of the German philosopher Georg Wilhelm Friedrich Hegel is relentlessly abstract, but the essentials of his holistic views can be conveyed briefly. In Hegel's ([1812, 1813, 1816] 1969) view, structures of thought and reality are ultimately identical, and nothing is in the last analysis real except the 'whole' envisaged as a complex system. The appearance of apparently separate things is not merely illusory, however. Each has some degree of reality in being an aspect of the whole (the 'Absolute'). For Hegel, what is real is rational and what is rational is real. But only when the apparent character of facts has been transformed by viewing them as aspects of the whole can they be seen as rational.

Hegel thought the nature of Reality could be deduced from the view that it must not be self-contradictory. In his view of logic, any ordinary predicate, if taken as qualifying the whole of Reality is self-contradictory. For Hegel, logic begins from 'being' and progresses towards its conclusion, that is, the absolute idea of truth itself (Scruton, [1995] 2002, p. 174). Hegel applies a triadic process of 'dialectic' comprising thesis, antithesis and synthesis. Through dialectic, we are impelled by the force of logic from any suggested predicate of the Absolute to the final conclusion of the dialectic that is, the 'Absolute Idea'. The implication is that nothing can be really true unless it is about Reality as a whole. Through the dialectic method, our views of Reality develop through the continuous correction of previous errors. All these errors arise from taking something finite or limited as if it could be the whole. It is impossible to reach the truth except by going through the stages of the dialectic.

Knowledge as a whole has its triadic movement. It begins with sense perception involving only awareness of an object. Next, through sceptical criticism of the senses it becomes purely subjective. Finally it reaches the stage of self-knowledge in which subject and object are no longer distinct. Self-consciousness is therefore the highest form of knowledge. The highest kind of knowledge is that possessed by the Absolute and because the Absolute is the whole, there is nothing outside itself for it to know. What is real in a person is his participation in Reality as a whole. As we become more rational, this participation is increased. The Absolute Idea is something like thought thinking about itself. For Hegel there is more reality (and more value) in wholes than in their parts. A whole increases in reality and value as it becomes more organised. Such is Hegel's conception, but it was Jan Christiaan Smuts, the South African statesman, who sought to link holism with evolution.

Smuts

Smuts (1927) coined the term 'holism' to suggest an integrative and pre-existing principle in the universe guiding evolution and the emergence of human consciousness. This principle was non-material and dynamic. Accordingly, natural wholes are regarded as more than the sum of their parts (Smuts, 1927, *passim*). Holism is a fundamental, real factor 'operative towards the creation of wholes in the universe' not an artificial construction of thought (ibid. p. 88). The explanation of 'Nature' therefore cannot be 'purely mechanical' and a mechanistic concept of Nature only has justification in the 'wider setting' of holism' (ibid. p. 89).

Smuts (1927) seeks to interpret matter, life and mind so as to 'present them as successive more or less continuous forms and phases of one great process'. They can also be presented as 'related progressive elements in one total coherent reality' (p. 51). While matter, life and mind are often viewed separately they intermingle in human beings who are compounded of all three. Darwin's theory of evolution implies that 'both life and mind have developed from matter or the physical basis of experience' (ibid. p. 8). Life is considered to have arisen in chemical substances more subtly structured than those of inorganic compounds (ibid. p. 49, paraphrased). Where matter and life differ is in 'the character of their activities' (ibid. p. 52).

The two fundamental structures of the universe are seen as:

- the atoms in 'the world of matter'
- the cell in 'the world of life'.

(Smuts, 1927, p. 62)

Metaphorically, the cell is 'the point where matter or energy aroused itself'. The cell became 'active from within, with activities and functions which reveal its inner character and nature' (ibid. pp. 65–66). Cells are considered to cooperate for a common purpose. The 'whole meaning and significance of Metabolism is that activities of the cell are not self-centred or self-regarding' (p. 79). Smuts sees 'structural order' as the characterising inorganic matter. He also argues that there is 'active co-operation and unity of action superadded as the characteristic of the organism' (p. 84). Mind is the third 'great fundamental structure of holism' (p. 233). Personality, built on the prior structures of matter, life and mind, is 'the latest and supreme whole which has arisen in the holistic series of Evolution' (p. 270).

Six stages are identified in which holism expresses itself in the 'progressive phases of reality'. The first is 'definite material structure or synthesis of parts in natural bodies' – a chemical compound, for example. Next is the 'functional structure' of living bodies, as in a plant. Thirdly, there is specific co-operative activity 'coordinated or regulated by some marked central control', as in an animal. Next is conscious central control, culminating in personality. Penultimately come group organisations, such as the State, in which human associations become 'super-individual'. Finally, there are holistic ideals or 'absolute Values' operating as creative factors on their own account (Smuts, 1927, p. 109).

The whole in each individual case is 'the centre and creative source of reality' (ibid. p. 120). There is an infinity of wholes, 'comprising all the grades of existence in the universe'. Holism is the general term to include all wholes under one concept. It is in this sense that holism comprises 'all wholes in the universe' (ibid.).

Other uses of the term 'holism'

Some uses of the expression 'holism' differ from those of Hegel or Smuts. Where holism is used in a more general and looser sense, it may be maintained that a part cannot be described or explained fully without reference to the whole of which it forms an element. Rain in a particular area cannot be accounted for or interpreted without reference to the wider weather fronts and trends of which it is a partial expression. Another understanding of holism is that an account of parts of a whole and their interrelations does not sufficiently provide an account of the whole. A car may be described in terms of all its component parts and their individual relationships, but such an account will fall short of including the overall functioning of the machine.

Holism sees the object of the human sciences in terms of structures and systems. The study of individual social agents is not the proper object of study and the structures and systems cannot be reduced to these individual social agents. In ecosystemic studies in the social sciences the ecosystem is regarded as a unity whose parts are interdependent. An ecosystemic approach to explaining behaviour is likely to look much more widely than the individual person and examine interrelationships between the person and their family, and the community. Gestalt psychology theorises that the organising principle of the brain is holistic. The tendency of the brain to make wholes is suggested in experiments in which complete forms are seen rather than discrete parts (Bruce, Green and Georgeson, 1996).

Evaluation of holism

Russell ([1949] 1996) rejects Hegel's argument that a part cannot be understood without reference to a whole. Russell takes the example of the statement, 'John is the father of James' (p. 673). Hegel would say that before one can understand that statement, one must know who John and James are. Even knowing who John is will involve knowing all the characteristics and relationships that constitute him, so we would tend towards an account of the whole universe, not just a statement about two people.

But if this were so there would be no point from which any knowledge could begin. In fact, in order to use the statement 'John is the father of James' one does not need to know everything about the people but only enough to identify them. If Hegel were right, concludes Russell ([1949] 1996), no word could begin to have meaning (p. 673). This is because we would have to know all the meanings of all the words in order to state the properties of what the word designates. Hegel thought (incorrectly) that if enough were known about a thing to distinguish it from all other things, then all its properties could be inferred by logic (Russell, [1949] 1996, p. 674). Russell also takes the view that even if Hegel's metaphysical argument were right, it does not necessarily follow that his ethical argument, that wholes are preferable or more valuable than parts, is correct (ibid. p. 671–673).

Scruton ([1995] 2002) maintains that much of Hegel's metaphysics develops 'independently of any epistemological basis' (p. 182). Hegel avoids the first person standpoint by a process of abstraction, which abolishes the individual and therefore leaves no room for a theory of knowledge. This makes it fatally vulnerable to sceptical attack so it has 'little to bequeath to us but its poetry' (ibid.).

Holism for Smuts (1927) does not rule out a mechanical view of the universe. Certainly the explanation of 'Nature' is not considered to be 'purely mechanical' but within a wider context of holism, a 'mechanistic concept of Nature has its place and justification' (p. 89).

In the vision of Smuts (1927) a great whole was a sort of tendency to completeness. Within that there were different levels of 'wholes' that could be recognised as coherent. Where a particular notion of a 'whole' is selected, for example in a systems view, it is not always easy to justify the reason why the boundaries of that supposed whole have been selected for the purpose of study or explanation. It is important that this is made clear at the outset. This relates to Russell's ([1949] 1996, p. 673) criticism that the apparent boundary of whole would be the whole universe. If one stops short of that rather ambitious goal, it is necessary to specify where and why.

As suggested, 'holism' may not imply the sense coined by Smuts (1927) but the expression may be used more loosely. In such usage, it may be argued that a part cannot be fully described or explained without reference to the whole of which it is an element. Or it may be said an account of parts of a whole and their interrelations does not sufficiently provide an account of the whole. In the social sciences, holism may imply that the object of the human sciences is structures and systems and that these cannot be reduced to these individual social agents. In ecosystemic studies in the social sciences it may be implied that the system forms a unity whose parts are interdependent.

Another way of considering the relationships between what appear to be parts and what appear to be wholes is to consider their interdependence. If whole and part are interdependent, then the whole may not be understood without reference to parts and the parts. Their relationship to each other may not be fully understood without relation to the whole. Holism can sometimes seem as though it is prioritising a perceived whole over a perceived part.

In ecosystemic studies, while it can be fruitful to look wider than individual and small group interactions, the definition of what is taken to be the 'whole' that is to be studied may not always be explained. The apparently arbitrary border at which the whole is delineated is sometimes difficult to justify. In psychology, holism has been criticised for offering 'vague and inadequate' laws and only descriptive principles without a model of perceptual processing (Bruce, Green and Georgeson, 1996, p. 110).

Holism in special education

A holistic and mechanistic paradigm

An article by Heshusius (1989, reprinted 2004a) takes a holistic perspective, with constructivist aspects. Heshusius is critical of what she describes as a 'Newtonian mechanistic paradigm' in special education. She contrasts a holistic paradigm to a mechanistic paradigm. The holistic metaphor is not of a machine but a human being. In a holistic paradigm, assumptions 'directly emerge from human knowing and relationality' (Heshusius, 2004a, p. 42). The approach aims to 'transform our understanding into something qualitatively, and therefore fundamentally, different' (ibid.).

Heshusius refers to Gergen (1985) to the effect that knowledge, rather than being something people have somewhere in their heads, is more like a shared activity (Heshusius, 2004a, p. 43). For Heshusius, however, lodging everything within social interchange and nothing in a person's head is a 'too simplistic monism' (ibid.). But, she argues for the importance of 'conceptualisations that focus on social interchanges as a medium through which knowledge and knowing come about'. Human reasoning seems to comprise 'understandings that are constituted in the context of personal use and purpose' (ibid.).

A holistic process of motivation in education involves 'understanding students in *who they are*' (Heshusius, 2004a, p. 46, italics in original). It also involves letting students' instruction emerge 'in a dialectical manner in the process of coming to understand them and in assisting them to become empowered as persons'. Learning in this perspective involves working with the experiences students bring to education and making these 'the object of debate and confirmation' (ibid.).

Holistic education understands human behaviour as 'constructive, self-organising, and self-regulating' (Heshusius, 2004a, p. 50). Learning is regarded as understanding relations rather than 'pieces of knowledge'. It is the personal, social and cultural 'construction of meaning' by the child, based on who the child is and what he knows (ibid.). Progress is seen as 'transformative' and occurring when concepts are seen in new ways. Teachers, make use of children's 'natural curiosity and natural interests' (ibid. p. 51).

Assessment takes account of how the child thinks and reasons. It focuses on what children do over a period of time in 'natural, interactive settings'. More broadly, rather than testing and ranking, assessment involves 'documenting real life-processes and accomplishments' (ibid. p. 51). A holistic curriculum stresses for all learners interdependence 'among concepts and areas of study' and 'among individuals and the larger world around them' (ibid.).

More recently, Heshusius has stated that holistic principles 'are not a set of techniques or strategies'. Instead they are, 'a different way of looking at relations that make up life and learning, and out of which different educational practices, relations, and pedagogies emerge' (Heshusius, 2004b, p. 179). Observable outcomes, while expected to become different, are not 'a *direct* target for change' (ibid. italics in original). Heshusius draws a parallel with holistic medicine. Traditional medicine deals with 'specific symptoms typically in isolation from the rest of the patient's life' while holistic medicine is seen as an approach that 'heals, rather than treats symptoms, while in healing the symptoms are also "treated"'(ibid.).

Heshusius (2004b, pp. 181–182) distinguishes between positivist and holistic approaches to 'meaningful' curriculum content. In a positivist approach, she suggests, the curriculum content comes first and is used to measure a pupil's performance. The meaning and 'real life purpose' is, as it were, added afterwards. In a more holistic perspective, the real life meaning is primary and 'learning engagements *emerge* from that' (ibid. p. 181, italics in original).

The parallel with holistic medicine becomes clear. The positivist is seen as dealing with the superficial externals of learning, the vehicle of the curriculum, (the symptoms) rather than the meaning to the child (parallel with the process of healing). Therefore meaning is not developed. By contrast, the holistic educator deals with meaning for the child (real healing) and in doing so also ensures the child learns the activities (the symptoms).

Holism and interpretations of behaviour

A holistic approach would be conversant with a systems perspective of some situations. Where a child was considered to experience a disorder of conduct, a systems approach would suggest looking beyond the child to examine the context of the unacceptable behaviour. A child's school may be seen as a system in which a child can be envisaged as having a problem but where the problem may also be understood in relation to the school as a whole.

By contrast, a linear model of behaviour seeks a rationale to explain the apparent causes and effects of behaviour as an individual phenomenon. A systems approach, taking an interactional and holistic view, sees behaviour as existing within a context. Through a sort of circular causality, sequences of interactions are considered to contribute to the continuation of a 'problem'. It becomes more pertinent to ask *how* rather than *why* a problem happens (Dowling and Osborne, 1994, p. 5). If a parent, sibling or a teacher 'punctuates' the circle of interaction by focusing on a point in the cycle, this can create an impression of a linear cause and effect which may be unfounded.

A cycle of interaction may perpetuate regular conflict between a particular pupil and a certain teacher. The teacher may punctuate the circle at the point of a pupil's perceived rude and uncooperative classroom behaviour, seeing the problem as being predominantly within the pupil. The pupil may punctuate the circle at the point of the teacher's perceived negative and demeaning attitude towards him, seeing the situation as being largely precipitated by the teacher. Neither individual is considered 'correct', there being no absolute perspective from which behaviour can be viewed and evaluated. Certain components of a school system may sustain unacceptable conduct. If these elements of routine and procedure were modified, the school's aims might still be fulfilled without sustaining the conflict with a pupil.

Holism and reading

Holism can also suggest a certain view of teaching and learning of reading. Kauffman and Sasso (2006) are critical of holism, associating it with a constructivist philosophical position. They maintain, in the teaching and learning of reading, holism could suggest that language cannot be meaningfully analysed or taught in component parts and that words should not be segmented. This might be contrasted to direct instruction in sound and symbol correspondence (ibid. p. 73).

Evaluation of holism in special education

The analogy of traditional and holistic medicine

Heshusius (2004b) depicts holistic medicine as an approach that 'heals, rather than treats symptoms, while in healing the symptoms are also "treated"' (p. 179). This is a revealing analogy suggesting, on Heshusius's part, a distrust of science as well as a lack of understanding of medicine. It would not be easy to find a physician who took the view that medicine is about dealing only with the symptoms of a condition or a disease. Symptoms are an indication of a condition or a disease. Once this has been identified – as far as is possible through taking account of the symptoms – it is the disease, not the symptoms that are treated.

Consider the example of haemophilia A. In severe cases, symptoms include frequent spontaneous bleeding from early in life (Kumar and Clark, 2005, p. 472). If a physician were to treat the symptoms, anything that might appear to arrest the bleeding might be considered sufficient. But in fact the cause of the condition is known to be a reduced level of Factor VIII:C, a blood–clotting agent. It is this that is treated by administering factor VIII concentrate by intravenous infusion (ibid. p. 473). This intervention is a treatment of the condition, not just the symptoms. The focus in 'traditional' medicine in this example is on healing in the sense of tackling the cause of the condition, not purely on treating symptoms.

Holistic medicine seeks to look more widely than some approaches to traditional medicine and is also focused on healing. But the debate is surely about what are the boundaries of investigation and study (as well as treatment). Perhaps physicians keep both issues in mind. If possible they will directly tackle the biological source of symptoms. Where causes are not fully known, a physician may prescribe medication that reduces unpleasant symptoms, as with the common cold. With certain viruses, medication may be prescribed to combat symptoms, allowing the body to defend itself against the virus.

Positivistic and holistic education

If this analogy is taken back to the issue of positivistic and holistic education, it can also be instructive. It implies that more positivistic traditional approaches to education tackle only the external superficialities of learning and development (the 'symptoms'). It does not address the important and more central issues of learning and development in the context of the whole child. By contrast, it is implied that holistic approaches take a broader view of a pupil into account, and in doing so enable the more meaningful learning and development to take place. Consequently, the outcomes are the 'symptoms' of learning and development, and these are enhanced in the process of recognising the whole child.

But it is not clear why these approaches are presented as intractable dichotomies. Indeed, both might offer useful ways of thinking about children and learning. Whether one takes a positivist or holistic approach, the curriculum will include content that has to take account of what society thinks is valuable – being able to read, for example. The positivist might prioritise externals such as phonic reading and supplement this by reading in context and for meaning. The intention is to educate the child to read for meaning but part of the road to that objective may be to learn the mechanics. The holistic educator might focus more on holistic approaches to reading (such as sight vocabulary) but would presumably have to supplement this by working on the mechanics of reading. A holistic educator may have an orientation towards the relationship between parts and whole, but would not deny the parts.

The first approach has the advantage of building confidence in the child who can quickly learn to read phonetically regular words, but it has to be supplemented by reading for meaning. The second method has the strength of conveying early that reading is for meaning, but needs to be supplemented by phonetic learning. In practice, good teachers skilfully draw on both strategies to get the benefits of both.

For Heshusius (2004b), the core problem with the positivist paradigm is a need to 'reduce all complexity to simple units of measurement', 'reduce wholes to no more than the sum of parts', 'see the act of knowing as identical to the act of control' and 'see oneself as being a privileged knower and the prestige that comes with it' (p. 212). It is to avoid such a standpoint, that Heshusius prefers the holistic perspective. The reason that holism is seen as especially important in special education appears to be that it is perceived that special education is much more concerned with positivist perspective and behavioural approaches than general education. Therefore there is a tendency to provide special children with a more limited education than other children. Another limitation might be the use of measurement. It is suggested the normal curve leads to ranking children in a hierarchical order according to a particular factor. This could mislead if it does not offer insight into how a child learns and how an educator should teach.

If this is the case, a holistic perspective might act as a corrective to curricula that might be too narrow and insufficiently attuned to children's interests. A holistic view might help ensure that learning is not too exclusively skills-based and overconcerned with elements and parts.

Assessments made at one point in time may be helpful in indicating to employers and others how a student can marshal knowledge and skills in a concentrated period of time. But assessment could be extended to include more naturalistic evaluations. In other words, a holistic perspective might help ensure against possible weaknesses of a positivist perspective.

Implications for thinking and practice of holism in special education

Someone taking a holistic view in special education may be critical of a perceived overly scientific view of special education. She may see holistic principles as offering a different way of looking at relations that make up life and learning, leading to different educational practices, relations and pedagogies.

A holistic curriculum may be preferred, stressing for all learners interdependence among concepts and areas of study and among individuals and the larger world around them. Real-life meaning would be primary, and learning engagements would emerge from that. Someone advocating holism may consider that the holistic educator deals with meaning for the child and in doing so also ensures the child learns the activities. Both pedagogy and the curriculum would (to use former descriptions popular in the 1960s) be more child-centred.

An advocate of holism may see assessment as taking account of how the child thinks and reasons, focusing on what children do over a period of time in natural, interactive settings. Assessment would document real-life processes and accomplishments. This would suggest that students develop a portfolio of work to show what they can do and that they would be assessed continuously rather than in a single examination.

A holistic educator may view understanding as made in the context of personal use and purpose. She might take the view that instruction should be allowed to emerge dialectically from coming to understand students better and helping them become empowered as individuals. Learning would involve working with the students' previous experiences and debating and confirming these. Human behaviour would be seen as constructive, self-organising and self-regulating. She might regard learning as understanding relations, the personal, social and cultural construction of meaning by the child based on who the child is and what he knows.

Someone taking a holistic perspective may see progress as transformative and occurring when concepts are seen in new ways, suggesting teachers make use of children's natural curiosity and natural interests. In the teaching and learning of reading, she may prefer a whole-word strategy, and consider that language cannot be meaningfully analysed or taught in component parts and that words should not be segmented.

She would be likely to take a holistic view of behaviour and its context rather like that of a systems approach. A holistic educator would want to ask how rather than why a problem happens. She might look at components of a school system that may sustain unacceptable conduct, looking to modify them.

Resources and their use would be likely to reflect a view of learning as whole rather than in small parts. In the teaching of reading this would suggest a resistance to phonics resources and more of an emphasis on whole-word reading and 'reading for meaning'. In mathematics, resources might be aimed at developing insights rather than learning step-by-step techniques, perhaps without understanding their overall meaning and context.

Therapy might fit into a holistic view of educational provision. For example, psychodynamic psychotherapy might be seen as exploring past events and present behaviour and building a relationship with a therapist. Related to this might be an expectation that at various points in the therapy, holistic insights will illuminate past and present concerns and behaviour.

Relationships may be identified between holism and constructivism. To some extent, holism looks beyond individuals and at the environment and other factors that help explain how individuals learn and develop. Holism may suggest that the individual constructs knowledge through interacting with environmental influences. It is to constructivism that the chapter now turns.

Constructivism

In philosophy, constructivism is an approach to epistemology (the branch of philosophy concerned with the nature and scope of knowledge). Constructivism espouses the view that knowledge is produced or constructed. Objects in an area of enquiry are constructed; they are not already there in some preordained completeness, 'waiting' to be discovered. The epistemology of constructionism implicates 'the knower and meaning-maker in the process of knowing and understanding' (Paul, Kleinhammer-Tramill and Fowler, 2009, p. 4). What is known depends on 'the observing, interpreting and knowing mind' and is 'created rather than discovered'. The relationship between the creating mind and what it is investigating is 'vague and unspecified' (ibid.). In constructivism, there is a 'fundamental coherence of fact and value'.

Piaget

The work of the Swiss biologist and researcher into child development, Jean Piaget, was concerned with structures and indeed his work may be related to a structuralist perspective (Piaget, 1970). His theory of cognitive (intellectual) development can also be seen as constructivist in that he regarded development as involving a process of adaptation to the environment. Piaget developed a stage-related theory of cognitive and affective development (Piaget and Inhelder, [1966] 1969; Piaget, 1970).

For Piaget, cognitive development involves gradual, progressive adaptation, for which the child was innately prepared, and which leads to adult reasoning. The process of adaptation involves a reciprocal interaction between the child and his environment. In order to survive, the child acts on his environment through physical activity to control aspects of it. He comes to be able to act appropriately towards aspects of the environment, and to this extent begins to understand them. The knowledge the child has can 'assimilate' features of the environment. However, the environment also acts upon the child's cognitive structures ('schemas'). It does this by presenting new features, requiring the cognitive structures to change to 'accommodate' them.

Essentially, assimilation concerns interpretation, and accommodation has to do with the adaptation of cognitive schemes (general concepts). A baby may explore an object that is soft and pliant and *assimilate* its properties. Later, he may manipulate a similar looking object that happens to be hard and resilient and will *accommodate* these features. In cognitive development, the individual moves towards adaptation in which schemas most closely represent an external reality in which he can operate. The motivation to learn comes from the disparity between an existing schema and incoming information, which requires the child to accommodate it.

Assimilation and accommodation are the mechanisms of 'equilibration'. Equilibration is a self-regulatory process allowing external experience to be incorporated into internal structures (Gallagher and Reid, 1981, p. 233). Piaget sees learning as an 'internal process of construction' (ibid. p. 2), by which knowledge is gained through direct experience of the environment. But learning also occurs from interplay between maturation, experience and equilibration (p. 172).

Piaget identified typical ways of responding, considered to be associated with qualitatively different sequential stages of cognitive development. He believed this sequence to be universal and invariable because it was determined by maturational factors. Piaget's stages were considered to occur at approximate ages: sensorimotor stage (0–2 years), pre-operational stage (2–7 years), concrete operational stage (7–11 years), and the formal operational stage (11–12 years onwards).

To take one example, in the sensorimotor stage (Piaget and Inhelder, [1966] 1969, pp. 3–27), the baby initially exhibits reflex survival behaviours such as sucking and grasping. These develop into the formation of a very basic notion of causality and his role in making things happen. These 'cognitive sub structures' constructed by the child form a basis for subsequent perceptive and intellectual development (ibid. p. 3).

Vygotsky

Interpretations of Piaget's theory can suggest that maturational 'within child' factors largely account for slower than typical cognitive development. On the other hand, Byelorussian psychologist Lev Vygotsky emphasises the importance to intellectual development of a child interacting with others who are more advanced thinkers (Vygotsky, [various dates] 1978).

Aspects of Vygotsky's work inform current debates on the relative contribution of individual factors and social/cultural factors in special education (Minick, 1987; Wertsch, 1985). Vygotsky's view of psychology and of special pedagogy highlights cultural influences on development (Knox and Stevens, 1993, p. 5, translators' introduction).

Two strands of development are identified: the biological or natural and the historical-cultural. The historical-cultural strand is internalised through the use of psychological 'tools' such as concepts, signs and symbols, and language. This strand is superimposed on natural behaviour and substantially transforms it so that natural behaviour is grounded in the structures of personality. Where there is a failure of biological function, another line of development, helped by socio-cultural 'tools', can operate. This enables other biological functions to circumvent the weak point and form a psychological superstructure over it. In this way, the disability or disorder does not come to dominate the whole personality (Knox and Stevens, 1993, pp. 12–13, translators' introduction).

While Vygotsky accepts that blindness and deafness are biological, he recognises that education must cope with their social consequences (Vygotsky, [1925–1926] 1993, p. 66; [n.d.] 1993, p. 107). A child should be educated, not as a blind child, but primarily as a child, so that special pedagogy does not become completely focused on the disability and disorder alone (Vygotsky, ([1924] 1993, p. 83). Vygotsky argues for recognising a child's strengths, not only his weakness (Vygotsky, [1925–1926] 1993, p. 68; [1927] 1993, p. 56). Constructing the educational process on the basis of compensatory drives involves ensuring the child's strengths are concentrated on compensating for the 'defect', and selecting in proper sequence tasks that will over time shape the entire personality 'from a new standpoint' (Vygotsky, [1927] 1993, p. 57).

Vygotsky's concept of a zone of proximal development, described in *Mind in Society*, has attracted particular attention (Vygotsky, [various dates] 1978). Vygotsky distinguishes between two judgements of a child's developmental level. The first is that determined by his independent problem solving. The second is the level of potential development established through problem solving with adult guidance. The zone of proximal development is the difference between these two levels of development. The implication is that a child's learning can be enhanced if he is presented with activities within his zone of proximal development.

Focusing on language, Gergen (1995) identifies three assumptions relating to a social constructionist view. First, meaning in language is achieved through social interdependence, language being a social medium for making meaning. Secondly, meaning in language is dependent on the context, so that children are socialised into already existing meanings and languages. Thirdly, language primarily has a communal function (pp. 17–40).

In constructivist research, data is regarded as inseparable from the theorising agent or theory in the sense of 'the construction that interprets and gives the data meaning'. Objectivity is not possible and indeed is not always 'a desirable goal' (Paul, Kleinhammer-Tramill and Fowler, 2009, p. 4). Constructivism has been defined as 'a nonpositivist perspective grounding several qualitative approaches to research' (ibid.). Constructivism, associated with qualitative methods, has been contrasted to positivist approaches and related quantitative methods, although it has been maintained there is much common ground in constructivism and positivist methods (Padgett, 2004, pp. 5–7). Grounded theory (Glaser and Strauss, 1967) originated as a positivist perspective but has more recently been developed in a constructivist orientation (Clarke, 2004; Charmaz, 2006; Alvarez McHatton, 2009, pp. 127–141).

Evaluation of constructivism

Constructivism is appealing to those attracted by the view that the world may not be out there waiting to be perceived but may be created in an interactive way by the individual perceiving it. It accounts for differing perspectives and supports a negotiated perspective of knowledge and reality. Yet there is a difficulty in determining which of several differing perspectives might be the most supportable, and recourse to a more positivist view of the world seems difficult to avoid under such circumstances.

Evaluation of Piaget's ideas

Among criticisms of Piaget's theory is that sensorimotor cognition, contrary to Piaget's hypotheses, can be argued not to be redeveloped in the mental realm. Instead, sensorimotor knowledge appears to be augmented by further experience either through action or through language. Logical development may also depend on a child's ability to reflect metacognitively on his knowledge and on the extent to which he can inhibit competing knowledge that is interfering with his applying the logic (Goswami, 2008, p. 386).

'Neo-Piagetian' perspectives, (Morra et al., 2007) tend to be informed by neuropsychology. They take a constructivist approach and regard cognitive development as divided into qualitatively different stages. But they tend to relate increasingly complex stages with the child's information-processing system rather than with logical properties.

The ages Piaget considered to be typical of his various stages may be somewhat conservative (Wood, 1998). Repeating some of Piaget's experiments indicate that the language the experimenter uses – and how the child perceives what is being requested of him – influences outcomes. Some young children can reason at a more advanced level than Piaget had been able to demonstrate (Donaldson, 1978). Similarly, Piaget may have underestimated the capacity of newborn infants for imitating and remembering, evidence for which was not available in Piaget's time (Goswami, 1998). Within the 'sensorimotor stage', the age at which infants develop cognitive representations has been shown to be much earlier than Piaget indicated (Goswami, 2008, chs 1 and 2).

Piaget did not regard language as having a facilitating effect on thought. However, the interaction of language and thought is now considered influential in cognitive development. Although Piaget's theory embraced interaction between the child and the environment, the environment seemed to take a rather passive role. The potential for modifications in the child's environment to enhance development may not have been given sufficient attention. While Piaget regarded the child's maturation as being largely a matter of unfolding development, modern interpretations allow for the importance of structuring the environment to encourage such development.

Evaluation of Vygotsky's ideas

Regarding social constructivism, an aspect of Vygotsky's writings has been the focus of attention for supporters of a social constructivist view. This is the aspect concerning the intellectual development of a child interacting with others who are more advanced thinkers. In particular the notion of a zone of proximal development (Vygotsky, ([various dates] 1978) has attracted much interest. Indeed Vygotsky's view of psychology and of special pedagogy does place importance on cultural influences on development (Knox and Stevens, 1993, p. 5, translators' introduction).

However, other aspects of Vygotsky's work sometimes receive less attention. He maintains (Vygotsky, [1927] 1993) that a child with a disability or disorder develops differently from peers (p. 30). The child's development represents a creative physical and psychological process involving compensation and adaptation. Via this process a child's personality is shaped through restructuring adaptive functions and forming new processes brought about by the disability or disorder. This creates new, circumventing paths for development (ibid. p. 34 paraphrased). Importantly, while typical development can be conditioned by culture spontaneously and directly, atypical development cannot (p. 42 paraphrased).

Consequently in special pedagogy, a special child's cultural development involves a particular line of development, guided by distinctive laws, and with specific difficulties and means of overcoming them (p. 43 paraphrased). Those citing Vygotsky in support of exclusively social constructivist views relating to special pedagogy appear to ignore or be unaware of his recognition of the importance of biological influences as well as cultural ones.

Constructivism in special education

The importance of meaning

This section examines the perspective of constructivism in special education, drawing on Poplin's earlier articles (Poplin, 1988a, 1988b) and on the views of Danforth and Smith (2005).

An advocate of constructivism in special education is Mary Poplin of Claremont Graduate University, California. In two articles, published in the same edition of *The Journal of Learning Disabilities* in 1988 (Poplin, 1988a, 1988b), she argues against a 'reductionist' approach, a positivist perspective emphasising behavioural learning theory. As an alternative to reductionism, Poplin favours an approach based on structuralist philosophy, constructivist theory and holistic beliefs.

Poplin suggests schools need to concentrate on helping students 'develop new meanings in response to new experiences rather than to learn the meanings others have created' (Poplin, 1988a, abstract). This she argues (Poplin, 1988a) implies changes in the principles of learning in designing classroom instruction. Principles drawn from the structuralist, constructivist and holist literature imply a different classroom environment, where instruction is from students' perspectives rather than through 'preferred methodologies, mandated curricula, and student assessments and diagnoses' (ibid. abstract). More recently, Poplin and Cousin (1996) have argued for a more eclectic view, drawing on strengths of both constructivist and positivist insights.

As an approach to teaching and learning, constructivism has been described as assuming that 'knowledge is actively made rather than passively taken in' (Danforth and Smith, 2005, p. 6). Students are seen as bringing the 'total of their experiences' to the classroom. When a lesson is taught, students 'bring all their meanings and identities to the interaction with the course content'. This interaction 'yields a wide variety of emotional responses and intellectual results'. Teachers seek to engage pupils in an 'ongoing dialogue of meaning' and in a 'shared interaction that opens up channels of thought and communication' (ibid.). Constructivist theories of learning and knowing assume that reality is interpreted. Meaning does not reside in a simple objective way in the world, but in 'the interaction between our minds and the stuff onto which we project our meaning' (ibid. p. 35).

A constructivist orientation

Danforth and Smith (2005) seek a constructivist approach to what they call 'troubling students'. In fact, they draw on a constructivist interpretation of Piaget's work (pp. 36–38), social constructionism (pp. 38–39) and critical theory (pp. 44–48). They call this 'critical constructivism' (pp. 6–7 and *passim*).

Danforth and Smith (2005) describe constructivist/constructionist pedagogy as encompassing several features (pp. 39–44). There is an emphasis on cognitive structures. Learning is seen as an 'ongoing process of interaction between self and environment' and involves a 'qualitative change in the learner's thinking' (p. 40). Teachers focus on how students 'make sense of their texts or contexts' (ibid.). Students are given opportunities to construct meanings and to share these constructions. This gives the teacher opportunity to 'interpret students' understandings' and connect with students' meanings to help mediate students' learning (ibid.).

Connection is emphasised. Constructivist pedagogy involves pupils 'actively making connections' between present knowledge and new learning (ibid. p. 41). It encourages learning 'social engagement with others and within contexts'. Learning occurs through engagement, and language is 'the currency of engagement'. Social constructivism concentrates on learning as 'a social process' (ibid.) including group discussions. Teachers are not seen as 'experts in all contexts' and it is not assumed there is 'only one "real world"' (ibid. p. 42). Indeed 'diverse meanings, cultures, perspectives and ways of learning are extremely valued' (ibid.).

In a constructivist approach, relationships, contexts and cultures are emphasised. Teachers, parents, board members and (crucially) students are invited to participate 'in creating meaning, choosing curriculum, and having input on decisions that affect the class' (ibid.). However, this is not meant to negate the teacher's responsibility to pupils to be in a 'position of authority in the room' (ibid. pp. 42–43). Multiple views 'can be represented side by side' as there is not only 'one "real world"'(ibid. p. 43). Constructivist pedagogy is viable 'in an emerging global society that includes an endless array of meanings, contexts, languages and cultures' (p. 44). It does not so much teach students facts about the world, but 'engages meanings in relationship to various worlds' (ibid.).

Furthermore, it suggests that instead of searching for a single 'right' answer, learners ask 'right within what context, for whom, and at what moment in time' (ibid.).

Regarding knowledge and power, it is suggested that constructivist approaches for learning 'provide a foundation for social change by making conscious the ways in which knowledge is socially constructed' (ibid. p. 47). 'Reification' is considered a process by which subjective views are made to seem objective truths. 'Dereification' is promoted by 'making conscious our participation in constructing the truths that structure our social realities' (ibid. p. 47, and following the views of Berger and Luckmann, 1971).

A constructivist approach to 'troubling students'

Among applications of a constructivist approach, Danforth and Smith (2005, p. 177) cite the 'Keeping Every Youth Successful' programme in St. Louis County. It comprises a range of support services for students from Kindergarten to Year 12 having emotional and social difficulties, aimed at helping them remain in the general education building. 'Keeping Every Youth Successful' is an ecological approach seeking to link preventative efforts across different settings, including the classroom and the home.

It links interventions between individuals and their families to changes in 'environment and systems' (Danforth and Smith, 2005, p. 181). 'Keeping Every Youth Successful' alters 'process in the system' by involving many agents of change, including teachers and classmates. It conceptualises individual and family functioning 'in terms of interactions between and among the broader social environments' (ibid.).

Danforth and Smith (2005, pp. 180–200) provide a vivid description of this innovation. A feature of teachers involved with the project was the way they viewed themselves as influencing the world around the child. This included the classroom, teachers' attitudes, and teachers' practice, as much as the child himself. Teachers often supported children with behaviour difficulties in the general classroom, reporting that their work consisted less in assisting the student and more in working on themselves (Danforth, personal communication, February, 2010).

Other approaches may have constructivist elements or orientations. These include peer mentoring and close and supportive partnership with families. Circle of Friends (Forest and Lusthaus, 1989) is a way of encouraging networks of social support in general education classes for pupils with cognitive impairments.

Evaluation of constructivism in special education

Among difficulties for a constructivist position is that of demonstrating the moral basis on which some constructed meanings and truths are preferred to others, and the reluctance to draw on positivist notions of truth and meaning.

In writing about knowledge and power in relation to constructivist theory, Danforth and Smith (2005) state constructivist approaches for learning 'provide a foundation for social change by making conscious the ways in which knowledge is socially constructed' (p. 47). They describe 'reification' (following Berger and Luckmann, 1971) as a process by which subjective views are made to seem objective truths (Danforth and Smith, 2005, p. 47). 'Dereification' is helped by 'making conscious our participation in constructing the truths that structure our social realities' (ibid. p. 47).

Yet if 'knowledge is socially constructed' (Danforth and Smith, 2005, p. 47), how is knowledge which tells Danforth and Smith (e.g. pp. 44–45) they should listen to women, homosexuals and bisexuals, individuals with disabilities, and poor people more justified than the socially constructed knowledge that tells others they take account of the views of white, heterosexual, middle-class, non-disabled males? Educational practices of the past are described as being characterised by 'deep-seated racism, sexism, classism, and ableism' (ibid. p. 45). But how does constructivism demonstrate that these views are not merely other people's socially constructed truths? In other words, it is unclear how constructivism of itself provides a moral grounding for challenging 'truths' held by others with whom one might disagree. This lack of moral compass is linked to the reluctance of constructivism to draw on positivist 'truth'. In this sense, a constructivist is likely to accept that all truth is on shaky ground.

For example, Danforth and Smith (2005, pp. 47–48) discuss an example from Kohl (1994) concerning a Texas school that had children of Mexican decent. Their textbook stated that the first people to settle Texas came from New England and Virginia. Mexican children 'felt insulted' by this as if it negated the claims of their ancestors to have settled in Texas first (Danforth and Smith, 2005, p. 47). If these two apparent truths, that Mexicans settled first or that New Englanders settled first, were merely socially constructed, there would be no deciding between them. It is because, in positivist terms, there is a truth out there that goes beyond socially constructed knowledge, that such claims can be tested and decided upon.

However, to say that something is socially constructed is not however to say that it is not real or does not have real consequences. Social construction does not dispense with all claims to truth or evidence. In the case of the settlement of Texas, the textbook in question contradicted what, at the time it was being used in classrooms, was the best knowledge that historians had been able to establish.

The dependence on positivist views of reality and truth are evident in Danforth and Smith's (2005) reference to the non-behavioural model of Consistency Management and Cooperative Discipline (Freiberg, 1999). This model, state Danforth and Smith (2005, p. 73) has been 'researched extensively in controlled studies'.

Implications for thinking and practice of constructivism in special education

Someone who supports a constructivist approach may see reality as interpreted by individuals and meaning as made in the interaction between our minds and that on to which we project our meaning. She may view knowledge as being actively made. Constructivist approaches for learning might be seen as offering a foundation for social change. This would be by making conscious the ways in which knowledge is socially constructed and our participation in constructing the truths that structure our social realities.

Curriculum content might be broadly similar to that of any school, but the way that content is conveyed is likely to be more exploratory and less directly didactic than in some schools. Given that diverse meaning and views are likely to be considered valuable, the curriculum might be more varied than usual. Different student views and opinions – about music or art, for example – may be accepted rather than closing exploration too early by conveying the teacher's own preferences.

A constructivist may consider that multiple views can be represented together. She might believe that instead of searching for a single right answer, learners should question the notion of 'right' in different contexts, for different people and for different times. Although there may be times when understanding and skill development will need to be assessed, this may be done in an ongoing way, reflecting the gradual development of knowledge and skill rather than its sudden mastery.

A constructivist educator may wish to help students develop new meanings in response to new experiences. Efforts may be made to ensure instruction is from students' perspectives. She may regard students as bringing their experiences, meanings and identities to the interaction with the course content, leading to various emotional responses and intellectual results. A constructivist teacher may seek to engage pupils in an ongoing dialogue of meaning, in a shared interaction opening up channels of thought and communication. She might see learning as an ongoing process of interaction between self and environment, involving a qualitative change in the learner's thinking.

She would tend to give students opportunities to construct meanings and share these constructions. At the same time she would interpret students' understandings and connect with their meanings to help mediate their learning. Constructivist pedagogy will tend to be seen as involving pupils actively making connections between existing knowledge and new learning. The teacher may see learning as occurring through engagement, with language as a facilitator for this. Learning through group discussions is likely to be valued. A constructivist may value diverse meanings, cultures, perspectives and ways of learning and might emphasise relationships, contexts and cultures.

Resources and their use would tend to reflect the view that meanings are made. Consequently the environment would be likely to be rich in learning resources so that experience of these can be used to help the student build their own meanings. There would tend to be less telling and more experiencing and discussing.

Organisation would tend to be more democratic than is perhaps usual. Someone supporting a constructivist perspective may consider that students should be invited to participate with others in creating meaning, choosing the curriculum, and influencing decisions affecting the class.

She may support peer mentoring and close and supportive partnership with families, and approaches such as Circle of Friends that encourage networks of social support in general education classes for pupils with cognitive impairments.

Concerning pupils with emotional and behavioural difficulties, a constructivist might support particular approaches and might be reluctant to see emotional or behavioural disorders as being largely within the individual.

She might argue for the importance of drawing on a range of support services to link preventative efforts across school, home and other settings. She may favour linking interventions between individuals and their families to changes in 'environment and systems'. Agents of change might include teachers and other class members. She might see individual and family functioning in terms of interactions between and among the broader social environments. The teacher's way of influencing the world around the child (classroom, teachers' attitudes and teachers' practice) would be considered important.

Thinking points

- Can you think of examples in special education where holistic and positivist approaches might be compatible, and is the teaching of reading one such example?
- What do you consider to be the weaknesses and strengths of a constructivist approach to special education?

Key texts

Holism

Smuts, J. C. ([1926] 1999) *Holism and Evolution: The Original Source of the Holistic Approach to Life* (edited by Sanford Holst), Thousand Oaks, CA: Sierra Sunrise Books. This seeks to link holistic ideas with Darwinian theory.

Gallagher, D. J., Heshusius, L., Iano, R. P. and Skrtic, T. M. (2004) *Challenging Orthodoxy in Special Education: Dissenting Voices*, Denver: Love Publishing. In this book is a reprinting of Heshusius's 1989 article 'The Newtonian Paradigm, Special Education, and Contours of Alternatives: An Overview' and a chapter by Heshusius entitled, 'From Creative Discontent Toward Epistemological Freedom in Special Education: Reflections on a 25-year Journey'.

Constructivism

Burr, V. (1995) *An Introduction to Social Constructionism*, New York: Routledge. This is a basic introduction.

Danforth, S. and Jo Smith, T. (2005) *Engaging Troubling Students: A Constructivist Approach*, Thousand Oaks, CA: Corwin Press/Sage. This book draws eclectically on constructivist theory, social constructionism and critical theory to outline an approach for 'troubling' students.

Further reading

Hegel, G. F. W. ([1812, 1813, 1816] 1969) *The Science of Logic* (translated from the German by A. V. Miller), London: George Allen & Unwin. In this text, Hegel discusses 'being', 'nothing' and 'becoming' and many of the other topics touched on in this chapter.

Karpov, Y. V. (2005) *The Neo-Vygotskian Approach to Child Development*, New York: Cambridge University Press. This book critically presents Neo-Vygotskian attempts to integrate child development (cognitive, motivational and social) with the role of children's activity as mediated by adults in development.

Singer, P. (2001) *Hegel: A Very Short Introduction*, Oxford: Oxford University Press. Given the difficult and abstract nature of Hegel's writing, this introduction is a good entry point.

Chapter 7

Underlying structure and its dismantling

Structuralism and poststructuralism

Structuralism

The development of structuralism

Structuralism developed in the mid-1900s, spreading to a wide range of disciplines, particularly in the social sciences. Having emerged in linguistics, it influenced architecture, economics, literary criticism, social anthropology, sociology and psychoanalysis. Previously, the French philosopher Sartre's popularisation of existentialism had been pre-eminent, in which a self-directing individual could shape his own world (Sartre, [1947] 1957). In some respects structuralism was a reaction to this, giving the structures of society a more determining role. In France, under the influence of the anthropologist Lévi-Strauss and the psychoanalyst and psychiatrist Jacques Lacan, the intellectual centre of interest shifted from existentialism to structuralism (Dosse, 1967).

Yet the development of structuralism may be better understood as having different motivations and implications in different disciplines: in economics its origins and application differ from those in architecture. Its adaptability to different areas of study certainly aided the spread of its influence, yet structuralism attempts to apply a single methodology to the human sciences and so unify them. In each discipline, whether linguistics or social anthropology, the conceptual system is interrelated so that each concept determines and is determined by the others in the system.

Saussure

An important figure in the development of linguistics is the Swiss linguist Ferdinand de Saussure. Structuralism places particular emphasis on aspects of Saussure's *Course in General Linguistics* (Saussure, [1915] 1966). In discussing the 'nature of the linguistic sign' (pp. 65–70) Saussure distinguishes:

- The sign
- The signifier
- The signified.

Language is presented as a system of 'signs' comprising a 'signifier' (for example a spoken word, 'tree') and a 'signified' (the concept, tree). The sign does not gain its meaning from being directly linked to the external object or 'referent' to which it refers (the real tree). Signs gain their meaning through the similarities or differences to other signs in the system. Saussure ([1915] 1966) coins the term 'semiology' to refer to a potential science that 'studies the life of signs within society' (ibid. p. 16).

In Saussure's work, a distinction may be made between *'langue'* and *'parole'*. *Langue* refers to social aspects of language organised into a system to convey ideas. Signs that make up *langue* are arbitrary and only agreed by convention, and it is the differences between signs that give them their meaning. *Parole* refers to individual aspects of language or the 'manifestations of *langue* in individual speech acts' (Macey, 2000, p. 224). At the level of *parole*, the linguistic innovations of individuals can modify *langue* but only by becoming elements of a system over which individuals have no control. Dialectic between *langue* and *parole* drives linguistic evolution (ibid.).

The Prague Linguistic Circle

Saussure influenced the linguistics of the Prague Linguistic Circle (the 'Prague School') founded by a small number of linguisticians in 1926 and dissolved in 1950. They developed the functionalist notion that the so-called meaning of linguistic units is the function they have in the language system.

A key figure was the Russian linguist Roman Jacobson, a founder member of the Moscow Linguistic Circle and a longstanding associate of the Prague School. His study of sound patterns and phonology led to a theory of the 'phoneme', a phonological unit with a particular function that cannot be further reduced to smaller units with similar functions. For example /d/ and /b/ are phonemes conveying the difference in meaning between 'dig' and 'big'. There are a small and limited number of phonemes having distinctive features and these can be arranged in binary oppositions, which can explain the workings of language. This analysis of phonology is therefore compatible with Saussure's notion that language comprises a system of differential signs.

In examining aphasia (loss of speech function), Jacobson contrasted:

• contiguity disorder
• similarity disorder.

In contiguity disorder an individual is unable to combine simple units into more complex ones. Jacobson associated contiguity disorder with metaphor and a paradigmatic dimension of language. A paradigm is a set (for example phonemes) from which lexical items are selected and is sometimes compared with a meal menu.

An individual with similarity disorder has difficulty selecting the suitable unit and might say 'cat' for 'dog'. Jacobson associated similarity disorder with metonymy and the syntagmatic dimension of language. A syntagm is the combination of units (for example a sentence) and is sometimes compared with a meal in which menu items having been selected are put together.

In Jacobson's structural view, language is organised around the poles of:

*   metaphor (which can be mapped on to the dimension of the paradigm)
*   metonymy (which can be mapped on to the dimension of syntagm).

(Jacobson and Halle, 1956)

A structuralist view of language then is that it is not a means of expression at the will of the speaker. The speaker does not commandeer language and make it link with external objects to provide meaning. Rather language exists as a binary system independently of the observer. It is not a tool to express the thoughts of the speaker but is itself a precondition of thought and social existence.

Lévi-Strauss

Lévi-Strauss in an essay 'Structural Analysis in Linguistics and Anthropology' published as a chapter of *Structural Anthropology* (Lévi-Strauss, [1958] 1977) envisaged a revolutionary potential of the contribution of structural linguistics to social sciences. With visionary optimism, he states, 'Structural linguistics will certainly play the same renovating role with respect to the social sciences that nuclear physics . . . has played for the physical sciences' (p. 33).

Lévi-Strauss seeks a level of conceptualising that allows structures to be identified. These include aspects of kinship and elements of mythologies. Once these concepts are found, it becomes possible to identify structures of which even the participants may be unconscious. For Lévi-Strauss, 'The term "social structure" has nothing to do with empirical reality' rather it concerns 'models that are built up after it' (ibid. p. 279). Structure is a method to be applied to any kind of social studies.

A structural view in sociology

Sociological theories are sometimes broadly considered as typifying a structural view or a social action view. Structuralism in sociology approaches analysis assuming that the social environment structures people's actions. Differences in the way structures operate are thought to determine the way people behave.

Marcel Mauss, the French sociologist and anthropologist, made important contributions to what became known as structural anthropology. Emile Durkheim (Mauss's uncle) developed a model of social analysis focusing on structures and functions in society, a contribution that can be seen as a precursor to structuralism in sociology. Talcott Parsons, the American sociologist who established the Harvard University sociology department, helped develop and extend the structural perspective in sociology, advancing theories sometimes described as structural-functionalist. Meighan and Harber (2007, pp. 285–298) provide a summary of the structuralist view in relation to the sociology of education.

Piaget and structuralism

Structuralism links to constructivism. In structural anthropology Lévi-Strauss ([1958] 1977) searches for a level of conceptualising that allows structures such as kinship to be identified. Once these concepts are established, an observer can identify structures unknown even to the participants. 'Social structure' does not therefore refer to empirical reality but to subsequent models (ibid. p. 279, paraphrased). Through conceptualising or constructing an analysis of observations, structures can be hypothesised. In this sense structuralism can be constructivist.

In his book *Structuralism*, the Swiss biologist, psychologist and philosopher Jean Piaget ([1968] 1971) discusses a range of disciplines. These include mathematical and logical structures, physical and biological structures, psychological structures, linguistic structuralism, structuralism in philosophy, and economics, law and anthropology.

For Piaget ([1968] 1971) structure draws on the key ideas of wholeness, transformation and self-regulation (p. 5). *Wholeness* involves 'structures' (wholes) and 'aggregates' (composites formed of independent elements) (p. 7). While structures may still have elements, these are subordinated to laws which define the system or structure as a whole. All structures from mathematical groups to kinship systems are, 'systems of *transformation*' (p. 11, italics added) and elements of structure themselves undergo 'transformation or change' (p. 12). *Self-regulation* entails 'self-maintenance and closure' (p. 14). Transformations inherent in a structure 'never lead beyond the system but always engender elements that belong to it and preserve its laws' (ibid.). Structure then concerns wholeness, and involves transformation and self-regulation.

Piaget discusses three possible origins of structures in the context of the development of intelligence. Structures may be given, derived, or dependent on the subject. Structures may be *given* rather like 'eternal essences'. This suggests 'innatism', perhaps similar to predetermination, but because hereditary origins are regarded as biological it is unclear how the structures might have been first formed. *Derived* structures may arise from the physical world, as Gestalt psychologists (e.g. Köhler, 1947) propose, or arise in history, as the French historian of ideas Michel Foucault suggests (Foucault, [1961] 2006; [1963] 2003; [1966] 2002; [1969] 2002; [1975] 1991; [1976] 1998; 1980). This implies a theory of contingent emergence. Structures *dependent on the subject* imply a constructivist account (Piaget, [1968] 1971, p. 60).

Evaluation of structuralism

Structuralism has been widely influential. Saussure ([1916] 1966) influenced the Prague Circle, which developed a functionalist notion that the 'meaning' of linguistic units is the function they have in the language system. Jacobson's analysis of phonology is compatible with Saussure's notion that language comprises a system of differential signs. Lévi-Strauss ([1958] 1977) recognises the potential contribution of structural linguistics to social sciences (p. 33), seeking a level of conceptualising that reveals structures that may remain unrecognised by the participants (p. 279). Durkheim developed a model of social analysis focusing on structures and functions in society and Talcott Parsons helped extend the structural perspective. Piaget ([1968] 1971) discusses structuralism in a wide range of disciplines. At the zenith of structuralism, it appeared that structure was a method applicable to any kind of social studies.

Structuralism reached its greatest influence in the middle of the 1960s, after which criticisms of poststructuralism and other factors seem to have dimmed its radiance. A suggested turning point was the Johns Hopkins University conference on 'The Languages of Criticism and the Sciences of Man' in 1966. In a discussion session at this conference, Derrida referred to his decon-struction as a criticism of structuralism (Derrida, 1966). Other criticisms of structuralism involved doubts about its political uses (Macey, 1994).

Appraisals of structuralism may seek to criticise it for what it is not. As structuralism looks not so much at the content of social transactions but at their structure, it can be perceived as missing what is more important. On the other hand, in anthropology, Lévi-Strauss argues that structures can reveal meanings unrecognised by the very participants acting within the structures.

The implication, of course, is that such hidden meaning can be very impor-tant. Some distinctions are challenged. Lévi-Strauss drew a difference between nature and culture, which was intended to help cross-cultural analysis. But the adequacy of this position is open to question. An area of contention is that the position takes a universal view of nature and culture as if each can always be recognised as distinct. Such a universalism can obscure the many cultural configurations of 'nature'.

Structuralism and special education

Psychology and structures

Piaget drew on structuralism as a method in his psychology. For Piaget as a constructivist, construction is a precondition of structure. His interest in episte-mological (knowledge) categories of cognition – space, quantity and causality, for example – led to a 'structuralist' semiotic analysis of symbolic forms. (Semiotics concerns the study of signs and their processes such as designation, symbolism and metaphor.) Arguing that structure must be integrated with notions of development, Piaget supported genetic structuralism. He took a dynamic view of learning in which what is perceived is modified by existing structures of knowledge through 'assimilation'. The knowledge structures are themselves modified to 'accommodate' the perceptions.

In *Structuralism*, Piaget ([1968] 1971) considers the mathematical 'group' as a structure (Piaget, [1968] 1971, pp. 17–18) consisting of a set of elements such as the integers, positive and negative, and an 'operation' – for example, addition (ibid. p. 18). Structuralism in relation to logic is concerned with recovering what is 'beneath' the operations codified by axioms (ibid. p. 31). That is, it concerns the underlying features of operations. Piaget argues that there are physical structures, which while they are independent of us, 'correspond to our operational structures' (ibid. p. 43).

In a living organism, structure is seen as 'a systematic whole of self-regulating transformations' (ibid. p. 44). The organism is both a 'physico-chemical system among other such systems and a source of a subject's activities' (ibid.). If we knew our own organism thoroughly enough it could provide the key to a general theory of structure because it is both a complex physical object and the originator of behaviour (ibid. paraphrased).

Psychological structures may be traced to Gestalt psychology (Köhler, 1947) which is concerned with the 'wholeness' of perception. But Piaget's theory is structural in its use of principles of 'equilibration' (Piaget, [1968] 1971, p. 57). In considering the origins and development of intelligence, Piaget (ibid. p. 60) rejects the notion of *contingent emergence* as being 'pretty nearly incompatible with structure', certainly logico-mathematical structures (ibid. p. 61). He does not embrace the idea of *preformation*, where structures are seen as static, 'closed and autonomous wholes' (ibid. p. 61). He prefers a formational or constructional hypothesis, in which structures are seen as operational 'transformational systems' deriving from one another by largely abstract 'genealogies'. Self-regulation requires self-*construction* (ibid.).

Relationship between structure and construction

In the context of the development of intelligence then, Piaget argues for a formational hypothesis. Human structures are generated in a way that constantly passes from 'a simpler to a more complex structure' (Piaget, [1968] 1971, p. 62). There are certain givens, from which the construction of logical structures 'takes off'. However, the data do not 'contain' what is in the course of construction derived from them or based on them (ibid.). These initial structures, Piaget calls 'general coordinations of actions'. These are the connections common to all sensorimotor coordinations (ibid. pp. 62–63). Piaget identified stages of sensorimotor development involving behaviour which has innate roots but becomes 'differentiated by function' (ibid. p. 63). Such behaviour shows the same functional factors and structural elements.

At the sensorimotor level, development involves the functional factors of 'assimilation' and 'accommodation'. These are processes by which the child adapts to the environment and maintains equilibrium between the external and 'internal' worlds.

The structural elements are: certain order relations, subordination schemes, and correspondences. *Order relations* concern 'the order of movements in a reflex act, in a habitual act, in the suiting of means to ends' (Piaget, [1968] 1971, p. 63). *Subordination schemes* refer to the subordination of comparatively simple schema to more complex ones, for example the subordination of grasping to pulling (ibid. paraphrased). *Correspondences* are involved in 'recognitory assimilation' in which an experience is recognised to be similar to previous experiences and is assimilated into the child's cognitive structure (ibid.).

As the primary assimilation schemes become 'mutually co-ordinated', equilibrated structures that make up for a certain degree of reversibility become established (Piaget, [1968] 1971, p. 63). For example, a 'spatialised and objectivised' form of causality enters into intentional acts, such as getting at items by using supports (ibid. p. 64).

For Piaget, structuralism is essentially a method (Piaget, [1968] 1971, p. 136). It is not exclusive, nor does it suppress other dimensions of investigation (ibid. p. 137). It is intimately associated with construction. Piaget states, '*There is no structure apart from construction*' (ibid. p. 140, italics in original).

Piaget and child developmental stages

Piaget's stage-related theory of child development involves cognitive (especially logical) development and affective development (Piaget and Inhelder, [1966] 1969; Piaget, 1970). Cognitive or intellectual development was envisaged in terms of gradual and progressive adaptations. The child was innately prepared for these and they led to adult reasoning. This process of adaptation involves a reciprocal interaction between the child and his environment.

More may be said about the important processes of 'assimilation' and 'accommodation'. In the context of child development, *assimilation* involves a child bringing in some experience into what he already knows so that cognitive structures are developed by the 'outside' experience being incorporated into the cognitive structure. *Accommodation* involves a child modifying his thought structures because a new experience does not fit into what he already knows. He adjusts his previous way of thinking. Underlying these processes is a tendency for the child to match experiences with cognitive structures so that there is a balance or equilibrium between the two.

Piaget identified typical ways of responding, considered to be associated with qualitatively different sequential stages of cognitive development. The sequence was believed to be universal and invariable because it was determined by maturational factors. Piaget's stages were considered to occur at approximate ages as follows:

- The sensorimotor stage (0–2 years)
- The pre-operational stage (2–7 years)
- The concrete operational stage (7–11 years)
- The formal operational stage (11–12 years onwards).

In the sensorimotor stage (Piaget and Inhelder, [1966] 1969, pp. 3–27), the baby begins by exhibiting reflex survival behaviours, such as sucking and grasping. Subsequently, the infant forms a very basic notion of causality and his role in making things happen. These 'cognitive sub structures' constructed by the child form a basis for subsequent perceptive and intellectual development (ibid. p. 3).

In the pre-operational stage (ibid. p. 128), thinking is still limited by egocentricity. The child's judgements are based on: sensory evidence, a logic lacking reversibility, and a focus on one aspect to the exclusion of others. Children's responses in various experiments were taken to indicate they are unable to recognise that matter maintains or 'conserves' its volume even in different forms.

The two operational stages (concrete and formal) involve the use of organised systems of mental actions that interrelate. They transform reality through 'internalised actions' grouped into 'coherent, reversible systems' (ibid. p. 93). In the concrete operational stage, complex and systematic mental problem solving (in which mental representations are used) can take place in relation to concrete and actual events. After the age of 11 or 12, in the formal operations stage, concrete operations are restructured and subordinated to new structures enabling the child to reason hypothetically (ibid. p. 152). The child becomes able to use the form of logical systems to create and test hypotheses about real or imagined events. For example, in a scientific task, a child will be able to work out, using a balance scale, the rule relating weight and the distance from the centre of the fulcrum.

Piaget and Inhelder ([1966] 1969) proposed sub-stages within the sensorimotor stage relating to modified reflexes and various reactions. These are:

- modification of reflexes stage (0 to 4 weeks)
- primary circular reactions (about 1 to 4 months)
- secondary circular reactions (about 4 to 10 months)
- the coordination of circular reactions (about 10 to 12 months)
- tertiary circular reactions (about 12 to 18 months)
- interiorisation of schemes (about 18 months to 2 years).

Piaget's work provides insights into cognitive impairment. He describes typical development of children, specifying usual chronological ages when certain indications of development are often noted and can be assessed. These ages are only broad indications but are considered typical and are expected to follow one another in a specified sequence.

Some educators maintain that these indicators of development can help inform understanding of the development of children who have cognitive impairments. These children may have a chronological age that is far above the level at which they are functioning. A young person of 14 or 15 years old may be functioning in a way more typical of a child of say one or two years old. It is argued that a study of the development typical of this younger age can help understanding of the student with cognitive impairment. Any parallels are not assumed to be exact, but are considered informative and may act as aids to establishing suitable provision, including pedagogy.

Evaluation of structuralism in special education

The views of Piaget and his co-workers have made a major structuralist contribution to special education. In Piaget's constructivist perspective the environment and the individual are taken into account and structures may be dependent on the subject (Piaget, [1968] 1971, p. 60). Yet a concern remains that the notion of mental structures may be a limiting view of human development. Such mental structures may suggest a constraint on development that could lower the expectations of educators.

Piaget's hypothesis that sensorimotor cognition is redeveloped in the mental realm has been questioned. It has been argued instead that it is important that sensorimotor knowledge is augmented by further experience, either through action or through language. A different emphasis is that logical development may also depend on two other factors – a child's ability to reflect metacognitively on his knowledge, and the extent to which a child can inhibit competing knowledge that is interfering with his applying the logic (Goswami, 2008, p. 386).

Some evaluations concentrate on the outcomes of Piaget's research. They question the ages at which some of Piaget's stages are said to emerge. Piaget's data included experiments indicating the child's stage, such as lack of 'conservation' of matter at the pre-operational stage. Later research has indicated that the language the experimenter uses – and how the child perceives what is being requested of him – influences the outcomes of these experiments. It is evident that some young children can reason at a more advanced level than Piaget was able to show (Donaldson, 1978).

Piaget may have underestimated the capacity of newborn infants for imitating and remembering. Within the sensorimotor stage, the age at which infants develop cognitive representations has been demonstrated to be much earlier than Piaget could demonstrate (Goswami, 2008, chs 1 and 2). Such evidence reinforces the concern that taking Piaget as the last word might lead to lower expectations for educators. However, these findings tend not to challenge the main thrust of the structural and constructivist nature of Piaget's theory.

Neo-Piagetian perspectives (Morra et al., 2007) are often informed by neuropsychology. Like the earlier Piagetian perspective, they take a constructivist approach to cognitive development and consider that cognitive development consists of qualitatively different stages. However, neo-Piagetians tend to relate increasingly complex stages not so much with logical properties as with the child's information-processing system.

Implications for thinking and practice of structuralism in special education

Someone influenced by structuralism might take a dynamic view of learning in line with that of Piaget. She may take the view that what is perceived is modified by existing structures of knowledge through 'assimilation' and that knowledge structures are themselves modified to 'accommodate' the perceptions. A structuralist may take a sequential view of child development reflecting Piaget's stages. She may modify such a view in the light of later findings in child development but may maintain the essential notion of progressive development integrating earlier stages. Most of the remainder of the present section concerns students with profound cognitive impairment. This is because aspects of Piaget's work have been adapted to inform provision for these students.

A structuralist may consider that Piagetian indicators of development can help inform understanding of the development of special children. The study of typical child development, it may be thought, can help understanding of the older student with cognitive impairment. Such study can be informative and may act as an aid to establishing suitable provision.

In line with these views, a structuralist may value certain developmental approaches and implications to learning and development. She may take care not to assume development is limited and too tightly related to sequential steps. At the same time she may seek to use knowledge of regular child development to inform understanding of the development of atypically developing children.

A structuralist may have an interest in and a commitment to so-called developmental curricula. Someone taking a genetic epistemology view may consider it helps shed light on provision for pupils with profound cognitive impairment. She may take the view that Piaget's theory can help an understanding of very early development that can illuminate work with children with profound cognitive impairment in encouraging sensory and motor development. She might consider that sensorimotor development underpins later development in typically developing children and that a pupil with profound cognitive impairment is likely to spend a considerable time responding and exploring in ways typical of this stage.

Someone taking a structuralist view may take account of proposed substages within the sensorimotor stage (Piaget and Inhelder, [1966] 1969), namely modification of reflexes stage; primary circular reactions; secondary circular reactions; the coordination of circular reactions; tertiary circular reactions; and interiorisation of schemes. Accordingly, she might look at a range of responses of the pupil in different settings and with different activities and materials and consider whether the pupil's responses are best characterised as being typical of a certain sub-stage.

Certain questions would arise. Is the child showing 'modification of reflexes' such as mouthing different objects? Is there evidence of 'primary circular reactions' connected with the child's own body? Using careful observation, she might assess the sub-stage at which the pupil appears to be functioning. Although Piaget considered the sub-stages as naturally evolving, later views accept the possibility of encouraging and accelerating progress through education.

Such a thread of the curriculum would be seen as providing an underpinning of very small steps of development to try to recognise and celebrate increments of development of children and young people with, for example, profound cognitive impairment. It might be linked to similar small-steps assessments.

Taking this view, a structuralist might seek to provide activities to consolidate progress in that sub-stage. If the pupil is demonstrating 'secondary circular reactions' she might encourage these and widen them to different reactions, objects and situations. If the apparent 'secondary circular reactions' are obsessive in nature they have the potential to hinder learning and development. So she might offer opportunities to extend the repertoire. The secondary circular reactions might be developed in potentially meaningful and appropriate situations, such as throwing and catching a ball with a partner in a physical education session or mixing ingredients in a cookery session. The teacher can then consider whether encouraging activities typical of the next sub-stage might be suitable.

Resources associated with a structuralist view of profound cognitive impairment, for example, are likely to reflect the importance of responses at very early stages of development. Examples are sensory rooms, computer-operated switches, or aids to very early communication, such as objects of reference.

An approach to organisation reflecting a structuralist perspective that can help the learning of students with profound cognitive impairment is creating a 'responsive environment' (Ware, 2003), important in the development of social, intellectual and communicative development. This involves creating an environment in which pupils with cognitive impairment 'get responses to their actions, get the opportunity to give responses to the actions of others, and have the opportunity to take the lead in interaction' (p. 1). A particular type of organisation is 'room management', in which groups of pupils and adults are assigned to one of three roles: individual helper, group activity manager, or mover (Lacey, 1991). The individual helper might be involved with one pupil at a time on intensive work, varying the time depending on the pupil, the task and other factors. The group activity manager makes sure that the other pupils are occupied, perhaps with a game or some other activity not focused intensively on skill building. The mover ensures the smooth running of the group, dealing with visitors, preparing materials, or tidying away.

Therapy for students with profound cognitive impairment is likely to be closely integrated with other aspects of provision. Speech and language therapy, physiotherapy and occupational therapy are likely to be an integral part of the curriculum and part of the provision for learning and development.

Poststructuralism

It has already been pointed out that the zenith of the influence of structuralism coincides with the rise of poststructuralism. Poststructuralism is sometimes equated with postmodernism and identified as a thread in various forms of critical thought. It is associated with several positions. There is reluctance to set discourse in any theory with metaphysical origins. Enlightenment thinking, or the 'Enlightenment project', is treated with suspicion. Poststructuralism is sceptical about overly scientific approaches and, in some interpretations, views meaning as unstable and plural. Poststructuralism is often related to the ideas of Derrida, especially deconstruction.

Derrida's Of Grammatology *and its structure*

An introduction to some of Derrida's concerns is *Of Grammatology* (Derrida [1967] 1997). Grammatology involves the scientific study of writing systems. In *Of Grammatology*, Derrida examines texts by several authors, including Saussure, Lévi-Strauss and Rousseau, in exploring the relationships between speech and writing. One theme is that previous analyses of language have given speech a preferential place over writing and that speech has been depicted as more primary. Writing has been seen as a derivative of speech. The assumed closeness of speech (logos) to meaning leads Derrida to use the term 'logocentrism' for what he sees as the prioritisation of speech.

Of Grammatology comprises two parts. Part 1 introduces Derrida's position. This includes a criticism of what he sees as 'logocentric metaphysics' (Derrida [1967] 1997, e.g. pp. 8, 43) and an introduction to the enterprise of 'deconstruction' (ibid. e.g. pp. 14, 19, 24). It includes commentary on an aspect of Saussure's ([1915] 1966) *Course in General Linguistics*.

Part 2 concerns analysis of several texts relating to Derrida's thesis. In his chapter 'The Violence of the Letter', Derrida considers 'The writing lesson', a chapter from Lévi-Strauss's *Tristes Tropiques* (Lévi-Strauss, [1955] 1961) concerning the introduction of writing to the Nambikwara people. In a chapter ". . . That Dangerous Supplement . . ." Derrida ([1967] 1997, pp. 141–164) examines an aspect of Rousseau's *Confessions* (Rousseau [1769 and published posthumously in 1782] 2005). A substantial amount of the remainder of Part 2 deals with Rousseau's *Essay on the Origin of Languages* (Rousseau [n.d and posthumously published in 1781] 1986).

Derrida's reading of Saussure

A brief examination of Derrida's reading of Saussure will serve to point out some key terms and concerns. Saussure ([1915] 1966, pp. 65–70) in the *Course in General Linguistics* presents language as a system of 'signs'. A sign comprises a 'signifier' (e.g. a spoken word, 'tree') and a 'signified' (the concept, tree). The sign does not gain its meaning from being directly linked to the external object to which it refers (the real tree), but through the similarities or differences to other signs in the system. Saussure ([1915] 1966) discusses the relative importance of language and writing (pp. 23–25). He states that writing exists 'for the sole purpose' of representing language (p. 23). Sometimes people may attach more importance to the 'written image of a vocal sign than to the sign itself' (p. 24). But this Saussure considers a mistake, rather like believing that more can be learned about a person by looking at a photograph of them than at the real person. He prioritises the spoken over the written word.

Derrida examines the implications of Saussure's argument that the sign is 'arbitrary'. The signifier (the spoken word) is considered to have no necessary relationship with what is signified (the concept). Derrida argues that this suggests a denial of the possibility of any natural attachment. If a sign is arbitrary and does not refer to reality in any fundamental way, one sign could not be more natural than another. A spoken sign could not be more natural than a written one. But Saussure suggests that the spoken word has a more intimate bond with thought than the written word and, as Derrida points out, this runs counter to the notion of the arbitrariness of the sign. In short, 'The thesis of the arbitrariness of the sign must forbid a radical distinction between the linguistic and the graphic sign' (Derrida, [1967] 1997, p. 44).

Also, speech is itself structured by distance and difference just as is writing. A word is characterised by distance in being separated into a signifier (phonic sounds) and a signified (a mental concept). Furthermore, Derrida views language as a system of differences where meaning is conveyed not by some quality of a single word but by its difference from other words. He uses the term *différance* to convey both difference and deferring. Derrida calls the quality of speech that can be characterised by distance and difference *différance*, simultaneously indicating 'the production of differing/deferring' (Derrida, [1967] 1997, p. 23).

Deconstruction

Derrida's enterprise of 'deconstruction' involves a close analytic reading of a text to demonstrate it is not a coherent entity. Derrida frequently uses deconstruction to examine internal contradictions of discourse. It is helpful to specify common features of deconstruction. However, to do so can be problematic because the method involves an encounter with particular texts and modifies itself accordingly.

In the texts already cited (Saussure, Lévi-Strauss and Rousseau) Derrida seeks to deconstruct opposites. In selecting an aspect of Saussure's course, Derrida examines the notion of the arbitrariness of the sign to suggest there can be no clear distinction between the linguistic and the graphic sign. In focusing on Rousseau's work, Derrida looks at speech and writing in parallel with the consideration of presence and absence, maintaining that speech and writing are intimately interrelated.

More broadly, Derrida ([1967] 1997, e.g. p. 49) is concerned with the 'metaphysics of presence' which he regards as a central feature of Western philosophy. This is the notion that the subject can express itself fully in speech. Logocentrism is seen as presenting speech as the fullest form of expression and writing as a supplement to speech. Derrida suggests that if this is so, then something must be absent from speech that requires supplementing. Speech in its origins is lacking something.

Derrida's notion of *différance* is used to suggest that language and meaning has no point of origin. Meaning is always produced by the difference in signs and is always deferred endlessly. The endless process of *différance* is considered to unsettle the oppositions so central to structuralism.

An aspect of deconstruction then is to permanently disrupt the structure into which the deconstructor has intervened. The term 'supplement' in the consideration of Rousseau is an example. As it examines binary opposition, deconstruction exposes a 'trace'. This trace is a rupture within metaphysics. The trace does not appear and 'no concept of metaphysics can describe it' (Derrida, [1967] 1997 p. 65). However its path in the text can be brought to recognition by deconstruction. Two aspects of deconstruction are therefore a demonstration that binary opposites in which one of the pair is prioritised is untenable, and the revelation of the trace.

Evaluation of poststructuralism

Poststructuralism places great emphasis on discourse and involves a very close analysis of discourse which can be illuminating. However, poststructuralism can be regarded as an over-concentration on discourse and a view of discourse as being at the centre of things. A possible consequence is that the human body and sense experience can be demoted or reduced to a collection of discursive significations. The symbol can become more important than bodily experience and how the body is constituted. Such a view suggests that a phenomenological perspective might be diminished if one were to focus only on discourse. Merleau-Ponty ([1945] 1982) might be considered to support a phenomenological alternative.

Evaluation of some of the ideas in Of Grammatology

Derrida's examination of aspects of texts can be penetrating. His analysis of Rousseau's writing, including *Confessions*, is revealing. Consider Derrida's chapter, 'That Dangerous Supplement' ([1967] 1997, pp. 141–164). Here Derrida examines Rousseau's rhetoric on writing in relation to a desire for presence. The particular focus is *Confessions* (Rousseau [1769 and published posthumously in 1782] 2005). Rousseau views writing as a less immediate – therefore inferior – representation of speech. Relatedly, speech is a more direct expression of the self. But it becomes clear it is more difficult for Rousseau to express himself in speech. He finds his presence more faithfully represented in writing. Rousseau's physical absence enables the presentation of truth but his presence confounds it. Through his assumption of the need for absence, Rousseau is able to reappropriate the lost presence. But the attempted reappropriation subverts itself because its starting point is not presence but a lack of presence. One cannot desire presence if one is already present.

For Derrida, the starting point is therefore what he calls a *différance*. Writing and speech can no longer just be opposed, but neither have they become identical. In this analysis, their identities are put in question. The logic of the supplement (both 'an addition' and 'a substitute') disturbs the balance of metaphysical binary oppositions. (In a different context, see also the reference to the logic of supplementarity, Derrida, [1967] 1997, p. 215). Speech is not simply opposed to writing. Writing is added to speech and at the same time replaces it. Speech and writing are neither opposed nor equivalent. They are not even equivalent to themselves but are their own *différance* from themselves. The doubleness of the word 'supplement' takes the signifying possibilities of the text beyond what is assumed to be Rousseau's conscious intentions.

The consideration of Rousseau's complex motives and actions is revealing. However, when Derrida moves from very close readings of particular texts to grand generalisations he is less persuasive.

Part 1 of *Of Grammatology* 'sketches in broad outlines a theoretical matrix' and 'proposes certain critical contexts' (Derrida [1967] 1997, p. lxxxix). In Part 2, these concepts are 'put to the test' (ibid.). Derrida starts from general ideas and then presents examples to illustrate or support them. However it is strange he chooses only obscure and limited texts; for example a very small aspect of Saussure's course is considered. It might be more convincing if the general ideas could be supported more comprehensively with well-known texts. That this is not done suggests a weakness in Derrida's thesis that Western thought is in thrall to logocentrism. Derrida recognises the particularity of his illustrations, explaining references to Saussure's 'project and texts' as a 'privileged example'. He states that he will try to keep in view that the 'particularity of the example does not interfere with the generality of my argument' (p. 29). Nevertheless, because the examples are limited, Derrida is open to the criticism that the generalisations are weak.

With regard to the focus on limited aspects of texts, Foucault in the 1972 edition of *History of Madness* points to the potential tyranny of deconstruction. He argues that Derrida's criticisms tend to be based on very small fragments of text and that deconstruction is a 'pedagogy that inversely gives to the voice of the masters that unlimited sovereignty that allows it indefinitely to re-say the text'.

Kenny (2008) compares Derrida (unfavourably) with J. L. Austin, the Oxford philosopher. Austin introduced many technical terms to bring out the differences between different types of speech acts and their elements. Each term is lucidly defined and illuminated by examples. Derrida also introduces many new terms such as 'supplement' and 'trace' but, in contrast to Austin, Derrida is less willing to define them. He seems to view the 'very request for a definition as somehow improper' (Kenny, 2008, p. 91). The relevance of his illustrative examples is 'rarely clear' so that banal aspects of language assume 'an air of mystery' (ibid.). Kenny challenges Derrida's claim that Western philosophy has been phonocentric, citing the emphasis placed in law and business on getting things in writing and the great efforts of modern societies in promoting literacy.

So weak is Derrida's charge of phonocentrism that it 'has to be based on a number of eccentric texts starting with an ironic passage in Plato's *Phaedrus*' (ibid.). Kenny's judgement is that in his early work, Derrida 'showed evidence of great philosophical acumen' (ibid. p. 92). However, of his subsequent work, Kenny is dismissive. He finds it unsurprising that Derrida's fame 'has been less in philosophy departments than in departments of literature, whose members have less practice in discerning genuine from counterfeit philosophy' (ibid. p. 96).

Poststructuralism and special education

The general application to special education of poststructuralism reflects the broad definition of it as equated with postmodernism. This includes reluctance to ground discourse in any theory with metaphysical origins, suspicion of the Enlightenment project, scepticism about scientific approaches and a view of meaning as being unstable and plural. These may lead to positions from which positivism is criticised and has similarities with postmodern stances. The focus in this section is the implications of Derrida's deconstruction for perspectives of disability and of special education.

For some writers, deconstruction may be seen as a tool that can be detached from the texts on which it works. Those holding such a view might attempt to deconstruct certain concepts associated with special education, examining commonly used terms usually considered opposites, such as 'able' and 'disable'. This would not be done using an existing piece of writing where inconsistencies might be examined but would involve only a consideration of isolated words.

Silvers (2002) suggests 'normalcy' and 'disability' need not be antithetical. She argues, 'The privilege of being normal is that one has a claim on having one's commonness respected. The equivalent, and compatible, privilege of being disabled is acknowledgement of a claim to having one's difference respected'. In this way, Silvers suggests, normalcy and disability are not antithetical but concordant (p. 238). A common way of perceiving the use of two terms is found and it is suggested that in this respect they are not different but similar. In the example of 'normalcy' and 'disability' the common reference point, it is suggested, is 'privilege'. This implies a claim in both the case of 'being normal' and 'being disabled'. If both are associated with privilege and claim then there should, it is suggested, be an equal response in the sense that for a 'normal' person their commonness is respected, and for a disabled person their difference is respected. If normalcy can be respected then, in this line of argument, disability can be respected.

In questioning the perception of binary opposites, postmodern approaches can encourage a re-examination of opposites such as 'disabled' and 'able bodied'. It might be accepted that some aspects of the knowledge, understanding and skills of a child with a disability or disorder are less well developed than a typically developing child. This is part of the definitions of disabilities and disorders. However, this does not necessarily imply that all the experience of disability has to be constituted as a negation of ability. The experience of disability has its own realities also. Titchkosky (2002) states 'it is still common to regard the disabled body as a life constituted out of the negation of ablebodiedness and, thus, as nothing in and of itself' (p. 103). It is this sole perspective, that disability is inevitably the negative opposite of normality, that poststructuralism seeks to question.

Plurality in regarding disability can lead to recognition of different perspectives, including positivist ones, but also ones that take account of personal interactions in mapping out disability. As Titchkosky (2002) says, 'In this diversity, it is possible to map disability as opposition, as a medical thing'. However, she continues, it is possible to map disability in a different way, as 'an interactional accomplishment' (p. 109). The alternative way of 'mapping' disability suggests a focus on what an individual can do in interacting with his environment, rather than what he cannot. The focus is also on accomplishment rather than difficulty. At least this way of thinking opens up the possibility of viewing disability in some respects as an accomplishment instead of always regarding it as solely a difficulty.

Danforth and Rhodes (1997) adapt aspects of deconstruction to special education. They suggest that the acceptance of concepts such as 'disabled' hinders moves towards more inclusive schooling. This is in part because the concept 'disability' already assumes the identification and separation of one group of children from another. The 'dis' part of disability already marks out the difference from the 'ability' part of the term. The authors regard disability as a social construct that can and should be challenged. They state that in failing to contest the 'disability construct' those who would wish to support mainstreaming are effectively supporting the 'devaluation and stigmatization' of these students (p. 357). By developing an approach questioning the term, 'disability', it becomes possible to better advocate inclusion.

The use and acceptance of the terms 'ability' and 'disability' suggest 'moral and political categories'. The authors see deconstruction as a way of opening up the binary logic supporting the separation of children into such 'moral and political categories based on "ability" and "disability"' (ibid. p. 358). Danforth and Rhodes (1997) attempt to deconstruct the binary pair 'ability' and 'disability'. They see the term 'ability' as the preferred or dominant part of the binary opposites and 'disability' as the less valued part. If the terminology of 'mental retardation' were rejected, they maintain, the construction of 'retardation' would be challenged and would lead to greater respect for children previously so labelled.

Danforth and Rhodes (1997) link 'deconstruction' and the 'social construction' of disability in their own way, recognising this approach might be one that Derrida might 'baulk at' (p. 353). They maintain that if disability is socially constructed unjustly, it can be 'socially constructed in a more respectful and egalitarian way'. This depends on finding or persuading enough people to 'steer the momentum of sociocultural activity in that new direction' (p. 359). They suggest that both social constructionism and deconstruction assume that different forms of disability 'are not physical absolutes'. They are in fact, 'social designations that are made by people in interaction and relationships' (ibid.).

However, deconstruction offers 'a strategic, political means to promote local change in daily professional work' (Danforth and Rhodes, 1997, pp. 359–360). If society 'somehow' lost the vocabulary of mental retardation, 'the constructed reality of mental retardation would no longer continue in its present form' (ibid. p. 360). The new terms that emerged could be politically and morally advantageous, allowing people previously labelled to be treated with a greater respect than at present.

Evaluation of poststructuralism in special education

Poststructuralism is concerned with language and discourse. It sees discourse as a primary factor, leading to the charge that poststructuralism reduces everything to discourse, diminishing sentient reality. In the context of an understanding of disability, Hughes and Patterson (1997) criticise poststructuralism as 'discursive essentialism', demoting the human body to the 'multiple significations that give it meaning'. The body and sense experience disappear into language and discourse, losing their 'organic constitution' in the 'pervasive sovereignty of the symbol' (pp. 333–334).

Danforth and Rhodes (1997) maintain that if the world is socially constructed and language reflects and shapes this, changing language might change perceived reality. However, such a position does not reflect their affinity to Derrida's deconstruction. More relevant to Derrida's line of thought is their questioning of the ability/disability dichotomy. The border between ability and disability is where 'the assumed differentiation of the human categories . . . collapses on itself, where the practical logic of sorting children into distinct and meaningful types breaks down' (p. 360).

Danforth and Rhodes (1997) criticise a diagnostic practice in which a parent and a school appeared to define reading performance differently and therefore disagreed whether the child had a reading difficulty (pp. 361–362). One party took a fairly mechanical view of reading and the other a more contextual one. Danforth and Rhodes see the 'deconstructionist purpose' of this as pointing out that the two opposing definitions of reading, 'throw a paradigmatic monkey wrench into the process of diagnosing a reading disorder' (ibid.).

The authors correctly point out difficulties in always agreeing on a definition of reading performance. However, the way they proceed from this truism to the act of dismantling the assessment process lacks justification. Certainly, if an assessment involves criteria on which parties do not agree they are unlikely to be in harmony on the outcome of the assessment. But this does not inevitably require ditching the criteria. It might suggest working to develop wider criteria or both parties coming to agree on the same criteria.

Danforth and Rhodes (1997) attempt to deconstruct ability/disability by opening up its 'binary logic'. But the conclusion that the terminology of 'mental retardation' might be rejected lies beyond the remit of deconstruction. Their case might be better substantiated through reference to labelling theory, although still open to challenge. The authors intimate that dropping certain terminology could lead to greater respect. But if there was no use of such terms, who would know whether greater respect was being demonstrated and to whom? If there was no language in which to identify disability, what would happen to the evidence-based practice that is premised on types of disabilities and disorders being identified? It is one thing to point to possible problems of logic in extended discourses, but quite another to suggest abolishing terms that might help identify children who could benefit from special education.

More generally, deconstruction can suggest how meaning in special education might be open to challenge. However, it does not point to direct consequences for special education. To leap from questioning the stability of meaning to banning words is difficult to justify and does not bode well for informed debate. Challenging meaning by exploring supposed dispersed meaning among words is an interesting exercise. But there is a danger that the relationship between words and phenomena is ignored. To say this link is direct and simple may have pitfalls. However, to move to a position of discursive essentialism is equally problematic. To ignore the physical reality of phenomena and to think analysing meaning changes the world can be naive and lead to poor decisions. The steps by which Danforth and Rhodes (1997) move from thinking they had thrown a 'paradigmatic monkey wrench' into concepts of assessment to suggesting dismantling an assessment process is only one example of this danger.

Implications for thinking and practice of poststructuralism in special education

A poststructuralist view of special education rejects it in a fundamental way. Therefore it is difficult to consider poststructuralism according to what it might mean for special education in relation to curriculum and assessment, pedagogy, resources, organisation and therapy. The point of contact between postmodernism and special education, if there is one, is through the use of language.

Someone supporting a poststructuralist view of special education may be critical of positivist approaches. She may take a particular interest in the language associated with special education. She may seek to 'deconstruct' words associated with special education and disabilities and disorders. A poststructuralist may argue that terms such as 'normalcy' and 'disability' need not be antithetical but may be seen as concordant in the sense of being linked with respect. She might argue that although there may be differences as part of the definition of words like 'normalcy' and 'disability', this does not necessarily imply that all the experience of disability has to be constituted as a negation of ability.

Plurality in regarding disability might be seen as leading to recognition of different perspectives. These perspectives might include positivist ones and ones that take account of personal interactions in mapping out disability. Disability in this light may be seen as interactional, focusing on accomplishment rather than difficulty. A poststructuralist may argue that acceptance of concepts such as 'disabled' holds back more inclusive schooling. This is because the concept assumes the identification and separation of one group of children from another.

A poststructuralist might consider 'ability' and 'disability' to have moral and political implications. If so, deconstruction might open up the binary logic supporting the separation of children into such categories. Rejecting the terminology of 'mental retardation' would challenge the construction of 'retardation', leading to greater respect for children previously so labelled. She may take the view that disability can be socially constructed in a more respectful and egalitarian way, if enough people concur.

She may regard different forms of disability as social designations made by individuals in interaction and relationships. Deconstruction may be thought to promote local change in daily professional work. A poststructuralist might believe that, if old terms were dropped, new terms could be adopted that are more politically and morally advantageous. This might allow people previously labelled to be treated with a greater respect than at present.

Such views may lead to investigating the language of policy documents connected with special education. The purpose of this might be to see if assumptions that are unrecognised are evident and if these suppositions and those who drafted the documents can be challenged. A poststructuralist may examine documents that appear to be supportive of mainstreaming but that still assume the language and concepts she might associate with separate education. Where those drafting such documents seem unaware of such contradictions, discussion may take place to highlight the anomalies.

Thinking points

- Does the notion of mental structures necessarily lead to a limiting view of human development, and does this inevitably in turn imply lower expectations of educators?
- Can you provide examples of instances where the language used in debates about special education appears contradictory when analysed and examples where the power of language might be overestimated?

Key texts

Structuralism

Piaget, J. ([1968] 1971) *Structuralism* (translated from the French by Chaninah Maschler), London: Routledge & Keegan Paul. This closely argued text, as well as expressing Piaget's position, provides a useful background to the development of structuralism in different disciplines.

Poststructuralism

Derrida, J. ([1967] 1976) *Of Grammatology* (translated from the French by Gayatri Chakravorty Spivak), Baltimore and London: Johns Hopkins University Press. A good point of entry into Derrida's work, this book has an engaging chapter on 'That Dangerous Supplement' referring to Rousseau.

Danforth, S. and Rhodes, W. C. (1997) 'Deconstructing Disability: A Philosophy for Inclusion', *Remedial and Special Education* 18, 357–366. Uses the term 'deconstruction' rather loosely.

Powell, J. (1997) *Derrida for Beginners*, New York: Writers and Readers Publishing. This, as the title suggests, offers an introduction to some of Derrida's ideas.

Further reading

Hawkes, T. (2003) *Structuralism and Semiotics* (Second edition), New York and London: Routledge. A clear discussion of the nature and development of structuralism and semiotics.

Marshall, J. (Ed.) (2004) *Poststructuralism, Philosophy, Pedagogy*, Netherlands: Kluwer Academic. Concerns the history and conceptual development of poststructuralism and some implications for education.

Chapter 8

Working things out and bestowing meaning

Pragmatism and symbolic interactionism

Pragmatism

American pragmatism and some key figures

The general usage of the word 'pragmatism' gives a clue to its philosophical meaning. In everyday parlance, to be pragmatic indicates being practical or carrying out an activity towards a practical end. In order to get things done, it suggests not being too tied to particular views that might constrain action. The philosophical use of the term is similar, although it concerns not only efficacy but also truth.

Pragmatism as a form of philosophy is often described as a distinctly American contribution (Stuhr, 2000). It is centrally concerned to argue for a particular theory of truth. This theory is that a proposition is true if holding it to be true is advantageous or practically successful. Accordingly, a true belief is one that leads to successful action. Haack (1996) seeks to define the general core of pragmatism. He does this in terms of the method expressed in the maxim by which 'the meaning of a concept is determined by the experiential or practical consequences of its application' (p. 643).

A recent introduction to pragmatism places particular emphasis on the contributions of, among others, Charles S. Peirce, William James and John Dewey (Stuhr, 2010). In the present section, pragmatism is traced through: the writings of Charles S. Peirce and William James; John Dewey and the Chicago School of Pragmatism; and Richard Rorty and 'neo-pragmatism'.

Charles S. Peirce

Peirce, the American philosopher, logician and polymath, referred to his philosophy as 'pragmatism' because it links belief and action. He later called his philosophy 'pragmaticism' to differentiate it from what others called 'pragmatism'. Two articles offer an introduction to his ideas. In 'The Fixation of Belief' (Peirce, 1877 in Moore, Peirce and Fisch, 1986) Peirce claims that the scientific method is superior to other methods of overcoming doubt by 'fixing' belief. 'How to Make Our Ideas Clear' (Peirce, 1878 in Moore, Peirce and Fisch, 1986) argues for the pragmatic notion of clear concepts.

For Peirce, the whole meaning of a clear conception consisted of the entire set of its practical consequences. A meaningful conception, in other words, must be relatable to a collection of possible empirical observations under certain conditions. The whole meaning of such a conception consists of all the specifications of possible observations. Pragmatism then offers rules for clarification of the meaning of certain terms or ideas. Through enquiry it is possible to determine the best beliefs through a sort of self-correcting process. For certain kinds of concepts to have meaning, their application would have to make an observable difference to something. The conditional way in which this position is expressed is important and the phrase 'would have to' is intended to indicate this. If one were to try to clarify the meaning of the term 'soft' one might begin by saying that for a substance to be considered soft, it would be pliable in the hands. The application of the term 'soft' would be expected to indicate a difference in observable reality. If this was not so, it would not be possible to ascribe meaning to the concept. This leads to a view of science that it is fallible and not forever secure and unchallengeable.

William James

The American philosopher and psychologist William James is, with Peirce, credited with developing pragmatism. James ([1907] 1995) in *Pragmatism: A New Name for Some Old Ways of Thinking*, developed from a series of lectures, states a tenet of this philosophy (second lecture). This is that in order to 'attain perfect clearness in our thoughts of an object' we need only to 'consider what conceivable effects of a practical kind the object may involve'. These effects are the sensations we might expect and what reactions we must prepare. Our conception of these effects is then for us, 'the whole of our conception of the object' (ibid.).

This tenet is applied to the conception of truth in the sense of the agreement between a belief and reality. That which counts as agreement with reality depends on the sort of belief with which one is concerned. If common sense beliefs are true, when they are acted upon they spring no surprises. But truths evolve as new information challenges old beliefs so that they have to be accommodated.

Values and value judgements become objective when sentient beings care for one another, developing and accepting an interpersonal standard. In *Essays in Radical Empiricism*, James ([1912] 2003) argues that external phenomena are directly perceived. He maintains that some issues, such as whether or not there is a god, or whether there are objective values, cannot be settled by common sense or by science or by the sort of agreement that emerges in ethics. They require a 'will to believe'.

Russell ([1949] 1996) describes James's view of the function of philosophy as elucidating Peirce. The function of philosophy is to find out what difference it makes to a person if one or another worldview is true. In this way 'theories become instruments, not answers to enigmas' (p. 727). Ideas become true to the extent they help one to gain satisfactory relations with other parts of one's experience. An idea is true so long as believing it is profitable to one's life. Truth is not made true by events but rather truth happens to an idea (ibid. pp. 727–728).

John Dewey

John Dewey, probably the best-known philosopher in the United States in the twentieth century, studied at Johns Hopkins University, where Peirce was one of his teachers. In his earlier work, Dewey accepted a form of idealism. Subsequently he rejected idealism and adopted views which he described variously as experimentalism and pragmatism. He founded the Chicago School of Pragmatism during the ten years he worked at the University of Chicago (1894–1904). Among the original group was the philosopher George Herbert Mead, who developed ideas leading to the approach of symbolic interactionism.

Dewey took the view that the pursuit of truth is not disinterested. Thinking is seen as a matter of problem solving. Later still, he was concerned with religion, art and other matters. He is perhaps best known as a theorist of education, and in Chicago, founded a laboratory school where curriculum and pedagogy reflected his educational theories (Dewey, [1899] 2001; [1910] 2009; [1916] 1997). Given that Dewey argued that human thinking was essentially a matter of problem solving, education involved providing children with the greatest range possible of problem-solving skills. A social setting was very important, and the problem-solving skills included moral skills.

In his pragmatism, Dewey does not regard the individual as standing outside the world and observing it. Rather the individual is an agent engaged in interacting with the world. He focuses on a process he calls 'inquiry', which is a form of mutual adjustment between an organism and its environment. Inquiry is the transformation of an indeterminate situation into one that is determinate in the distinctions and relations that constitute it. This transformation is such that it changes the elements of the original situation into a coherent whole. Russell ([1949] 1996) suggests that Dewey's conception of inquiry is part of a general process of making the world more organic and that 'Unified wholes' are to be the outcome of enquiries (pp. 733–734).

Dewey's theory is summarised by Russell ([1949] 1996) as stating that the relationships of an organism to the environment may be satisfactory or unsatisfactory to the organism. When unsatisfactory, the situation may be improved by mutual adjustment. When alterations improving the situation are largely on the side of the organism, the process is one of 'inquiry' (ibid. p. 734). Whether a belief is good or bad depends on whether the activities generated in the organism holding those beliefs have consequences that are satisfactory or unsatisfactory to the organism. In other words, belief is judged by its effects. A belief is true or has 'warranted ascertainabilty' if it has certain kinds of effects (ibid. p. 736).

Richard Rorty

American philosopher Richard Rorty takes a philosophical standpoint sometimes described a 'neo-pragmatism'. He states that:

> Truth cannot be out there, cannot exist independently of the human mind, because sentences cannot so exist, or be out there. The world is out there, but descriptions of the world are not. Only descriptions of the world can be true or false. The world on its own, unaided by the describing activities of humans, cannot.
>
> Rorty (1989)

Rorty (1979) argues that the problems of epistemology relate to picturing the mind as seeking to mirror an external reality that is independent of the mind. A foundationalist has to accept that some beliefs are self-justifying or foundational. This is because if one belief only depends on another that also depends on another we have a problem of never reaching a foundational belief, a problem of infinite regress. Rorty suggests we have to discard the metaphor of the mind as mirroring nature. He rejects the view that knowledge has objective foundations that can be described by a theory of knowledge. For him, knowledge does not comprise ideas that faithfully mirror the external world. Knowledge is judged by the accuracy of its representations and in this sense is seen as what works for us (Rorty, 1979).

But it is recognised that there is a difficulty in specifying non-relatively who the 'us' are in relation to this neo-pragmatic position. Relativism therefore remains a central matter. Action can only be understood within an interpretative community, so the meanings and outcomes of action break down beyond these settings. What works for one person or group may not work for another. Some commentators see such apparent absolute relativism as controversial.

John McDowell (1994) challenges Rorty's view of the relation between agent and world as merely causal. He maintains that this view is incompatible with a notion concerning our concept of a creature with beliefs. This is that this involves the idea of a rational constraint of the world on our epistemic states (that is our states of knowing).

Evaluation of pragmatism

James ([1907] 1995), in the second lecture of his series, points to the advantages of a pragmatic method. He sees it a method of 'settling metaphysical disputes that otherwise might be interminable'. These are questions such as whether the world might be one or many, guided by fate or free, or material or spiritual. The pragmatic method tries to interpret each notion by tracing its practical consequences. One asks what difference it would practically make to anyone that a certain notion rather than another one is true. If it is not possible to discern a practical difference, the alternatives mean practically the same thing. Consequently the dispute is pointless. In a serious dispute, James maintains it ought to be possible to show some practical difference that must follow from one side or the other being correct.

Among criticisms of pragmatism as a philosophy is that its view of truth is out of kilter with what the term 'truth' is normally taken to mean. This in itself is not necessarily an insurmountable obstacle. Many aspects of philosophy that are illuminating are counterintuitive. Plato's idealist conception of the world that there are ideal types of what we perceive as phenomena is a very odd notion at first meeting but has engaged philosophers in debate for centuries.

But it is the implications of Dewey's view of truth that is open to challenge too. In logic and in his theory of knowledge, Dewey places great store on inquiry rather than on the traditional notion of truth. This inquiry is considered to reshape subject matter so that it is unified. It is not always clear what the underlying notion is that allows this.

Russell ([1949] 1996) examines Dewey's conception of truth and inquiry along such lines. Despite professed admiration of Dewey and despite being in complete agreement with him in many of his views, Russell cannot agree with a fundamental feature of Dewey's philosophy. Russell has to dissent from Dewey's doctrine of 'substituting inquiry for truth as the fundamental concept of logic and theory of knowledge' (p. 730). He finds Dewey's definition of inquiry as being concerned with the 'objective transformation of objective subject matter' to be 'plainly inadequate' (p. 733).

Russell ([1949] 1996) wonders if Dewey's views have some hidden 'metaphysic' similar to that of Georg Wilhelm Friedrich Hegel, the philosopher and a founder of German Idealism. Russell does not accept that inquiry should be expected to lead to a unified whole, unless it is on the basis of 'an unconscious Hegelian metaphysic'. In such a metaphysic, appearance may be 'confused and fragmentary' but the reality is always 'orderly and organic' (p. 734). If such a metaphysic does underlie Dewey's philosophy, Dewey, it is suggested, seems unaware of it.

For Russell ([1949] 1996), a difficulty with Dewey's theory is that it breaks the relationship between a belief and the facts that would commonly be said to verify it. For Dewey, it appears that a belief about some past event is to be classified as good or bad 'not according to whether the event took place' but according to 'the future effects of the belief' (Russell, [1949] 1996, p. 735). But there is a problem of how one knows the consequences of believing something (in Russell's example whether he had coffee that morning). Until the consequences of holding the belief are known, it is not feasible to know whether it is a good or bad belief. Russell finds this situation 'absurd' (ibid.).

Pragmatism and special education

Albrecht (2002), writing about American pragmatism and disability studies, suggests that pragmatism, being a diverse philosophy, 'has had a pervasive influence on American social science and subsequently on disability studies' (p. 20). Pragmatism, it is argued, exerted this influence because it offered 'a conceptual framework for thinking about the critical issues confronting social scientists'. It also suggested 'the types of data and analysis that should be used to construct arguments' (ibid. p. 22).

Among the ways that pragmatism has influenced sociology, Albrecht mentions the influence of neo-pragmatism – that of Rorty, for example. In this respect, Albrecht maintains that pragmatism has moved towards 'recognition of the importance of subjective experience, relativistic and culturally different conceptions of behaviour, paradigm shifts in the gathering and interpreting of information and competing communities of discourse' (Albrecht, 2002, p. 23). Rorty, it is said, 'dismisses claims to objectivity as wishful thinking' and argues that 'our standards of evidence and our scientific and social policy practices are cultural conventions' (ibid. p. 23). This seems a far cry from the pragmatism of Dewey and the early pragmatists. As Albrecht points out, 'In reviewing this broad range of pragmatic positions and their uses, it is noteworthy that there are not merely different, but radically opposed forms of pragmatism' (ibid. p. 23).

In considering the adaptation of the philosophy of pragmatism to special education, the contribution of Tom Skrtic (1995, 2004) is sometimes quoted. In order to understand Skrtic's position however, it is necessary to recognise the contributions to his arguments of postmodern threads as well as the influence of American pragmatism.

For example, Skrtic (1995) in *Disability and Democracy* draws not just on pragmatism but also on postmodern influences. He indicates the book's postmodern orientation, in particular the influence of Derrida, in the intention to 'deconstruct' special education. When Skrtic refers to special education, he usually means the separate education of special children from other children within ordinary schools or educating special children in special schools. He therefore includes in his definition of special education not only special children educated in separate special schools but also students educated separately for substantial amounts of time in ordinary school.

He suggests special education in this sense developed in response to a failure of ordinary schools to educate all children. Special education is only required in Skrtic's view because of inflexible school organisation and rigid professional culture and practice in mainstream teaching. Special education is concerned with problem solving, innovation, flexibility, and developing new programmes.

This 'adhocracy', Skrtic believes, contrasts with the 'bureaucracy' of mainstream schools. This distinction gives a pointer to the structures and professional awareness required in public education if it were to successfully prepare all future citizens for democracy.

However, having indicated Skrtic's use of certain postmodern suggestions, it can be said that his main source is American pragmatism. Drawing on the ideas of John Dewey (e.g. Dewey ([1899] 1976), Skrtic employs 'critical pragmatism' to investigate presumptions he believes have constrained professional discourse and practice. Using this method, Skrtic seeks to construct, 'deconstruct' and reconstruct educational practice and discourses. He argues that the adhocratic approach makes possible certain organisational conditions necessary to educate diverse pupils. Skrtic suggests that public education can be for the education of all children if it changes in two ways. First it should adopt adhocratic school organisation as the condition of critical practice. Secondly, it should employ critical pragmatism as a mode of professional discourse.

Here critical pragmatism refers to the use of pragmatism to evaluate and modify professional discourse. Instead of a rigid professional culture, critical pragmatism, it is suggested, would lead to greater questioning of this culture. It would lead to mainstream schools adopting the problem solving, innovation, flexibility and new programme development that typify the best special schools.

This appears to imply several things. Problem solving would be applied to the real everyday situations in which teachers find themselves and would not be an abstract pursuit. To this extent, problem solving is in line with the instrumental approach advocated by Dewey. The creativeness of such problem solving would be built into pedagogy. In other words, each situation would present a challenge to be met and for which there would be no predetermined blueprint. Problem solving would relate in this way to innovation as solutions are found. Flexibility would emerge as teachers adapted to challenges and were aware that there is no one-size-fits-all approach.

Flexibility would help assure responsiveness to the particular learning requirements of different students. New programme development would draw together aspects of creative responses that worked and apply them in what appeared to be similar situations. It could not be guaranteed that programmes would work on children who were different to the ones for which they had been developed. Consequently, educators would need to be vigilant that any such programmes remained effective. This would be part of the overall approach of problems solving, flexibility, innovation and further programme development.

More recently Skrtic (2004, pp. 357–359) has elaborated on some common features of critical pragmatism and broad critical theory associated with the Frankfurt School. Briefly, 'critical theory' in relation to the Frankfurt School refers to neo-Marxist critical theory originally associated with the Institute for Social Research at the University of Frankfurt am Main. Its influences included Marxism and aspects of the theories of Sigmund Freud. Among its theorists are Adorno, Horkheimer and Marcuse. (For an outline of the work of the Frankfurt School, please see Chapter 5 'Historical materialism and critical theory' in the present volume).

Skrtic's own version of critical pragmatism draws on social pragmatism relating to the work of John Dewey, George Herbert Mead and the Chicago School of American Pragmatism (ibid. p. 357). This approach to pragmatism (like critical theory) aims to be interdisciplinary and to integrate philosophy and empirical science (ibid. p. 358). Seeking social change, it draws on ethical and social theory informing 'norms of justice, liberty . . . and participatory democracy' (ibid.).

In Skrtic's view, critical pragmatism requires 'a particular form of historical reflection'. This is reflection that avoids two poles. The first is the 'transhistorical stance of traditional foundationalism'. The second is the 'relativism of pure contextualism' (Skrtic, 2004, p. 359). The concern here seems to be that where traditional foundationalism is the touchstone, advocates seek to rise above historical context. Where 'pure' contextualism is adopted, there is a danger of over-subjectivism.

Skrtic seeks to avoid both of these positions. He highlights from Dewey's social philosophy aspects of historicism. First, the only foundation for ethical and political ideals is the 'history of their meaning' (ibid.). Dewey does not appeal to 'timeless standards beyond the contestation of contemporary political discourses'. Secondly, Dewey's historicism is 'sensitive to context' which in turn depends on an appreciation of history (ibid.).

Evaluation of pragmatism in special education

Skrtic does not outline his use of Dewey's philosophy in sufficient detail to make it clear how he would view potential criticisms of the pragmatic position. Indeed, Skrtic (2004) draws rather loosely on a combination of views. His critical pragmatism is informed by social pragmatism relating to the work of Dewey, Mead and the Chicago School of American Pragmatism (p. 357). Yet this approach faces the same difficulty that pragmatism more generally encounters, that of instrumentalism.

Instrumentalism takes the view that theories, especially scientific ones, are not true or false but are more correctly regarded as tools. These tools are mainly useful to help with predictions, in making a transition from one set of data to another. The particular effectiveness of some theories above others in this respect gives justification for their acceptance, rather than whether or not they are supposed to be true.

The instrumentalism of pragmatism seems to turn away from usual notions of truth and breaks the relationship between a belief and the facts that would be said to verify it. It appears to support a conception that depends on inquiry being guided by an unacknowledged Hegelian metaphysic.

Skrtic's (2004) views seek social change and draw on ethical and social theory informing 'norms of justice, liberty . . . and participatory democracy' (p. 358). Such a starting point indicates that the intention is a philosophical approach that seeks change and is emancipatory. In Skrtic's view, critical pragmatism requires a form of historical reflection avoiding the transhistorical and the relativistic (p. 359). Skrtic follows Dewey in suggesting that the only foundation for ethical and political ideals are the 'history of their meaning' and seeks to be 'sensitive to context' (ibid.).

Continuing his eclectic stance, Skrtic moves to Derrida's method of deconstruction to examine tensions between adhocracy and bureaucracy. Derrida's use of 'deconstruction' involves a close analytic reading of a text to show it is not a coherent entity. Often, he uses deconstruction to examine internal contradictions of philosophical discourse. It is difficult to specify approaches to deconstruction because it involves an encounter with particular texts and modifies itself accordingly. Several of Derrida's early books demonstrate the process (Derrida, [1967] 1973; [various dates and 1967] 1978; [1967] 1977). As a political practice, it has been suggested that deconstruction could question the logic whereby particular systems of thought and their expressions as political structures and social institutions keep their force (Eagleton, 1996a, p. 128).

Skrtic does not explain the way in which he draws on Derrida's method. However, if a common thread can be discerned in Derrida's approach it is a very close examination of hidden contradictions at the heart of the text. It appears this is Skrtic's procedure. Skrtic uses deconstruction to focus on an apparent contradiction at the heart of special education. This is that special education requires adhocracy but is positioned in a setting encouraging bureaucracy. Conceptually adhocracy and bureaucracy are incompatible. Procedurally, there has to be organisational change for special education to be realised. Nevertheless, Skrtic does not develop the practical implications that might be involved in these changes. Nor does he indicate the likely content of any reflective critical development emerging from critical pragmatism.

However, the implication of Skrtic's perspective seems to be that the practices that could emerge from teachers working together to solve problems will be authentic. The practices will represent the 'truth' because they will be designed to work. Their effectiveness will indicate that teachers have identified the problem and its solution correctly, in line with pragmatic philosophy. The difficulty remains though that none of these solutions is suggested as a general possible solution. They are expected to emerge from the act of problem solving.

This seems to miss the opportunities that are afforded by broadly applied evidence-based practice. This of course assumes that where problems have been solved in one situation and with one group of children, that these can be generalised to similar situations and similar groups of children. There are difficulties with this approach too because it is not always easy to determine which aspects of a child group or which aspects of a situation are those that contribute to effective practice.

Nevertheless, evidence-based practice has led to useful interventions – for pupils with autism, attention deficit hyperactivity disorder and many other disorders and disabilities (Farrell, 2008; Fonagy et al., 2005). The approach of pragmatism, despite its supposed focus on what 'works', seems to miss the opportunity to use evidence-based findings and instead concentrate on perpetual exploratory pedagogy. Yet pragmatism and evidence-based practice at least have a shared concern with outcomes. Pragmatism looks to the consequences of holding beliefs to inform its view of truth. Evidence-based practice in special education looks to the outcomes of interventions not to determine their truth but to judge their efficacy.

Implications for thinking and practice of pragmatism in special education

Someone taking a pragmatic view of special education might seek to avoid the limitations of foundationalism or subjectivism. She may take the view that the only foundation for ethical and political ideals is the 'history of their meaning' and being 'sensitive to context'. More specifically, she might focus on possible reasons for separate provision. She may understand special education as concerning not only special children educated in separate special schools but also students educated separately for substantial amounts of time in ordinary school. A pragmatist may regard special education as having developed in response to a failure of ordinary schools to educate all children. She might consider that special education is only required because of deficiencies in mainstream schooling – inflexible school organisation and rigid professional culture and practice.

A pragmatist may take the view that flexibility would help assure responsiveness to the particular learning requirements of different students. New programme development would draw together aspects of creative responses that worked and apply them in what appeared to be similar situations. Generalisation of approaches could not be guaranteed so she would remain vigilant that any such programmes remained effective. This would be part of the overall approach of problem solving, flexibility, innovation and further programme development.

Someone advocating pragmatism might investigate presumptions believed to have constrained professional discourse and practice, that is, pedagogy. She might use pragmatism to evaluate and modify professional discourse and challenge this culture. She would be likely to work in a mainstream school to use problem solving, innovation, flexibility, and new programme development. She may apply problem solving to the real everyday situations in which teachers find themselves. The creativeness of such problem solving would typify pedagogy. She might regard each situation as a challenge with no predetermined blueprint. Problem solving would relate to innovation as solutions are found. Flexibility would emerge as teachers adapted to challenges, aware that there is no uniform approach.

The roots of special education and the apparent necessity for it would be seen as a reflection of rigid organisational responses in mainstream schools. Consequently, a pragmatist may look to changing such rigid organisation in order to include pupils presently outside the mainstream. Special education may be seen as concerned with problem solving, innovation, flexibility, and developing new programmes. She may take such 'adhocracy' as pointing to the structures (and professional awareness) required in public education if it were to successfully prepare all future citizens for democracy. She may argue that adhocracy allows certain organisational conditions necessary to educate diverse pupils. Public education could be for all children if mainstream schools were adhocratic in their organisation. She would value interdisciplinary working. In such working she would try to bring ethical positions and social views together with empirical evidence.

A pragmatist might view resources as being at the service of the flexibility and innovation necessary for mainstream schools to provide well for special pupils. Resources would be seen in the wide sense and would include flexible staffing, opportunities to collaborate and develop new and ongoing responses to the requirements of students. Learning resources that might be thought of as part of special schooling would be available within mainstream schools as necessary. These might include aids to communication, support services such as audiology for deaf children. Such services and support might be provided peripatetically at certain times a week.

It is unclear in a pragmatic approach how therapy would be regarded. Someone taking a pragmatic view of special education might see therapy as part of the flexibility and innovation that should be developed in mainstream schools. She might therefore seek to develop provision for therapy within the flexible organisation of the mainstream school.

Symbolic interactionism

There are many varieties of symbolic interactionism, but some general orienting observations may be made. Symbolic interactionism is a sociological perspective of the self and of society. Humans are seen as living their lives in a symbolic environment. Symbols are defined as social objects derived from human culture, and the meaning of these symbols is shared and developed in interaction with others. Language and communication enable symbols to act as the means by which reality is constructed. For symbolic interactionists, reality is regarded as mainly a social product. The sense of self, society and culture emerge from symbolic interactions and they are dependent on symbolic interactions for their existence. The physical environment is interpreted through symbolic systems in the way it is made relevant to human behaviour.

From pragmatism, symbolic interactionists developed the view that experience is a social phenomenon. In a symbolic interactionist perspective, individual experiences are invested with meaning through being socially formed. Meaning is shared and in the process it is constructed. Individuals respond to others according to the meaning they place on others' actions. Symbols, interpretation, and an effort to ascertain meaning are believed to mediate human interaction. The pragmatic theme is apparent in the view that some ideas are found to work better than others and the poorer ones tend to be rejected while better ones are retained. Social interaction is the forum in which meanings are negotiated, challenged and modified, helping to assure their rational basis.

Just as there are different stances within symbolic interactionism, so there are debates about how its antecedents might be traced (Reynolds, 1995, p. 6). The role of pragmatism suggested in the present chapter is only one of the antecedents. However, as Reynolds (1995) notes, 'If forced to single out the one philosophical school of thought that most influenced symbolic interactionism, one would be on safe ground in concluding that pragmatism provides its primary intellectual underpinnings' (p.11). Furthermore, pragmatism, especially as shaped by Dewey, would become, 'the *primary* philosophical foundation of *symbolic interactionism*' (ibid. p. 19, italics in original). Among the contributions of pragmatism to symbolic interactionism were 'its arguments that it is senseless to draw hard distinctions between mind and matter or between society and the individual, as well as its theories of the existential basis of mind, intelligence and self' (ibid.).

Cooley, Mead and Blumer

Symbolic interactionism developed mainly from the work of Charles Cooley, George Herbert Mead and Herbert Blumer. Cooley was an American sociologist who taught economics and sociology at the University of Michigan. He was influential in emphasising the role of others in how humans develop their concept of the self. His notion of the 'looking glass self' (Cooley, [1902] 1983) suggests that individuals in part regard themselves as they believe others see them. Self-concept and our own feelings emerge from how individuals believe other people see and evaluate them.

In other words, self-concept involves an interaction between the way we see ourselves, and the way others perceive us, or more accurately, the way we think others perceive us. One's self-concept is built up in close groups that Cooley called 'primary groups', which included the family and play groupings, and which are the source, Cooley argued, of one's ideals and morals (Cooley, [1909] 1998). Cooley did not regard an individual and society as separate phenomena but as different aspects of the same thing.

The American philosopher George Herbert Mead was a professor at the University of Chicago, whose ideas were influenced by pragmatism and behaviourism. Mead wrote many articles and book reviews but published no books. After Mead's death, books were collated relating to his lectures in social psychology at the University of Chicago and from other sources.

In *Mind, Self and Society* ([1934] 1967), Mead considers how individual minds and selves arise from social processes. He considers social processes to be prior to the processes of individual experience. Mind arises within the social processes of communication. Communication processes involve the 'conversation of gestures', which have an unconscious effect, and language, in which communication takes place through significant symbols.

Although Mead did not use the term, his theories led to the development of symbolic interactionism, which has been influential in sociology and social psychology. It was Herbert Blumer who first used the expression 'symbolic interactionism' as he developed Mead's ideas, laying the foundations of subsequent distinctive symbolic interaction approaches.

Among Blumer's concerns were the notions of meaning, language and thought. Meaning is central to human behaviour in that humans behave towards other people or things in the light of the meaning they have given to those people or things. It is through language that individuals negotiate meaning through symbols. Through thought, each person's interpretation of symbols is modified. Thought based on language constitutes a mental dialogue. It requires that the individual imagine the point of view of another person. The three premises of symbolic interactionism for Blumer were that:

- individuals act towards things according to the meaning the things have for them
- these meanings derive from social interactions with others
- these meanings are dealt with and modified through an 'interpretive process' used by the individual.

(Blumer, 1986, p. 2, paraphrased)

Evaluation of symbolic interactionism

Symbolic interactionism as represented by the Society for the Study of Symbolic Interactionism (www.symbolicinteraction.org) has been credited with influencing the sociology of emotions, deviance and criminology, collective behaviour and social movements, feminist studies, sociological versions of social psychology, communications theory, semiotics, education, nursing, mass media, organisations, and the study of social problems. Other areas influenced by the perspective include health and illness and the sociology of sex. More broadly, it has had an impact on social psychology and micro sociology.

Among the symbolic interactionist concepts that are widely used are: the definition of the 'situation', 'identity work', 'emotion work', the 'looking glass self', and the 'total institution'. Of these, the most influential is the notion of the 'looking glass self' which has already been discussed. Symbolic interaction tends to use qualitative research methods to study areas such as social interaction and individual selves.

Limitations of symbolic interactionism can be inferred from the areas that it has influenced. Absent from these are concerns with macro sociological matters and social structure. However, it can equally be argued that approaches such as structural functionalism that address macro sociological matters are less suited to the areas influenced by symbolic interactionism.

Some implications of symbolic interactionism have been criticised. In describing symbolic interactionism, Armstrong (2003) raised the point that social interaction is taken to provide the 'rational structures for the mediation and resolution of different interpretations' (p. 24). He states that this might be argued to indicate a critical pragmatism in which analysis has a particular focus. This focus is 'comprehending the social, political, cultural and epistemological practices through which meaning is created' (ibid.).

Yet, Armstrong points out that at the theoretical level the approach might offer little to extend historical analysis beyond 'a reductionist focus on social interaction' (ibid.). Such a reductionist focus, Armstrong suggests, lacks the analytical tools to extend beyond 'an appreciation of the practicalities of "what works"'. It is less able to 'explore how these workings are constructed within a wider societal context of social experience of and social action' (ibid. p. 26). What works is understood only with regard to 'the practicalities of what is enforced', leaving historical understanding 'trapped in the ideological restrictions of present day concerns' (ibid.).

In brief then, Dewey's theory is criticised for breaking the relationship between a belief and the facts that would commonly be said to verify it. Symbolic interactionism is criticised because its conception of what works is understood in terms of the practicalities of what is enforced. Consequently for symbolic interactionism, historical understanding is constrained by the ideological restrictions of contemporary concerns.

Symbolic interactionism and special education

Haack (1996) defines pragmatism in terms of the method expressed in a maxim. This is that 'the *meaning* of a concept is determined by the experiential or practical consequences of its application' (p. 643, italics added). As Albrecht (2002) points out, the interactionist perspective in sociology was influenced by Dewey and elaborated by Mead and Blumer at the University of Chicago into what became symbolic interactionism (p. 27). Others used symbolic interactionism in medical sociology and qualitative research methods. Albrecht (2002) characterises symbolic interactionism as highlighting 'subjective experience and the interpretation of social reality' (p. 27).

In disability studies, the perspective has been used to ask certain questions – for example, 'What is the subjective experience of disability?' and 'How do others perceive, define and react to disabled people?' (ibid.). It is stated that social interactionism is 'well equipped to analyse how social problems, behaviour and institutions are socially constructed' (ibid. p. 28). Work informed by 'the social construction of disability, the political economy of disability, and analysis of the disability market place' may not be dominant themes in disability research. Nevertheless, they make a significant contribution to the understanding of disability 'on the societal and structural levels' (ibid. p. 31).

Turning to symbolic interactionism and special education, it has been used as a background orientation for some time. Bogdan and Kugelmass (1984) report a project drawing on the approach. Finding variations in who were considered to require special education provision and why, the authors maintain that perceptions were crucial. They state that 'the ways children are perceived, including whether they are thought of as handicapped, and how they are educated vary from school district to school district, from school to school, and from place to place within a given school' (ibid. p. 175).

The authors suggested two theoretical approaches might help in clarifying and understanding the situation in which identification and consequently interventions appear unreliable. These approaches were 'ecological theory' and 'symbolic interactionism'. Ecological theory is concerned with the interaction between individuals and their environment. Symbolic interactionism concerns the social nature of meaning.

Within symbolic interactionism, Bogdan and Kugelmass maintain, 'Objects like wheelchairs, people like resource teachers, and special education students, situations such as mainstreaming and behaviour such as reading and writing do not produce their own meaning. Rather, meaning is bestowed upon them' (ibid. p. 182). The authors do not deny that 'some students are more disposed to read than others, or that a child that is blind cannot see' (ibid. p. 183). But they argue that these concepts 'need to be understood' by examining the interplay between how different people 'come to define' these children in specific situations (ibid.).

Gunar Stangvik (1998) in 'Conflicting Perspectives on Learning Disabilities' discusses 'transactional approaches' to special education, and mentions additional contributions to theory including that of Mead and symbolic interactionism (p.147).

Symbolic interaction continues to inform research and can be combined with other views in research. For example Bentley (2005) sought to link symbolic interactionism with a 'Foucauldian genealogy'. This was to investigate disability and inclusion, and the interactions and meanings attached to them. Excluding and including interactions were identified within self-described inclusive practices.

Indications of 'excluding interactions' with an 11-year-old, nonverbal girl with Rett syndrome were suggested. Among these was that she was perceived in a medical context and considered different to others, which the author calls 'medical Othering'. She was treated as if younger than she was ('infantilisation'). Expectations of her were lower than for others ('academic exclusion through low expectations and limited participation'). Bentley points out that excluding interactions tended to support 'existing meanings' of disability and inclusion. 'Including interactions' were most often observed between the girl and peers with and without disabilities. These comprised 'medical sharing', 'age-appropriate expectations' and 'academic inclusion'.

Including interactions tended to transform existing meanings of disability and inclusion. The author suggested symbolic interactionist definitions of 'symbolic inclusion' and 'symbolic exclusion'. Symbolic inclusion was considered to apply to school improvement and social justice issues that are not confined to special education.

Derrick Armstrong (2003) has considered the possible contribution of pragmatics and of symbolic interactionism to special education. Writing about 'voices', he suggests some of these are excluded from special educational debate and theorising. Armstrong outlines two sources that he considers have addressed the problem of excluded voices (p. 23).

The first is the pragmatic philosophy of Peirce, James and Dewey. The second is sociological and psychological theories concerning 'everyday understanding and action' that have pragmatism as their philosophical starting place – symbolic interactionism, for example. Considering symbolic interactionism, Armstrong (2003) points out that where individuals debate and contest views and interpretations of reality, there may be 'significant differences between perspectives'. In such circumstances, social interaction itself is considered to provide the 'rational structures for the mediation and resolution of different interpretations' (p. 24). Armstrong goes on to examine difficulties with such a position and these will be considered below.

Evaluation of symbolic interactionism in special education

Regarding symbolic interactionism and disability, symbolic interactionism has informed medical sociology and qualitative research methods. It has been used to examine questions such as the subjective experiences of individuals with disabilities and the perceptions of disability of others who are not disabled. Related social construction views of disability similarly focus on subjective concerns. The difficulty of extending such perspectives beyond the perspectives and subjective experiences reported may limit the wider applicability of these views.

Albrecht (2002) points out that in disability studies, a symbolic interactionist perspectives has been used to ask questions about how others perceive and respond to disabled people (p. 27). Albrecht considers social interactionism to be equipped to analyse 'how social problems, behaviour and institutions are socially constructed' (p. 28). Work informed by, among other things, 'the social construction of disability' might contribute to the understanding of disability 'on the societal and structural levels' (p. 31).

However, such a perspective, like a predominantly social model of disability, can be criticised from two standpoints. On the one hand a social interactionist position can maintain that disability is only defined according to the factors such as negative attitudes and social restrictions that are considered to be layered on top of impairment. These, it can be argued, are socially constructed but are so by the circular definition of disability. On the other hand, the social interactionist view can regard disability and impairment as socially constructed, in which case it is open to the criticism of not taking enough account of the physical realities of impairment. The criticisms made by Shakespeare (2006, *passim*) of the social model of disability seem pertinent here.

Bogdan and Kugelmass (1984) suggest symbolic interactionism might help in clarifying and understanding the situation in which identification and consequently interventions in special education appear unreliable. For them, meaning is 'bestowed' on objects such as wheelchairs, on people like resource teachers and special education students, and on situations such as main-streaming (p. 182). The authors accept certain dispositions towards reading and the physical basis of sensory impairment (p. 183, paraphrased). But these concepts 'need to be understood' by examining the interplay between how different people 'come to define' these children in specific situations (ibid.).

There is something evasive in the view that some children have a disposition to read while others may not. Being able to read is more of an achievement than being 'disposed' to read and the fact of not being able to read is rather more than a concomitant of how others interpret this. Such an explanation seems even more limited in relation to certain disabilities and disorders. Clearly the way people interpret situations and other people might have an influence on the way they interact. But it is unclear how this illuminates the fact of physical disability or autism. Parents of autistic children might fail to understand that their child's condition is merely a 'bestowed' social meaning. It is unclear how social interactionism might contribute to better educating and caring for an autistic child.

In a case study, Bentley (2005) investigated disability and inclusion, and the interactions and meanings attached to them. Excluding and including interactions were identified within self-described inclusive practices. Among excluding interactions with a girl with Rett syndrome, were: 'medical Othering', 'infantilisation' and 'academic exclusion'. These tended to support 'existing meanings' of disability and inclusion. Among including interactions most often observed between the girl and peers with and without disabilities were 'medical sharing', 'age-appropriate expectations' and 'academic inclusion'. These tended to transform existing meanings of disability and inclusion. The author suggested symbolic interactionist definitions of 'symbolic inclusion' and 'symbolic exclusion'.

This underlines the difficulty of transferring insights from subjective individual studies. If the case study is representative, it might suggest looking carefully at the way educators and others interact with pupils. If it is an individual instance, it might suggest the adults involved have something to learn about the way they interact with a particular child. Yet more fundamentally, the case study appears to suggest that 'existing meanings' of disabilty (and inclusion) are associated with negative aspects. These negative responses were treating a child as if she is only a medical condition ('Othering'), treating the child like an infant, and excluding her academically. This is a position that might surprise teachers and others in special education who strive to do just the opposite in special settings including special schools. Educators who respond to the child as a whole, treat children according to their age and understanding (sometimes a difficult matter), and create learning opportunities to include the child in learning might not recognize the caricature presented by Bentley's case study.

Implications for thinking and practice of symbolic interactionism in special education

A symbolic interactionist would be likely to emphasise subjective experience and the interpretation of social reality. In the area of disability studies, she might be interested in the nature of the subjective experience of disability and how others perceive, define and react to disabled people. She is likely to favour qualitative research methods.

Someone taking a symbolic interactionist view in special education may be interested in why there are variations in who are considered to require special education provision and why, taking the view that the ways children are perceived are crucial. She might take the position that concepts are best understood by examining the interplay between how different people come to define special children in specific situations.

A symbolic interactionist may draw on that perspective to investigate disability and inclusion, and the interactions and meanings attached to them. She may consider that excluding and including interactions can be identified within self-described inclusive practices. Excluding practices might perceive a student only in a medical context, treating an older special student like an infant and having expectations of progress and development that are too low. Including interactions might be age-appropriate expectations and academic inclusion.

A symbolic interactionist may consider that things do not produce their own meaning but have meaning given to them. Aspects of pedagogy are examples. Literacy, numeracy, and social and personal skills are considered as forms of behaviour, each with their own meanings. Building confidence in social skills, for example, is likely to be viewed not as trying to build up a set of discrete actions that can be called 'social skills'. The enterprise is better conveyed by a student gradually investing with meaning various types of behaviour and coming to understand them in an interactive social context. This might suggest a social observational approach to encouraging social skills rather than a behaviour approach.

To a symbolic interactionist, resources such as wheelchairs or aids to communication are not taken to be external phenomena devoid of meaning.

Rather they have different meanings for different people. To one person a wheelchair may be a helpful aid; to another it may be an ever-present reminder of restrictions. People may also be considered as resources, and again they are likely to be viewed as invested with meaning. To create roles such as resource teachers or psychologists is to create networks of meaning that influence the way others – special children, for example – are seen. To speak of special children, of course, is also to set up certain meanings of which one needs to be aware.

Organisation reflecting a symbolic interactionist view is likely to place emphasis on students being able to express their views and being listened to. A symbolic interactionist may consider that some 'voices' are excluded from special educational debate and theorising. Where there are significant differences in views and interpretations of reality, social interaction may provide the rational structures for their mediation and resolution. She may see this as a way of helping ensure that special students have their perspectives heard and taken into account.

A symbolic interactionist may be suspicious of therapy. Like other aspects of special education, provision for therapy and what it means would not be viewed as necessarily innocent. Questions would be raised, such as: Why is it thought that therapy might be needed? Who is deciding this? What meaning does the special child place on therapy? Does the fact that therapy is thought to be needed reflect a particular view of disabilities and disorders, perhaps a negative view? On the other hand, a symbolic interactionist may take the position that within psychodynamic psychotherapy, for example, subjective experience and the interpretation of social reality can be usefully explored, leading to positive outcomes.

Thinking points

- To what extent can pragmatism offer a fruitful approach to special education and to what degree can it be linked to evidence-based practice?
- What is the justification for the view that meaning is 'bestowed' on objects such as wheelchairs, on people like resource teachers and special students, and on situations such as mainstreaming? What might be the consequences?

Key texts

Pragmatism

Stuhr, J. H. (2010) *American Pragmatism: An Introduction*, Oxford: Blackwell. Stuhr's text includes chapters on the thought of Charles Peirce, William James, John Dewey and George Herbert Mead. Other chapters concern the development of pragmatism and its varieties after Dewey, and a critical assessment of pragmatism.

Bernstein, Richard J. (2010) *The Pragmatic Turn*, Cambridge: Polity. This book maintains that many important recent philosophical themes are variations and developments of ideas associated with American pragmatism. It examines the work of philosophers influenced by pragmatism, including Jürgen Habermas and Richard Rorty.

Symbolic interactionism

Denzin, N. K. (1992) *Symbolic Interactionism and Cultural Studies: The Politics of Interpretation*, London and New York: Wiley-Blackwell. This book provides an account that has contemporary relevance, beginning with the origins of symbolic interactionism in American pragmatism and leading to relationships between symbolic interactionism and postmodernism.

Herman, N. J. and Reynolds, L. T. (1995) *Symbolic Interaction: An Introduction to Social Psychology*, New York: General Hall. This book includes Parts on 'Intellectual Antecedents of Symbolic Interactionism' and 'Varieties of Symbolic Interactionism and Leading Early Representatives' (including chapters on Cooley and Thomas, and on Mead, and Blumer). Part 5 considers contemporary developments.

Special education in relation to pragmatism and symbolic interactionism

Armstrong, D. (2003) *Experiences of Special Education: Re-evaluating Policy and Practice Through Life Stories,* New York and London: Routledge. The book includes thought-provoking sections on pragmatism and symbolic interactionism.

Skrtic, T. M. (Ed.) (1995) *Disability and Democracy: Reconstructing (Special) Education for Post-modernity*, New York: Teachers College Press. This book suggests that mainstream schooling can learn from special education to widen its remit.

Chapter 9

Psyche and language

Psychoanalysis – Freud and Lacan

Freudian psychoanalysis and later developments

Sigmund Freud

Freudian psychoanalysis refers variously to a 'theory of personality and psychopathology', a 'method of investigating the mind' and 'a theory of treatment' (Wolitzky, 2003, p. 24). Primarily Freud's aim was to develop psychoanalysis as a theory of the human mind, and his mature theories were developed over a considerable period during which they were substantially modified. The touchstone for Freud's work remains the *Standard Edition* edited by James Strachey, although other translations are easily available – for example, Ragg-Kirby's more recent one of Freud's *An Outline of Psychoanalysis* (Freud, S. [1940] 2003).

Among key concepts in psychoanalysis are the Ego, the Id and the Superego. The Id (rendered as the 'Es' by Ragg-Kirby) is the oldest of the forces or 'psychical provinces' containing 'everything that is inherited, everything present at birth, everything constitutionally determined' (Freud, S. [1940] 2003, p. 176). It consists of drives that have their origins in bodily organisation, which in the Id find 'a first psychical expression in forms unknown to us' (ibid.).

A form of organisation has developed mediating between the Id and the external world and which Freud calls the Ego (or Ich). The Ego deals with the external world – by adapting to moderate stimuli, for example. The Ego also deals with the internal world of the Id by various means, including deciding whether drives should be gratified or their excitations suppressed. The Ego strives for pleasure and avoids 'unpleasure' (p. 177). In the long period of childhood dependence on parents, a 'special authority' develops in the Ego in which parental influence persists. Freud calls this the 'Superego' (or Über-ich).

The action of the Ego is 'fully apt' if it reconciles the demands of the Id, the Superego, and reality. The Ego is the seat of rational perception, mediating between the demands of the Id and the demands of the Superego. Several processes produce the Ego. These include the differentiation of the Id as the psyche responds to outside reality. Because part of the Ego remains unconscious, it can communicate with the Id. Among the functions of the Ego is reality testing and the imposition of external norms on unconscious impulses and drives. The Superego forms as the child emerges from the Oedipus complex and casts off incestuous desires for the parent of the opposite sex, and internalises the father's prohibitions that make these desires taboo.

A little more may be said about the theory of drives. These are the forces considered to lie behind tensions brought about by the needs of the Id. They represent the 'physical demands on the psyche' (p. 178). Freud proposes that the multiplicity of drives can be traced to two basic ones: the Eros (also called 'libido') and the destruction drive (also called the death drive). Eros seeks to 'establish and maintain ever greater unities' (p. 179) while the destruction drive aims to 'dissolve connections' (p. 179). These two drives work with and against each other to produce a plethora of life-phenomena.

The entire amount of the libido is initially stored in the Ego in a state termed 'primary narcissism' (p. 180). This state continues until the Ego begins 'to invest its notions of objects with libido, to transform narcissistic libido into *object-libido*' (ibid. italics in original).

Relatedly, sexual life starts to manifest itself soon after birth. Sexual phenomena emerge in early childhood and increase, reaching a peak around the age of five years when they 'take a rest' in what Freud calls the 'latency period'. After this, towards puberty, the process blooms again. Events in the early period of sexuality become the subject of infantile amnesia (p. 182). Sexual phenomena are envisaged in stages:

- Oral
- Sadistic–anal
- Phallic
- Genital.

In the initial oral stage erotic activity is centred on the mouth. So-called 'sadistic impulses' begin at this stage with the cutting of the infant's teeth (p. 183). In the second, 'sadistic–anal' phase, gratification is sought in 'aggression and in the excretory function' (ibid.).

The third, 'phallic' phase is associated with the Oedipus complex. A boy, sexually attracted to his mother, may fear his jealous father will castrate him. As he comes to recognise the threat and identify with his father, the boy's Oedipus complex starts to fade. A girl may, in recognising she has no penis or in the 'inferiority' of her clitoris, experience her first disappointment in rivalry, with future consequences in character development (pp. 183–184). The complete organisation of the fourth, genital phase occurs at puberty. Any inhibitions in the development of this phase express themselves as 'the manifold disruptions to sexual life' (p. 184).

Three qualities are attributed to psychical processes; that they are: unconscious, pre-conscious, or conscious (p. 188). The purpose of psychoanalysis with adults is to provide treatment in which the patient can express his self-observations without censorship. This allows the analyst to deduce the patient's 'repressed unconscious material and to extend the knowledge his *Ich* has of his unconscious by sharing it with him' (p. 202, italics in original). In this process, the patient sees the analyst as the reincarnation of an important person from his past. He transfers feelings originally associated with the past figure to the analyst. Part of the treatment is for the analyst to use and reveal these feelings to help the patient to recognise and resolve conflicted wishes.

Pine (1990) conceptualising the development of psychoanalysis, succinctly describes Freud's theory as concerned with unconscious motivation in which libidinal and aggressive drives are considered to be the prime movers of mental life and behaviour. Wolitzky (2003) provides a lucid outline of Freudian theory and practice.

Freud's clinical work (Freud, S. [1940] 2003, pp. 175–236; 1923) was almost solely with adult patients. He reported a well-known case study on a child 'Little Hans' (Freud, S., 1909) as 'Analysis of a phobia in a five-year-old boy'. In fact, although Freud did see the boy and the boy's father, treatment was largely carried out by the father, a follower of Freud's, under instructions that Freud set out in a series of letters.

Klein, Winnicott and Bowlby

Pioneering work in analysis with children was undertaken by Freud's daughter Anna (Freud, A. ([various dates] 1998). However, for the purposes of the present chapter, the focus is on the work of three other psychoanalysts: Melanie Klein, Donald Winnicott and John Bowlby.

All of these innovators made important contributions to the understanding of childhood emotional disorders and their treatment. Sigmund Freud had hypothesised that children aged around 5 or 6 struggled with deep incestuous wishes. Klein (Klein, 1932; ([various dates] 1964; [1957] 1975), through her clinical work and observation of children, considered she was extending Sigmund Freud's ideas. She believed children aged around 2 or 3 (and even infants) experienced fantasies of incestuous union and of frightening punishments, but that the fantasies were in a much more primitive form.

Klein believed children could be analysed through interpreting their play rather as, with an adult, free association is analysed. By contrast, Anna Freud (Freud, A., 1945; [various dates] 1998) and her followers believed very young children could not be analysed because a child's Ego is insufficiently developed to cope with in-depth interpretations of instinctual conflicts (Mitchell and Black, 1995, p. 86).

Winnicott (1958, 1965) is associated with 'object relations' theory. Initially trained as a paediatrician, he developed theories of the early mother–child relationship and its connection with an individual's later development, whether this was healthy or dysfunctional. He focused on a state of 'false self disorder' affecting adult patients' sense of being a person, linking this to the patient's infant relationship with the mother. Winnicott referred to the infant's earliest state of mind as 'unintegration'. From this early, unintegrated drift of consciousness, the infant's needs and wishes emerge.

A 'good enough' mother creates a 'holding environment' in which the baby is protected without knowing it. Such a mother normally meets the baby's wishes and needs. But as the mother inevitably gradually emerges from her absorption with her infant, she does not meet the baby's needs as seamlessly as she did initially. The baby gradually comes to several related realisations: his desires are not omnipotent, his mother provides for him, and he is dependent on her. This experience of objective reality is added to the infant's experience of subjective omnipotence.

A 'transitional object' might be anything from a piece of cloth to a favourite toy, which becomes an extension of the child's self. It occupies a position between the child's two experiences of his mother that the child creates in subjective omnipotence and his mother acting for herself in the objective world. Transitional experience connects the subjective omnipotence aspects of the self to the world of other people's subjectivity. Where the mother cannot provide the child with a 'good enough' environment, the core of his personhood is arrested. He develops a premature concern with the external world constraining his own subjectivity and the true self becomes separated from a false compliant self. In later life, a holding environment might be found enabling the individual to develop authentic experience and a sense of self. In the analytic setting, the analyst provides the adult patient with this 'good enough' environment in which the patient's arrested development of self can be restarted so the true self can emerge (Mitchell and Black, 1995, pp. 124–134).

Like Winnicott, Bowlby also placed great importance on the bond between child and mother, which Bowlby termed 'attachment'. His theory of attachment relates to the biological survival of the species, and functions to secure the infant's safety in a loving environment (Bowlby, 1965, 1969, 1973, 1980). Bowlby proposed five instinctive responses that mediate attachment, leading to greater 'proximity' to the mother: sucking, smiling, clinging, crying and following. He argued that the child's attachment to the mother does not derive from the mother providing for the child's needs, but is instinctual and primary. His research into early experience of loss and separation indicated they lead to mourning.

This appears to support the importance of the primacy of the child's bond with the mother. Emotional security is built up through early childhood experiences and relates to the confidence the child has in the availability of attachment figures. Different forms of anxiety relate to basic anxiety about the separation from the object of attachment. All defences relate back to detachment in a 'deactivation of the fundamental and central need for attachment' (Mitchell and Black 1995, p. 137).

Evaluation of a psychoanalytic approach

Freud writes with conviction and in many ways with clarity, and he presents arguments followed by possible objections, so that the threads of the case can be very convincing. Among the strengths of a psychoanalytic approach is the dynamic nature of the psychoanalytic model. It has a flexibility and subtlety that seem necessary to depict the enormously complicated nature of mental life and behaviour. The notion that there are unconscious forces of which we are normally unaware is an attractive concept that seems to reflect the common experience of doing things individuals find difficult to explain. Such is the power of Freud's explanations and concepts that many have become part of common parlance, even though not always with a full understanding of the Freudian ideas.

The notions of the Ego, and the Superego, the power of infantile experiences and recognition of powerful unconscious forces are widely if loosely accepted in Western society. Aspects of Freud's theories, such as the exact development of the Oedipus complex, have been extensively debated. The developments instigated by those focusing more on childhood, such as Klein, Winnicott and Bowlby, are considered to have made important contributions to the understanding of childhood emotional disorders and their treatment.

Yet criticisms of psychoanalysis stem from the very permeating nature of the concepts, which seem at first glance to have an explanation for anything and everything. Scepticism towards psychoanalytic perspectives has been expressed in relation to the difficulty in testing meaningful hypotheses – relating to outcomes, for example. However, there is some evidence of the effectiveness of specific psychodynamic approaches. Focal dynamic psychotherapy is one example described later.

The most telling recent criticisms of Freud are those of Webster (2007). Among criticisms of Freud himself (and by implication of his findings) is his apparent proneness to being star-struck by charismatic healers such as Charcot and afterwards insufficiently interrogating their ideas. Criticisms of Freud's theories include that, from the beginning, they were based on likely misdiagnoses of hysteria. Anna O., the woman who Freud's colleague Breuer had treated, was viewed as suffering a psychological condition. But evidence indicates that Anna was not suffering from hysteria, neither was she cured (ibid. pp. 103–135).

Similar doubts are raised about the nature of the illness of another early patient, Frau Emmy von N. The mechanisms that Freud uses to describe the apparent functioning of the psyche are considered by Webster to be little more than pseudo-science, unknowingly immersed in the traditions of Judeo-Christian religious culture (ibid. pp. 168–181 and *passim*). Freud is seen as being fluent in 'mystical exegesis', which helps create the illusion of explanatory power (ibid. p. 295).

The development of psychoanalysis as a movement is presented in terms of religious dogma rather than a scientific movement, with Freud acting as a messianic figure. A possible alternative theory that scientifically begins to explain human behaviour without recourse to mysterious forces and pseudo-science might emerge from neo-Darwinism, argues Webster (2007).

Psychoanalysis and special education

General theorising

Marks (1999) brings together insights from social approaches to disability and psychoanalysis, as well as referring to the embodiment of disability and the work of Merleau-Ponty. She relates some aspects of psychoanalytic theory to disability, mainly drawing on various psychoanalytically related 'defences' such as projection (pp. 18–24). The term 'projection' is used in psychoanalysis to indicate mechanisms that transfer aspects of the psyche to the external world. It enables individuals to expel feelings or qualities they refuse to recognise in themselves, making these feelings and qualities seem aspects of the external world rather than part of oneself. Sigmund Freud ([1923] 1960) uses the word 'projection' in this sense while Anna Freud (1936) uses it to refer to one of the Ego's defence mechanisms.

Marks (1999) uses the notion of projection to suggest that a pupil who is badly behaved, or considered by others to be 'disturbed', 'may be acting as a convenient repository for all the rebellious feelings in the school' (p. 19). Health professionals, it is said, may be trying to sort out their own problems rather than being able to help clients. Marks quotes Skynner (1991, p. xviii) who suggests, 'The mental health professional automatically selects the ideal clientele in which to study himself or herself vicariously and discover what is missing' (Skynner, 1991, p. xviii). In other words, Marks explains of health professionals, 'the person who is unable to deal with their own rage, vulnerability or sense of shame may identify these characteristics in others, and remain disconnected with these disowned parts of themselves, through contact with stigmatised people' (Marks, 1999, pp. 109–110).

Therapy

Turning to treatment approaches, sessions of focal dynamic psychotherapy appear effective with children with mild anxiety disorder or dysthymic disorder (involving chronically depressed mood). One study concerned 58 children with mild anxiety disorder or dysthymic disorder treated through focal psychodynamic psychotherapy. This began with five sessions involving the whole family in which the therapist explored the dynamic formulation of the child's conflicts in terms of family relationships. Next came five sessions with the child only. In these, the therapist aimed to help the child make connections between his feelings and unconscious conflicts about the relationship with his parents. The final session included the whole family, and the therapist once more set out the dynamic formulation of the child's conflicts rooted in family relationships (Muratori *et al.*, 2002). Comparisons between the treatment group and a control group appear encouraging. Some 60% of children in the study were in the clinical range of the *Child Behaviour Checklist* (Achenbach and Edelbrock, 1983). In the treatment group, this was reduced to 34% at follow-up testing. In the control group in which children were referred for community treatment, the percentage increased to 65% (Muratori *et al.*, 2002).

Some approaches to music therapy, art therapy, drama therapy and movement therapy draw on psychodynamic perspectives. These 'arts therapies' may involve therapeutic interventions or programmes to promote wellness in the general population. The idea of the unconscious is said to be 'central to some areas of the arts therapies: their thinking and their methodology' (Jones, 2005, p. 126). Some arts therapists' work draws on 'ways of engaging with the unconscious which can bring about change or healing' (ibid. p.128). Art making and arts products within therapy are considered to relate to the unconscious in ways 'fundamental to the recovery of health, or the improvement or maintenance of well being' (ibid.). In the United Kingdom, research (Karkou, 1999a and 1999b, *passim*) suggests that among the main theoretical influences in arts therapies are Winnicott (1958, 1965) and Klein ([1957] 1975). Also, some orientations of play therapy are psychodynamic.

Where possible, the effectiveness of psychotherapies is evaluated in line with evidence-based practice. There is a perceived dichotomy between seeking to use objective approaches to assess the efficacy of arts therapies and the more fluid nature of therapeutic encounters, making developing evidence-based practice challenging. However, examinations have been made of ways in which drama therapists ascertain whether the client is 'getting any better' – experiencing improved well-being, for example (Valente and Fontana, 1997, p. 29). This might be suggested by client self-reports, projective techniques, and reports by other group members. In art therapy, evaluation may involve a review of pictures with the client, which may uncover previously unconscious 'connections and links' (Schaverien, 1995, p. 28).

To the extent that a psychodynamic approach implies underlying unconscious or subconscious forces influencing behaviour, connections with special education are tangential. Settings for special education may encourage more open communication from pupils and provide activities that may be communicative and expressive, such as drama, aspects of physical education, and play. But important differences exist between such activities and their therapeutic counterparts. Drama is not drama therapy and play is not play therapy. The aim of each is different and the training and perspectives of educators and therapists differ substantially.

Specialist settings and approaches

However, some very specialist settings use psychodynamic interpretations in day-to-day living and individual sessions. The Mulberry Bush special school in the United Kingdom (www.mulberrybush.oxon.sch.uk) draws on the work of its psychotherapist founder Barbara Dockar-Drysdale (1991, 1993) who developed her approach from the work of Winnicott (1958, 1965). The school works on the principle that its children have missed the 'building blocks' of nurturing experiences and seeks to offer them the opportunity to re-experience caring and clear relationships with adults and other children. Among the ways staff do this is through 'planned environment therapy', using opportunities associated with group living to give the child clear expectations, routines and rules about how to live and get on with others (Farrell, 2006, p. 66 gives a fuller description).

In ordinary school settings, the development of early intervention 'nurture groups' (Boxall, 2002) draws on Bowlby's attachment theory. These discrete groups are intended for children whose emotional, social and behavioural 'needs' cannot be addressed in a mainstream classroom. The intention is to return the children to mainstream classes as soon as appropriate. The group might comprise a teacher and an assistant and ten to twelve children. It is hypothesised these children have not had early experiences that would have enabled them to function socially and emotionally appropriately for their age.

The relationship between the child and the adults is seen as important to the child developing a sense of self. Social development is encouraged, concentrating on the emotional aspects of interactions between child and caregiver. Therefore, a nurture group emphasises emotional growth. It provides a range of experiences in an environment that provides security, predictable routines, clear boundaries, and repeated planned opportunities for learning (Boxall, 2002). The adults might 'model' suitable positive behaviour in a structure conversant with the child's developmental level. This provision aims to enable the child to develop an attachment to the adult, receive approval, and experience positive outcomes.

Evaluation of psychoanalysis in special education

Marks's (1999) suggestions of how psychoanalytic concepts might relate to disability are standard considerations. There may be underlying sources of the behaviour of children considered disturbed. They may be acting as 'a convenient repository for all the rebellious feelings in the school' (ibid. p. 19). But this seems more of a recognition that things are not always as they seem that could come from an agony aunt rather than from a student of psychoanalysis. Some health professionals may be disconnected from their own problems, and see their own unwelcome feelings in others, and this may limit their ability to understand clients better (Skynner, 1991, p. xviii; Marks, 1999, pp. 109–110).

But again this seems to concern a basic development of insight into motivation rather than anything necessarily supposedly unconscious. It is not clear what extra penetrating insight psychoanalysis offers. However, this may be because psychoanalytic concepts and pseudo-psychoanalytic concepts have permeated daily conversations to such an extent that they are barely noticed.

Furthermore it is difficult to see, in general and in particular circumstances, how it could be determined whether such suggestions are accurate or not. A child may be a repository of institutional rebellious feeling or he may not. He may be 'disturbed' (with inverted commas) as, presumably, the unhappy recipient of the unfair negative labelling of others. Or he may be disturbed (without inverted commas) in that his behaviour is far beyond what is age-typical or what a school can be reasonably expected to cope with unaided. The label therefore arises as a way of the school or parents saying they need support to educate a child and try to help him develop socially and personally.

A helping professional may seek out a helping profession because they lack insight into their own functioning. Or they may be able to deal with their own rage, vulnerability or sense of shame and not identify these characteristics in others. If the supposed underpinnings of such responses are unconscious defences, it is difficult to know how one could discern which was the more correct explanation of their choice of profession. Such suspicions are perhaps speculative correctives to the opposite assumption that every helping professional is driven by purely selfless motives.

The criterion of positivist evidence may not be applicable to theories developed by Freud and others. The individual and subjective nature of their remit may limit the degree that usual rules of evidence can be brought to bear. Yet Freud himself saw his work as scientific and amenable to examination and confirmation.

Where psychoanalytic perspectives have informed special education, the evidence of their suitability has been difficult to demonstrate. Professional judgement and personal testimony have often had to take the place of research evidence. This may not be a major criticism as the complexity of life changes within a psychoanalytic remit are unlikely to be as amenable to short-term objective research as the results of some other interventions.

To take only one example, the work of the Mulberry Bush School received an exemplary report (www.ofsted.gov.uk/oxedu_reports) from the agency responsible for inspecting schools in England. In 2008, the report found the school's overall effectiveness 'outstanding', with residential care, psychotherapy, family support and education 'very well co-ordinated'. The testimony of pupils who have left the school can also be cited. One such account is reported in Farrell (2006, pp. 42–43). A former pupil states of his time at the Mulberry Bush, 'I will never forget the life there and the profound impact it had on my life'. He speaks of 'the love of one teacher in particular' and of the other children there 'whose only crime was to be born to parents or situations that were at the very least toxic'. He says, 'Those of us who survived the brutality of the past will never forget it. But we can rise above it'. He states, 'Sitting in front of the big tree in front of the school with people whose names are lost to time, they could never have realised the difference they made' (ibid.).

Such testimonies do not fall easily into a model of evidence-based practice that can be widely applied. Yet they speak profoundly of individual life transformations. To the extent that such work can be traced through to psychoanalytic theory and practice, perhaps it is worthwhile to probe more deeply into an approach that can produce, even occasionally, such outcomes.

Implications for thinking and practice of psychoanalysis in special education

Someone supporting a psychoanalytic viewpoint may consider processes such as projection important. In a school or elsewhere, she may regard a pupil who is considered disturbed to possibly be the repository for rebellious feelings within the institution. She might take the view that mental health professionals may also be projecting some of their own rage, shame or vulnerability on to clients, misdiagnosing them and remaining disconnected from their own feelings.

There is a considerable difference between therapy and other curriculum provision – for example, between drama therapy and drama, or between play and play therapy. Nevertheless someone holding a psychoanalytical view of special education might consider several of the arts subjects relevant as modes of communication. This may suggest encouraging more open communication from pupils and providing activities that may be communicative and expressive such as drama, aspects of physical education, and play. The assessment of such contribution might be in terms of subject progress in skills and knowledge but also a judgement about the contribution to well-being and general communicativeness.

By its nature, a psychoanalytical approach concerns therapy more than pedagogy. However, it is important in a mainstream or special school where therapy is provided that it is planned into the whole curriculum. Arrangements may need to be made to ensure that the curriculum is viewed as a whole so that both therapy and education are balanced. Also, careful thought will be given to transition times as a pupil moves from a lesson to a therapy session or vice versa.

Among physical resources that may be used when a psychoanalytic approach is taken to special educational provision is that of items for play therapy, costumes or other materials for drama therapy, and instruments for music therapy.

Someone advocating a psychoanalytical viewpoint may work in a specialist setting which uses psychodynamic interpretations in day-to-day living and individual sessions. She might consider important nurturing experiences and offering children the opportunity for re-experiencing caring and clear relationships with adults and other children. This might be a special school or

therapeutic community. She might work through 'planned environment therapy', using group-living opportunities to give the child clear expectations,
routines and rules about how to live and get on with others.

In ordinary school settings, she might draw on attachment theory and be
involved with early intervention 'nurture groups' for children whose emotional, social and behavioural 'needs' cannot be addressed in a mainstream
classroom.

She may regard focal dynamic psychotherapy as effective with children with
mild anxiety disorder or dysthymic disorder, referring to evidence-based practice. She may consider psychoanalytical views of the unconscious as important
and take a positive view of psychoanalytically grounded approaches to music
therapy, art therapy, drama therapy, movement therapy, and play therapy.
Generally, someone holding a psychoanalytical perspective may consider that
such interventions can bring about healing and promote and maintain well-
being. She may examine evidence of the effectiveness of psychotherapies
through evidence-based practice, while recognising that there may be difficulties in using objective approaches to assess the efficacy of arts therapies and
aspects of therapeutic encounters. Evidence might include clients' views of
whether they are getting better or reviewing physical art products emerging
from therapy.

Lacan's theories

The imaginary and the mirror stage

Lacan ([various dates and 1966] 2006) in *Écrits* reconsiders Freudian theories,
and their possible relationships with language, with reference to structuralist
and poststructuralist theories of discourse.

In Lacan, the 'imaginary' refers to a state of being in very early infancy in
which it is not possible to have a distinction between subject and object and
subject and the external environment. There is no centre of self, and any
notion of self inter-permeates with objects. In the pre-Oedipal state, the child
has a symbiotic relationship with the mother's body, with no clear boundaries
between them. In 'Aggressiveness in Psychoanalysis' ([1948 and 1966] 2005)
Lacan refers to mental phenomena known as 'images' and to specific images
for which he uses the old term 'imago' (p. 85). Some of these represent the
'elective vectors of aggressive intentions'. They are images of 'castration, emasculation, mutilation, dismemberment, dislocation, evisceration, devouring and
bursting open of the body'. Lacan groups these as 'imagos of the fragmented
body' (ibid.).

Understanding of the later 'mirror stage' can be approached by envisaging
the child looking at itself in a mirror. The child sees a unified image of itself
which is both the child's self and not the child's self. There is still an 'imaginary' permeating of the self and the object, but the beginning of the ego and

constructing a centre of self emerge from this state. The sense of self is derived from finding that the self is reflected back by a person or object in the world. Such an object is both part of the self and not part of the self at the same time, so we both identify with it and find it alien.

The image the child sees in the mirror has a unity not experienced by the child as the child incorrectly recognises itself in the image which is alien. This is the sense in which Lacan uses the term imaginary – relating to images in which we make identification but at the same time misperceive ourselves. This continues as the child develops and grows up as the individual continues to make imaginary identifications with objects, so building up the ego. The ego then is a narcissistic process through which we develop a fictive sense of complete self by identifying with objects in the world.

Recall that Saussure ([1915] 1966, pp. 65–70) distinguishes the sign, the signifier and the signified. Language is a system of 'signs' comprising a 'signifier' (for example a spoken word, 'cat') and a 'signified' (the concept, cat). The sign gains its meaning not from being directly linked to the external object to which it refers (a real cat) but through the similarities or differences to other signs in the system.

The child looking at itself in the mirror may be seen as a 'signifier', capable of giving meaning. The image in the mirror is a kind of 'signified'. The image the child sees is in a sense the meaning of itself. Consequently, signifier and signified are united, as in Saussure's sign. Another metaphorical understanding of the mirror phase is the child as an item seeing a likeness of itself in another item, the reflection. In this state of 'plenitude', the child as a signifier sees a whole identity in the signified of the reflection. Signifier and signified, object and world are one.

In the lecture, 'The Mirror Stage as Formative of the I Function as Revealed in Psychoanalytic Experience', the mirror stage is depicted as a 'drama' which 'turns out fantasies that proceed from a fragmented image of the body' towards the 'armour of an alienating identity' (Lacan, [1949 and 1966] 2006, p. 78).

Lacan's interpretation of the Oedipal phase

In the Oedipal phase, the recognition of the father signifies sexual difference. Lacan uses the term 'phallus' to convey the signification of sexual difference. The entry of the father changes the unity of the mirror phase. Again this is interpreted in terms of language. In Saussure's linguistics the signs that constitute *langue* (social aspects of language organised into a system to convey ideas) are arbitrary and only agreed by convention. It is the differences between signs that give them their meaning.

In Lacan's terms, the entry of the father leads the child to recognise that identities come about by differences from others. A subject is what it is by virtue of excluding another. The child's discovery of sexual difference occurs at the time of the development of real language. The child unconsciously learns that signs gain their meaning by their difference from other signs and that a sign implies the absence of the signified object. Sexual developments parallel this.

The father's presence, symbolised by the phallus, leads the child to recognise that the place it must take in the family is defined by sexual difference. The role is also defined by absence and exclusion. The child must absent itself from the unity with its mother's body and must be excluded from being its parent's lover. The child's identity as a subject, the child comes to see, is made up by the relations of difference and similarity to other subjects. In this process, the child moves from the imaginary to the 'symbolic order'. The child enters the pre-existing roles and relations of family and society.

In this context, Lacan uses the term 'name-of-the-father' (nom-du-père) to convey the father of the Oedipus complex whose threat of castration marks the prohibition of incest. The 'no' of the father implies a play on the words 'nom' and 'non' as in 'non-du-père'. In a seminar held in 1955 on psychosis, Lacan presents the name-of-the-father as the fundamental signifier having two functions. It gives identity to subjects by placing them in a lineage and the symbolic order. It also underlines the prohibition of incest (Lacan, [1955 and 1956 and 1966] 2006, pp. 445–488).

In Freudian theory, the child after the Oedipal phase is conflicted between the repressed desires of the unconscious and the executive functions of the ego. In Lacan's theory, the child leaves the full imaginary possession of the mother's body and his unified self. He leaves this for the empty world of language in the symbolic order, where there is nothing but an endless chain of absence and difference. In Lacan's theory, the mirror world is traded for the world of language.

This brings in Lacan's use of the term 'desire' as the interminable movement from one signifier to another. Desire stems from a wish to rectify a lack of something. Language operates from such a lack, as signs designate real objects, which are absent, and words derive meaning from the exclusion of other words. Entering language precipitates desire and separates us from the 'real', which is beyond the symbolic order. Instead of unity with the mother's body, we have to make do with substitute objects ('objects little a'). No transcendental object or meaning fulfils our desire. Even the phallus as a 'transcendental signifier' is only an indication of what separates us from the imaginary and places in the symbolic order.

For Lacan, the unconscious is structured like language because it is more composed of signifiers (with likely multiple meanings) than signs (stable meanings). The unconscious is a shifting of signifiers whose signifieds may be inaccessible to us because they are repressed. The ego operates by repressing the constant shifting of meaning to temporarily fix words to meaning. However, meaning remains slippery and elusive. The subject continues as never one with itself and spread along the lines of discourse that make it up. The ego is a function of this dispersed subject.

Evaluation of Lacan's theories

Lacan can write with insight and subtlety as, for example, in much of 'Seminar on "The Purloined Letter"' (Lacan, ([1955 and 1966] 2006) before he gets lost in algebraic formulae. But Lacan is much criticised for his apparent obscurantism, of which parades of new terminology is a part – the 'imaginary', the 'mirror stage', 'phallus', 'law of the father', 'object little a', and so on. Nevertheless, Lacan's working out of the implications of pre-Oedipal and Oedipal stages and their interpretation in relation to language (Lacan, [various dates and 1966] 2006) has provided fertile ground for speculation about a range of areas, including psychoanalysis itself, literary theory, philosophy, feminism, and disability.

Derrida (1975) criticises Lacan for 'logocentrism' and 'phallogocentrism'. By logocentrism, Derrida means the tendency in Western philosophy to make speech the origin of truth and prioritise speech over writing. Speech in philosophy is presumed to be a complete means of expression available to a self-consciously rational subject. Writing is seen as a mere supplement to speech. The related term, 'phallogocentrism', combines 'phallocentrism' and 'logocentrism'. It was coined by Derrida (1975) to indicate his criticism that Lacan presents the 'word' as the site of truth. Lacan does this, Derrida suggests, because he makes the phallus the key signifier that dictates access to the symbolic order and determines sexual difference.

Sokal and Bricmont ([1997] 1999) make a more general point that Lacan's use of mathematical symbols is meaningless. It is presented as meaningful, with little indication that it is suggestive or metaphorical, yet is nonsensical. Sokal and Bricmont's criticism extends beyond Lacan to other postmodern writers. The criticisms include that such writers use scientific and pseudoscientific terms so loosely that they are vacuous, and that they use scientific terms without justifying their use or explaining their application. Dawkins (1998) in a review in *Nature* suggests Lacan's writing is full of scientific pretensions and that a philosopher caught 'equating the erectile organ with the square root of minus one' lacks any credibility.

Sokal and Bricmont ([1997] 1999), after providing examples of his misuse of mathematical and scientific concepts, criticise Lacan for the privilege he accords theory rather than observation and experiment. They point out that even if one assumes psychoanalysis has a scientific basis, it is a still a 'young science'. They suggest that before anyone launches into 'vast theoretical generalisations' about psychoanalysis, it might be wise to 'check the empirical adequacy of at least some of its propositions'. However, Lacan does not do this. Instead, his writings comprise 'mainly quotations and analyses of texts and concepts' (ibid. p. 34).

Others defend Lacan by suggesting that he is difficult to read and that scientists may lack the ability or have not devoted the time necessary to understand him – by not having a background in philosophy, for example. Bruce Fink, the main translator of the complete *Écrits*, suggests that Sokal and Bricmont miss the point that Lacan is using mathematical terminology metaphorically. He criticises Sokal and Bricmont for expecting 'clear meanings' as the only standard of serious writing (Fink, 2004, p. 130). This suggestion is difficult to sustain however. Sokal and Bricmont ([1997] 1998) consider whether Lacan is writing metaphorically and conclude that he is not. If he were writing metaphorically, one still has to consider what the metaphors convey. There is no indication what the supposed mathematical metaphors are meant to mean or suggest. A fair conclusion is that they are there for effect and were not understood by Lacan himself.

Also, it is difficult to know what Fink means when criticising 'clear meanings' as the only standard of serious writing. Of course clear meaning is not necessarily expected of serious poetry – or flippant poetry for that matter. The elusiveness of meaning and subtle suggestiveness is one of the charms of poetry. But in exposition it is rather a different matter. If a writer is introducing a theoretic framework, as Lacan wishes to do, then it is hard not to expect him to try to express his meaning clearly. In this, Lacan often disappoints, and all the talk that the reader ought to be cleverer in order to understand the seminars or essays rings rather false.

Lacan's theories and special education

Attempts have been made to relate Lacan's ideas to the study of disability. Not surprisingly, they have focused on what Lacan appears to be saying about the body. Shildrick (2009) recalls Lacan's discussion of the early imaginary and his mention of 'a fragmented image of the body' (Lacan, [1949 and 1966] 2006, p. 78). She refers to Lacan's mention of 'imagos' of 'castration, emasculation, mutilation, dismemberment, dislocation, evisceration, devouring and bursting open of the body' (Lacan, [1948 and 1966] 2005, p. 85). Shildrick (2009) suggests such images can remind us of the 'socio-cultural fantasies that have always surrounded disability' (ibid. p. 91). These forms of embodiment must be suppressed for the child to achieve the stability that marks out the 'normatively embodied subject' (ibid.). They re-emerge in the subject, however, as Lacan notes, in the form of aggressiveness.

Shildrick (2009) relates this notion to implications for a body that persists in its 'manifestation of dis-integration and disunity' (p. 91), that is, the disabled body. The disabled body may become a repository of anxiety. The anxiety may apply to bodily anxiety and also to the nature and being of disability and might attract a violent response. As individuals emerge into the symbolic order, the hold on order and control is fragile. The subject is 'insecure in its apparent normativity'. Disorder is held at bay by strategies that keep at a distance others 'whose own corporeality re-awakens intimations of a fundamental dis-organisation, and lack of self-completion' (ibid.). Faced with 'the reappearance of its pre-subjectival phantasies that should have been banished

– faced in substantive terms with the body of disability – the subject is endangered by the putative failure of its own boundaries of distinction and separation' (ibid. p. 92).

On the other hand, writing in the context of exploring disability, subjectivity and sexuality, Shildrick (2009) suggests a further interpretation. An idea of return to the disorganised body of the imaginary is associated with 'psychic danger' but its half-remembered pleasures 'also signify a seductive promise' (ibid. p. 96). So a response to disabled individuals may be to 'devalue or silence their sexuality'. Another response may be also a strand of voyeurism or identification 'that spills over into a fetishistic focus on disabled bodies precisely as sexual' (ibid.). Briefly then, the reaction of others to disability, according to Shildrick (2009), can be aggressive or fetishist.

Wilton (2003) draws on psychoanalytic theory to consider the meaning of disability in what he considers an 'ableist' culture and its relationships to death and sexuality. In psychoanalysis, disability has been used to stand as a symbolic substitute for castration, as understood by Lacan (and Freud). The implications of this formulation are that disabled bodies are culturally constructed as 'lacking'. Psychoanalysis provides insight into the origins of 'aesthetic anxieties' associated with disability in an ableist culture. It also offers insight into the way anxieties are involved in the geographic exclusion of 'different' bodies. Psychoanalysis is thought to indicate the illusory nature of the 'able-body' as a source of oppression.

For Corker and Shakespeare (2002a), a Lacanian view of disability might argue that 'the entire order of disabling culture' divides us into two states – impaired and normal, in the form of a hierarchy that privileges the latter. It does so through linguistic structures that are so deep that the 'tyranny of the normal' not only breaks up the impaired/'normal' dyad, but does so to the degree that any possibility of relationship to the normal is repressed in the unconscious as the imaginary. The entire concept of identity takes place through this repression of impairment, in such a way that people with impairments 'cannot affirmatively identify with others like themselves' (ibid. pp. 8–9).

Vanheule, Lievrouw and Verhaeghe (2003) look at intersubjective processes connected with burnout. Using qualitative data from interviews with thirty special educators, they examine Lacan's model of intersubjectivity and the way it might enable understanding of burnout and how people who experience burn out and those who do not might be differentiated. Lacan's distinction between imaginary and symbolic functioning allowed the researchers to make a difference between high and low scorers. High scorers functioned mainly in an imaginary way. Low scorers either interacted symbolically, or interacted imaginarily (with environmental factors having a protective function).

Evaluation of Lacan's theories and disability

Lacan presents the notion that, early in the imaginary, the infant experiences itself as fragmented (Lacan, [1949 and 1966] 2006, p. 78) and is exposed to frightening images such as those of 'castration' and 'mutilation' (Lacan, [1948 and 1966] 2005, p. 85). Acknowledgement of aggression is, of course, evident in Freudian theory. In *An Outline of Psychoanalysis*, Freud ([1940] 2003) refers to 'sadistic impulses' beginning at the oral stage with the cutting of the infant's teeth (p. 183). Also in the second 'sadistic–anal' phase, gratification is sought in 'aggression and in the excretory function' (ibid.).

Nevertheless, the basis of Lacan's suggestions concerning the frightening images is unclear. Shildrick's concentration on the fragmented and discontinuous early imaginary therefore draws on an aspect of Lacan that does not appear to build on Freud. This does not of course necessarily imply that Lacan's theorising at this point cannot be justified or supported elsewhere. However, there is no basis to enable a judgement to be made about the credibility of these notions. Furthermore, it is difficult to know what the response might be to such speculations.

Disturbing fragmented and discontinuous early imaginary images may suggest a reason if there is anxiety about and negativity towards disabled individuals. But such experiences are unconscious and therefore by definition normally inaccessible to the person affected by them. In Freudian analysis the shadows of the unconscious may be glimpsed through techniques such as dream analysis and free association, and internal conflicts may sometimes appear to be resolved through transference within the therapeutic relationship. But it is unclear what this implied about possible sources of anxiety concerning disabled people.

Shildrick (2009) draws on the ideas of Lacan ([1966] 2006; and especially Lacan, [1949 and 1966] 2006; Lacan, [1948 and 1966] 2006) to explore possible sources of responses to disability. Her discussion is focused on sexuality and subjectivity in relation to disability. However, her more generalised suggestions indicate a possible starting point for understanding negative and positive responses to disability in terms of early infantile experience and states. Shildrick herself however finds something of an impasse in the further development of Lacan's ideas in the context of her exploration of disability, subjectivity and sexuality.

Wilton (2003) uses Lacan's ideas to consider the meaning of disability and how disability has been used to stand as a symbolic substitute for castration, suggesting that disabled bodies are culturally constructed as 'lacking'. Psychoanalysis is thought to illuminate the origins of 'aesthetic anxieties' associated with disability, how anxieties are involved in the geographic exclusion of different bodies, and the illusory nature of the 'able-body' as a source of oppression. No external or confirmatory evidence is offered for these purely speculative ideas.

Corker and Shakespeare (2002a) suggest a Lacan-based view of disability in which 'disabling culture' privileges normal over impaired, through linguistic structures. It does so to an extent that potential relationship to the normal is 'repressed in the unconscious as the imaginary'. This repression of impairment influences identity such that 'people with impairments cannot affirmatively identify with others like themselves' (ibid. pp. 8–9). This is pure speculation and may or may not represent an accurate picture of psychic operations. There appears to be no way of confirming or disconfirming such views, which limits their value.

The criticisms of Sokal and Bricmont ([1997] 1998) about Lacan, for the privilege he accords theory rather than observation and experiment, seem to be worthy of consideration for speculation that builds on Lacan's speculation. Sokal and Bricmont ([1997] 1998) may have a point in criticising Lacan for 'launching into vast theoretical generalisations' rather than checking 'the empirical adequacy of at least some' of their propositions. If this is the case then the criticism applies with even greater force to subsequent ideas.

In a special education setting, Vanheule, Lievrouw and Verhaeghe (2003) at least attempt to relate speculation to interview results, although the implications of the findings – that those prone to burnout functioned imaginarily while those less prone to burnout functioned symbolically (or imaginatively with environmental protective factors) – are unclear.

Implications for thinking and practice of Lacan's theories in special education

The main application of Lacanian ideas is in trying to understand what might be the hidden (because unconscious) motives that lead some people to view disabled individuals negatively or with anxiety. They do not lend themselves naturally to considerations of the curriculum and assessment, pedagogy and other aspects of special educational provision.

Someone who draws on the views of Lacan in special education may take particular interest in how unconscious processes might influence the way able-bodied individuals perceive impairment and how people with impairments might perceive each other. Given that Lacan related the structure of language to that of the unconscious, it is not surprising that someone influenced by Lacan would be interested in language and perception as well as unconscious processes.

Someone interested in Lacan might focus on his discussion of the early imaginary and its fragmented images of the body. She might relate this to images sometimes associated with disability (particularly physical disability). The view may be taken that such fantasies have to be suppressed so a child can achieve the stability of normative embodiment, but that they can re-emerge in the subject in the form of aggressiveness.

A Lacanian may take the view that where a body continues as a form of disunity (that is a physically disabled body) that body may become a repository of anxiety. She may consider that this might evoke a violent response and that an individual identity responding to a disabled person may feel endangered by the putative failure of its own boundaries of distinction and separation. On the other hand, some responses to disability may be regarded as fetishist.

A Lacanian might examine the meaning of disability in a culture that priori-tises ability. She may consider that Lacan's views help to explain why disabled bodies are culturally constructed as 'lacking', and how aesthetic anxieties emerge associated with disability in an ableist culture. She may consider how anxieties are involved in the way disabled people might be excluded by the built environment.

She may argue that normality is placed in a hierarchy above impaired through deep linguistic structures. This leads to the normal being so dominant that the link between impaired and normal as a pair is broken. She may con-sider that any possibility of relationship of the impaired to the normal is repressed in the unconscious as the imaginary. The concept of identity takes place through this repression of impairment, so that people with impairments cannot affirmatively identify with others like themselves.

Thinking points

• Are the complexities of life changes within a psychoanalytic remit unlikely to be as amenable to short-term objective research as the results of some other interventions, or is this providing a leniency for psycho-analytic perspectives not afforded to other standpoints?

• How convincing do you find the speculations about attitudes to disability derived from Lacan's views, and to what extent do they rest on whether Lacan's views are credible?

Key texts

Freud, S. ([1940] 2002) *An Outline of Psychoanalysis* (translated by Helena Ragg-Kirkby), London: Penguin. Freud provides a condensed depiction of psychoanalysis as a method of treatment in this work.

Lacan, J. ([1966] 2006) *Écrits* (translated from the French by Bruce Fink, in collab-oration with Héloïse Fink and Russell Grigg, as *Écrits: The First Complete Edition in English*), New York and London: W. W. Norton. The previous widely used translation by A. Sheridan comprised about a third of the original, so the complete version represents a much fuller picture.

Further reading

Psychoanalysis

Gurman, A. S. and Messer, S. B. (Eds.) (2003) *Essential Psychotherapies: Theory and Practice* (Second edition), New York and London: Guilford Press. In this very well-edited book, the chapter by David Wolitzky is one of the best concise accounts of Freudian psychoanalysis available.

Mitchell, S. A. and Black, M. J. (1995) *Freud and Beyond: A History of Psychoanalytic Thought*, New York: Basic Books. In this readable introduction, chapters include: 'Sigmund Freud and the Classical Analytical tradition', 'Ego Psychology' (including an outline of the work of Anna Freud), 'Melanie Klein and Contemporary Kleinian Theory', and 'The British Object Relations School: W. R. D. Fairbairn and D. W. Winnicott' (with some reference to Bowlby).

Webster, R. (2005) *Why Freud Was Wrong: Sin, Science and Psychoanalysis*, Oxford: Isis-Orwell Press. That rare combination – a scholarly book that reads like a good novel. Webster points to problems with Freud's views, and argues that developments from neo-Darwinism might offer a stronger scientifically based theory of human nature.

Lacan

Goodley, D. (2010) *Disability Studies: An Interdisciplinary Introduction*, London: Sage. Chapter 8, on Lacan's ideas, is the best in this book. Other chapters discuss different models of disability, positivist and hermeneutic approaches to research, various sociologies of disability, critical psychology, poststructuralism, inclusive education and critical pedagogy, and critical theory.

Evans, D. (1996) *Introductory Dictionary of Lacanian Psychoanalysis*, London: Routledge. This book offers explanations of Lacan's terms, paving the way to a clearer understanding of his writing.

Sokal, A. and Bricmont, J. ([1997] 1999) *Intellectual Impostures: Postmodern Philosophers' Abuse of Science* (translated from the French by the authors), London: Profile Books. The chapter on Lacan is a thorough and convincing demonstration of how a little knowledge of mathematics can be an embarrassing thing. For anyone who is open to the suggestion that not every word Lacan wrote was profound or even meaningful, the chapter is also very funny.

Chapter 10

Shifting sands and power/knowledge

Postmodernism and historical epistemology

Postmodernism

'Postmodernism' is a slippery term, having different meanings in different contexts and when applied to various disciplines. By briefly examining some of this range of meanings and applications, it is possible to determine the common threads that appear, especially in postmodern philosophy.

In architecture, postmodernism rejects what are perceived as unwelcome elements of modern building design, such as high-rise slums, in favour of a more eclectic approach. Jenks (1977, 1996) refers to 'double coding' when he describes buildings that refer to and knowingly juxtapose different historical styles, an example being the Neue Staatsgalerie in Stuttgart.

In the arts, postmodernism represents a move away from modernism to the extent that modernism involves a search for truth and meaning. Postmodernism offers instead art which is ironic, playful, eclectic and unconcerned with reference. In literature, postmodernism has been associated with the names of Roland Barthes, Umberto Eco and Salman Rushdie in relation to metafictional literature, which draws attention to its own artificiality and deals playfully with the expectations of genre (Hutcheon, 1988).

Among common threads in these areas are: eclecticism, knowing irony, juxtaposition of varied elements and styles, playfulness, an attempt to disconcert expectations, and drawing attention to the nature of the artefact rather than implying an artefact is an adequate representation of something else.

In philosophy, the concern of this chapter, postmodernism has some of these features. For example, it is concerned with drawing attention to the limitations of philosophy and of discourse in a self-referential way. The term 'postmodern' also suggests two other features: that a period can be identified as 'modern', and that 'postmodern' follows this period. For the purposes of the present chapter the modern period is taken to be the period associated with Enlightenment thinking.

In this context, postmodernism is an attempt to move away from perceived problems with modernism, in particular relating to the values and aspirations of the Enlightenment. These are values and aspirations related to principles that inform positivism. The non-rational aspect of postmodern thought is traceable to radical strands of romanticism. Postmodernism seeks to 'challenge the hegemony of normativism' (Corker and Shakespeare, 2002a, p. 14). Postmodernism in philosophy can include a wide range of approaches, but the work of Jean Francois Lyotard may be taken as in many ways typical.

Speaking of postmodernity can have different implications. It can suggest a separation from the period of modernity and the so-called Enlightenment project. There is a difficulty placing postmodernism where this sort of meaning is implied. For those wishing to continue to develop the potential of the modern, there is no postmodernism, because the prospects of the modern are still to be worked out and fulfilled.

Habermas has maintained that modernity originally promised emancipation and a brave new world, but that this promise remained unfulfilled. Postmodernity developed as an irrational response to this perceived failure. Habermas's response is not to pursue postmodernism but to continue to work on the aims of modernism (Habermas, 1980). In a similar way, the Polish sociologist Bauman also suggests that the hopes of modernism were unrealised and that society should continue to look for new ways of liberation. He argues that intellectuals should eschew the emptiness of postmodern consumerism (Bauman, 1992).

Lyotard

Lyotard ([1979] 1984), in a report to the Canadian Government, *The Postmodern Condition: A Report on Knowledge* presented a review of the state of knowledge in highly developed societies. He argued that the influence of poststructuralism had altered the nature of knowledge, and that changes were therefore necessary. Scientific knowledge is distinguished from other forms, which are termed 'narrative' knowledge. At first sight, Lyotard suggests, scientific knowledge appeared to have supplanted narrative knowledge.

This was because scientific knowledge embraced an overarching narrative reflecting the values of humanism, which legitimated modern society. These perceived humanist truths include the view of history as progress, and that reason and the capacity for free individual action are universal. However, in Lyotard's view, the spread of secularism and the decline of political authority are challenging the dominance of scientific knowledge and fostering suspicion of grand narratives.

Wittgenstein introduced the notion of 'language games' as models of language aiming to show the workings of language and the process by which it is acquired. Language games indicate that no language is private because one's most private thoughts are only expressible in the language that is used by other individuals who participate in the language game. Language games also show that meaning is use. Lyotard uses Wittgenstein's notion of 'language games' (Wittgenstein ([1945] 2001, e.g. pp. 7–8) to suggest features of postmodernism.

Lyotard aims to show how coherent narratives: break up into many incompatible meanings; elevate the importance of particulars through diminishing the dominance of generalisation and unification; and detach philosophy from the influence of scientific method. He also argues that clandestine power relationships shape modern thought. This points to distrust of grand narratives as ideological constraints on individual thought and conduct. The prestige enjoyed by scientific knowledge, Lyotard believed unjustified. This prestige and the search for legitimation relate to philosophical and political narratives. Philosophical narratives emerge from German idealism typified by Kant. Political narratives stem from the French Enlightenment.

Yet, for Lyotard, scientific knowledge depends for its legitimation on philosophical and political narratives. In the view of science, these narratives do not constitute knowledge at all. This contradiction, he suggests, shows that science is interrelated to other discourses over which it has no privileged status. Also, there is a decline in the credibility of German idealism and French Enlightenment thinking. The fact that scientific knowledge depends on these for legitimacy weakens the legitimacy principle of knowledge, blurring distinctions between different areas of science.

Postmodern science concerns 'undecidables' and paradoxes, and evolves in a discontinuous way. Its 'model of legitimation' (Lyotard, [1979] 1984, p. 60) is based on reasoning that contradicts logical rules. It is counter to usual and established ways of reasoning.

Deleuze and Guattari

The French philosopher Gilles Deleuze is known for the breadth and variety of his work and for his collaboration with the psychoanalyst Felix Guattari. Deleuze's *Difference and Repetition* ([1968] 1994), is concerned to develop a physics and metaphysics of difference. Deleuze develops a criticism of what is seen as a traditional view of representation. In this view, a transcendental object is represented by intuitions and concepts. For Deleuze, representation is the actualisation of ideas by means of a process of 'differentiation'. The metaphysics is grounded only in the repetition of ideal problems which are themselves defined in terms of differences and which therefore amount to a non-ground. In *The Logic of Sense*, Deleuze ([1969] 1990) explores issues of meaning and non-meaning and develops a theory of meaning generated by the absence of meaning and revealed in paradoxes.

Deleuze and Guattari collaborated on several books. In *Anti-Oedipus: Capitalism and Schizophrenia* ([1972] 1983) they consider Freudian views. The book criticises the conception of desire reduced to the Oedipal triangle of father, mother and child. Rather desire is seen as polymorphous. They are concerned with the changing social body of desire. Desire is considered to take on as many forms as there are persons to implement it. It has to find new channels and different combinations to realise itself, forming a 'body without organs'. Schizophrenia is regarded as a form of becoming.

In *A Thousand Plateaus*, Deleuze and Guattari ([1980] 1987) continue the attempt to develop a new way of thought and writing. The introductory chapter developed from an earlier published piece (Deleuze and Guattari [1976] 1981) compares the multiplicity of desire to a rhizome ([1980] 1987, pp. 3–25). In biology, a rhizome is a plant which spreads in numerous directions and in which, in a sense, any point is connected to any other point. Unlike trees or their roots, 'the rhizome connects any point to any other point, and its traits are not necessarily linked to traits of the same nature' (ibid. p. 21).

Relatedly, the term 'deterritorialisation' moves away from hierarchical approaches to meaning where concepts and objects are seen as discrete units with singular identities. It approaches more identity which is multiple and rhizome-like. Meanings and operations are more fluid, so entities are interconnected and individual boundaries are not distinct. Territorialisation concerns maintenance, while deterritorialisation has to do with dissipation. (For example, see Deleuze and Guattari ([1980] 1987, pp. 9–10 relating deterritorialisation to the rhizome).

Their last collaborative work, *What is Philosophy?* (Deleuze and Guattari, [1991] 1996) sets out a view of philosophy as a process of creating concepts.

Evaluation of postmodernism

Postmodernism intends to challenge what it sees as the complacency of traditional views of perception and reality. The eclecticism, knowing irony, juxtaposition of varied elements and styles, playfulness, an attempt to disconcert expectations, and drawing attention to the nature of the artefact is all meant to unsettle the received view that an artefact is an innocent representation of reality. Where it is successful in this, established ways of seeing the world may be opened up to a new scrutiny.

Eagleton (1996b) recognises this potential. As well as offering some negative criticisms of postmodernism, he more positively suggests the influence postmodern thought might have on certainty, totality, purities, oppressive norms and foundations. He states that postmodernism has 'put the skids under a number of complacent certainties, prised open some paranoid totalities, contaminated some jealously protected purities, bent some oppressive norms and shaken some rather frail looking foundations' (p. 27). The benefits of this, as Eagleton sees it, is that postmodernism has 'properly disorientated those who knew only too well who they were, and disarmed those who need to know who they are in the face of those only too willing to tell them' (p. 27). In brief, postmodernism has led to a questioning of previously unchallenged certainties.

But to challenge apparent certainties requires that cogent arguments are put forward to undermine those positions and, ideally, that alternative interpretation are presented that can in their turn be challenged. Where this is lacking, postmodernism is not viewed in a positive light.

Habermas (1980, 1985) has criticised postmodernism for deserting the aspirations of modernity (which in his view have not been fulfilled) and for adopting an eclectic irrationalism. It has been described as a form of 'antirealist doctrine' antipathetic towards 'objectivity and knowledge' (Sasso, 2001, p. 178). Postmodernism is said to mistrust logical positivism and science and to give equal credence to 'alternative ways of knowing or constructing truth' (Kauffman, 1999, p. 248). It is characterised by rejection of the rationalist tradition of the Enlightenment, theoretical discourses unconnected with empirical tests, and a view that science is a social construction (Sokal and Bricmont, 1998, paraphrased). Alan Sokal, a professor of physics, maintains that postmodern views of science are merely 'intellectual posturing'. To try to demonstrate this, he submitted a spoof article to the cultural studies journal *Social Text* (Sokal and Bricmont, 1998). The article, 'Transgressing the Boundaries: Towards a Transformative Hermeneutics of Quantum Gravity', was planted with false arguments and absurdities and asserted physical reality was a social construct. It was accepted by the editors and published in 1996.

In the book, *Intellectual Impostures*, Sokal and Bricmont ([1997] 1999) identify in Lyotard's writing a mixture of statements that are banal, others that are incorrect, and others that are meaningless. They analyse a well-known passage alluded to earlier in the present chapter (Lyotard, ([1979] 1984) in which Lyotard concludes from research that, 'the continuous differential function is losing its pre-eminence' (p. 60). Lyotard continues:

> Postmodern science – by concerning itself with such things as undecidables, the limits of precise control, conflicts characterised by incomplete information, '*fracta*', catastrophes, and pragmatic paradoxes – is theorising its own evolution as discontinuous, catastrophic, nonrectifiable, and paradoxical. It is changing the meaning of the word *knowledge*, while expressing how such a change can take place. It is producing not the known, but the unknown. And it suggests a model of legitimation that has nothing to do with maximised performance, but has as its basis difference understood as parology.
>
> (Lyotard, [1979] 1984, p. 60)

The analysis of this paragraph as an example by Sokal and Bricmont ([1997] 1999) indicates various problems. Lyotard's reference to the 'catastrophic' as a reference to catastrophe theory does not support the notion that 'the continuous differential function is losing its pre-eminence' because catastrophe theory is based on mathematics concerning differentiable functions (Sokal and Bricmont, [1997] 1999, footnote 167). The passage brings together distinct branches of mathematics and physics which 'are conceptually quite distant from one another' (ibid. p. 128). It confuses the 'introduction of nondifferentiable (or even discontinuous) functions in scientific models with a so-called 'discontinuous' or 'paradoxical' evolution of science itself' (ibid.). The theories mentioned by Lyotard do produce new knowledge but generally without changing the 'meaning of the word' (ibid.). What they produce is known (not unknown) by definition. The 'model of legitimation' is not 'difference understood as parology' but the comparison of theories with observation and experiment. Indeed the intended meaning of 'difference understood as parology' is obscure.

Sokal and Bricmont (1998) in *Fashionable Nonsense* regard Deleuze's use of mathematical symbols and scientific terminology as inconsistent. Moving between accepted meaning and idiosyncratic use, such terms lose any meaning, becoming vague and unclear. Sokal and Bricmont do not turn their attentions to Deleuze's philosophy.

Among recent criticisms of Deleuze is that of Hallward (2006). He regards Deleuze's philosophy as being otherworldly. It aims for passive reflection upon the dissolving of all identity into the self-creation of nature. Hallward (2006) considers Deleuze's view that 'being' is always differentiating and is of necessity creative. This for Hallward leads to the position that Deleuze's philosophy cannot provide any insight into the material and actual conditions of existence. Indeed it is indifferent to them.

Postmodernism and special education

Heshusius and others

It was pointed out in Chapter 3 'Positivism and empiricism' that approaches in special education are often informed by positivist philosophy. Readers will recall that that chapter presented positivism as rejecting pre-scientific thought including religion, metaphysics and superstition and taking the general view that science makes continuing progress. Knowledge is seen as based on sense experience and enquiry in the hard sciences. In the social sciences, a positivist approach concerns describing and explaining empirical facts.

A postmodern view of knowledge, as indicated, eschews a positivist perspective. Postmodern special education, it has been suggested, recognises that special education is shaped by social and historical influences. Gerber (1994) states that postmodernism is typified by recognition, 'that social and historical forces contingently yet indeterminately impinge upon and shape the enterprise of special education' (p. 371). Furthermore, special education is not simply a description of special children and certain pedagogy. It is, in Gerber's words, 'not the simple sum of children who have disabilities or their instructional experiences in classrooms' (ibid.). This perspective, then, seeks to question the usual way of seeing things. What appears to be the natural order is shown to be only one of many ways in which the world might be perceived and arranged.

Heshusius (1991) criticises curriculum-based assessment and direct instruction in special education. In doing so, she suggests their underlying assumptions are parallel to the 'mechanistic, Newtonian paradigm'. This construction of reality, she maintains, has been questioned or shown to be incorrect in the light of the work of various well-known scientists. She argues that it 'has been challenged by Einstein, and has been further shown to be fundamentally incorrect by Bohr, Heisenberg, Bohm, and other contemporary scientists and philosophers of science' (ibid. p. 317).

More recently, Heshusius (2004a, p. 205) has sought to draw attention to the early development of science in its social and historical context. She points out that the procedures of science were not 'divine intervention'. In other words, scientific procedures were not given in their complete form by a divine power or in any other way, and this implies that they were a human construction. But the procedures of science did not involve all. They were not constructed during the scientific revolution 'by indigenous peoples, by persons with disability, by slaves, by females, by children, or by poor and uneducated men and women' (ibid.). The implication here is that scientific procedures were developed by a limited section of society, namely American settlers who did not have a disability, were free, male, adult, prosperous and educated. In short, scientific procedures were developed in a historical setting and in a certain social context. Scientific procedures are not, it is argued, the universal and detached set of practices it is thought. For Heshusius, science is seen as 'a historically and socially embedded construction' (ibid. p. 206).

Such arguments focus on the contested nature of science. From this position, proponents maintain that special education, to the extent that it depends on or draws on science, is failing to recognise the limitations of positivism. What appear to be disinterested and impartial scientifically based findings in special educational research, it might be argued, are historically and socially constructed. There are of course further arguments that the complexity of human beings precludes the application of scientific procedures to them.

A postmodern approach to special education tends not to offer an alternative to contemporary educational but mounts a criticism of positivist pedagogy. Its stance seems to be that present educational approaches are inappropriately scientific. The implication of the view of Heshusius (2004a, pp. 205–206) that the procedures of science excluded the participation of individuals with disabilities, women and others is that the foundations of science may be unfair and unjust.

Indeed, positivism and postmodernism have been contrasted as important approaches. There has been discussion of 'Discourse that espouses either a positivistic or a postmodern (relativistic) view to solve educational problems' (Sabournie, 2006, p. 63). It is recognised that 'philosophy of approach does not directly influence every aspect of special education'. However, a theoretical orientation 'will interact with what students with disabilities will receive as intervention in school, how teachers defend their pedagogy, and what teacher-trainers depend on to prepare present and future educators'. Postmodernism has also been equated with relativism (ibid.). It is in such contexts that the debate arises about whether postmodernity is a period following the conclusion of modernity or whether it cannot be meaningfully used because modernity is still continuing. This is perhaps another way of contrasting the modern, associated with the Enlightenment, scientific thinking and the usually accepted value of evidence, with the idea that all these have been superseded.

Another target of postmodernism is the way views of normality are presented so that they might appear to be the only way that things can be. This has been called 'the hegemony of normativism' (Corker and Shakespeare, 2002a, p. 14). Postmodernism tries to challenge such ideas by drawing attention to diversity rather than unanimity. This is a reflection of the theme in architecture and the arts in which juxtaposition and a rejection of determining underlying truth and meaning can be used to subvert conventional thinking.

With reference to special children, normativism may lead to viewing the usual as inevitable and superior. Typical levels and types of development become privileged over others. Consequently, individuals different to the norm can be viewed as lesser individuals, instead of different. This is sometimes expressed as viewing difference as deviance. The hegemony aspect of normatism emerges when the norm is unnoticed and unchallenged. It is simply accepted as the natural course of things that some ways of being are better than others.

In relation to postmodernism in a broad sense, the acceptance of the unusual, the ironic, the playful, all contribute to attempts to break down the usual ways of seeing things. Norms of fine arts, of architecture, and of development and being are all challenged.

Goodley and Allan's approach to Deleuze

Goodley (2007) in a paper that aims to be 'Deleuzoguattarian' suggests that disability studies tends to understand concepts such as 'exclusion', 'inclusion', 'impairment' and 'disability' as entities 'rooted in arborescent and hierarchical forms of knowledge' (abstract). These are, however, 'modernist misconceptions'. They can be challenged through 'understanding knowledge, practice, living and activism as rhizomatic'. This can create 'burrows for shelter and eventual breakout' (ibid.). Quoting some parents of 'disabled babies' Goodley 'maps out a vision of parents not blocked by the strata of disabling society' but instead 'enabled by lines of flight, resistance, flux and change' (ibid.).

Allan (2008) draws on Deleuze and Guattari more substantially, writing about inclusion. She presents the 'spaces' of schooling, teacher education and education law and policy as 'rigid, striated and hierarchical, with clear lines of demarcation' (p. 55). The market economy and the 'standards agenda' have 'laid down their roots and defined learning along linear and hierarchical lines which differentiate learners and exclude some of them' (p. 61). Accordingly, the ideas of Deleuze and Guattari might 'enable a reworking of educational spaces as smooth' (p. 55). This would be done by 'shifting power' and 'altering the way in which people can engage with these spaces' (ibid.). One of the aspects Allan (2008) focuses on is the notion of the rhizome (others are, deterritorialisation, difference and becoming).

The rhizome as a model of thought is seen as challenging 'conventional knowledge' which relies on the logic of binarism such as 'able/disable' (Allan, 2008, p. 59). Learning in such conventional ways is concerned with 'transfer of knowledge through a process of representation', which is hierarchical. Students are 'required to display their learning merely through repetition of these facts' (ibid. p. 60). Such learning is fractured and partial. Inclusion in these learning processes is 'partial, contingent and tied to individual's pathologies which in turn fragment and locate them within the striations of the school system' (ibid.). Instead of these tree-like structures, much better, states Allan, to have Deleuze and Guattari's notion of the rhizome. This avoids hierarchy, linear paths and other negative aspects of conventional learning and education. The rhizome for Allan has 'obvious metaphorical appeal'. It is much harder, as Allan recognises, to establish it 'as the model for thinking about learning and inclusion' (ibid. p. 61). Perhaps the rhizome can be 'deployed creatively – to subvert, subtract and invent' (ibid.).

In rhizomic learning, instead of seeking 'certainty, closure and *outcomes* in learning' (ibid. p. 109, italic in original) one would search for 'the undecidables, the incalculable, in which learning cannot be predicted' (ibid.). Being confounded to think laterally could help, as a film director was when his teacher played a recording of a song that led to his lifelong love of poetry. Active bodily learning might be a good thing (ibid.) the way one learns to swim. Learning should be concerned with 'more than the communication of subject content' (ibid. p. 110). We should have 'Good explanations of subject content, rather than the same ones repeated *louder*' (ibid. p. 111, italics in original). Children and young people 'need to be engaged actively, rather than being passive recipients of knowledge' (ibid.).

Evaluation of postmodernism in special education

It has been argued that aspects of postmodern thought could have the effect of reducing or denying a sense of agency for a disabled individual. Scully (2002), discussing medical encounters, makes a point with wider connotations, stating, 'a formulation of subjectivity as discursively constructed rather than a manifestation of an essential self tends to remove much of the grounds for individual autonomy – and this is already a too familiar position for the disabled person' (p. 58). Postmodern distrust or denial of 'a single, authoritative discourse' where this is taken to apply not just to subjectivity but to personal encounters leaves not just the physician unable to claim any special authority, but the disabled person too (ibid.).

Gross (1998, p. 48) argues that in the past science may have offered 'false universals'. However, these have been overthrown only by better science.

Heshusius (1991) does not sufficiently acknowledge that Newtonian physics and quantum physics continue to explain phenomena in their respective domains. It is not the case that Newtonian physics has been proved 'wrong'. It is more that limitations of the theory in specific circumstances have been identified, and work is taking place on theories addressing these limitations. In other words, science is proceeding by observation, experiment and theory, as would be expected. Gerber (1994) points out that Heisenberg's theories about the subatomic world 'are often misused metaphorically to argue the fundamental unsoundness of empirical methods of studying learning, individual differences, or education and schooling' (p. 376).

Kauffman (1999, p. 248) maintains that postmodernism presents a 'singularly egocentric' worldview because one's own experience is the only one that is knowable. He argues that the view that disability is a 'social construction' that one could 'eliminate (deconstruct, subvert, redefine)' is 'seriously at odds with the science of exceptionality' (ibid.). That postmodernism is at odds with another perspective, does not of course of itself discredit postmodernism. Nevertheless, Kauffman's argument is also that the consequences of the views of some proponents of postmodernism could have unfortunate practical consequences for special children.

Kauffman and Sasso (2006) have made more recent criticisms of postmodernism. It is, for them, 'intellectually bankrupt' and 'cannot be reconciled with a scientific view'. Its consequences if applied to any field including special education can be 'catastrophic' and it can lead to 'malpractice' (ibid. abstract, p. 65). Examples of suggested malpractice involve whole language reading (ibid. pp. 73–78), radical multiculturalism (pp. 78–82) and facilitated communication (pp. 82–84).

In their article however, Kauffman and Sasso (2006) bring together several approaches under the heading of postmodernism that it can be argued are more clearly open to evaluation separately. They include under the umbrella of postmodernism: 'poststructuralism', 'hermeneutics', 'critical theory' and 'deconstruction' (p. 65).

Postmodern perspectives would tend to miss opportunities afforded by evidence-based practice, such as the use of behavioural approaches for conduct disorder, because they are founded on observation, explanation and rational assessment of their effects. Of course, attempts to undermine positivist aspects of special education do not have to claim that the foundations of the physical sciences are illusory. Approaches suitable for the physical sciences may not always be transferable to social sciences, for example because of the complexity of human conduct, and the contradiction of being unavoidably within the human world and at the same time trying to assume a neutral perspective towards others.

Drawing on some ideas of Deleuze and Guattari, Allan's (2008) call for enabling learners to think and for teachers to try to inspire them sounds not at all contentious. It may not be a matter of either/or, as Allan at times seems to depict it. Some learning might have outcomes – for example, teaching swimming might lead to someone learning to swim – without too much shame being attached to the project. The standards 'agenda' might be pursued in reading to try to ensure a child is learning to read a word here and there rather than exploring the possibilities of reading too unproductively. Other learning opportunities could be quite open-ended, such as discussions and explorations in mathematics.

But it is difficult to see why it is necessary, if these views are to be propagated, to invoke the work of Deleuze and Guattari. They could be suggested simply as examples of good teaching that may well be widely accepted. If there is evidence of pupils being inspired by something, why not pursue it? How such approaches would enable a child – for example, with profound cognitive impairment or autism or severe conduct disorder – to be included in a mainstream school lesson is unclear. It might be that such an identification would be seen as part of the hierarchical paraphernalia of special education and would be rejected out of hand anyway as too arboreal and not rhizomic enough.

Implications for thinking and practice of postmodernism in special education

Someone supporting a postmodern view in relation to special education may challenge current approaches, and may be suspicious of a positivist perspective. Special education may be thought to be shaped by social and historical influences. She may question the whole notion of the way special children and distinctive pedagogy is assembled as special education, taking the view that the response is only one of many possible ones.

Regarding inclusion, a postmodernist might regard schooling, teacher education and education law and policy as rigidly hierarchical, in line with a focus on standards which define learning in a linear way which differentiates learners and excludes some.

Therefore a curriculum that over-emphasises standards and outcomes is likely to be viewed negatively. A broad curriculum which takes full account of all areas of development is likely to be more favourably viewed. Similarly, ongoing and portfolio-type assessments might be more acceptable than single-time high stakes examinations and testing. She may be critical of curriculum-based assessment and direct instruction in special education, seeing their underlying scientific construction of reality assumptions as mechanistic and unjustifiable.

A postmodernist may be critical of the enterprise of science, pointing to its human construction and its historical social exclusiveness, including the exclusion of disabled people, females, children, the poor and others. She may argue that what appear to be disinterested and impartial scientifically based findings in special educational research are historically and socially constructed, and perhaps also that the complexity of human beings precludes the application of scientific procedures to them. She may emphasise that present educational approaches are inappropriately scientific, implying that the procedures of science excluded the participation of individuals with disabilities, women and others, and that the foundations of science may be unfair and unjust.

A postmodernist might challenge conventional knowledge that relies on able/disable distinctions. She may eschew approaches to learning that are concerned with merely the transfer of knowledge through a process of representation. She might avoid approaches that are hierarchical, based on the repletion of facts, partial, and that over-emphasise certainty, linear paths, and outcomes. She may prefer a multifaceted model for thinking about learning and inclusion that can subvert and invent. She may seek a way of learning that involves the undecided, the incalculable, and in which learning cannot be predicted. She might encourage lateral thinking and active bodily learning. She might argue for good explanations of subject content and engaging pupils actively.

Given the orientation towards mainstreaming that seems to follow from postmodern ideas, the deployment of physical and human resources to facilitate mainstreaming is likely to be considered central.

Someone supporting a postmodern view is likely to support mainstreaming rather than separate special schooling and may question the whole identification and assessment of children and young people as having disabilities and disorders. The way views of normality are unreflectively presented as inevitable may be questioned. She may challenge such ideas by drawing attention to diversity rather than unanimity. With reference to special children, 'normatism' may lead to viewing the usual as inevitable and superior so that typical levels and types of development become privileged over others. She may be cautious of the consequence that individuals can be viewed as lesser instead of different and that the norm becomes accepted as the natural course of things because some ways of being are considered better than others.

She might seek to avoid ways of thinking that reflect hierarchical forms of knowledge and that might lead to unhelpful concepts such as 'exclusion', 'inclusion', 'impairment' and 'disability'. Instead, she may seek more de-centred and non-hierarchical ways of thinking allowing resistance and change in response to rigid modes of thought and perception. A postmodernist might argue for shifting power and altering the way in which people can interact. She may take the view that inclusion is partial and constrained to individuals' pathologies.

It is unclear what a postmodern view of therapy might be. If a view is taken that much of the identification of disabilities and disorders may be spurious, the case for therapy seems to be diminished.

Historical epistemology

Historical epistemology is a term applied to the work of Michel Foucault, Professor of History of Forms of Thought at the Collège de France and editor of *Critique*. His ideas have influenced a wide range of areas, including law, medicine and penology. Foucault avoided or discouraged classifications of his work, stating, 'Do not ask me who I am and do not ask me to remain the same: leave it to our bureaucrats and our police to see our papers are in order' (Foucault, [1966] 2002, p. 19). Despite this reticence and celebration of fluidity, it is possible to identify themes that develop in Foucault's work. For present purposes, this requires discussing his particular use of the term 'archaeology' and his expression 'epistémè', and outlining his conception of the relationships between power and knowledge.

In various books and essays, Foucault examines the conditions that allowed the possibility of ways of knowing and the historically contingent practices that shaped them. Concerned with periodic changes in perception and knowledge and the relationships between knowledge and power, Foucault analysed the historical development of forms of knowledge with regard to various areas: sexuality, punishment, medicine, the humanities and madness.

Regarding sets of presuppositions of thought relating to the humanities, medicine and so on as historically situated, he referred to them as 'epistémès'. Through these presuppositions, Foucault argues, rational order is recognised in a specified period and in a given society. However, while epistémès are necessary for reality to be interpreted and discussed, they remain obscured. Through what Foucault calls 'archaeology' (and 'genealogy') these presuppositions can be unearthed, allowing underlying structures of thought to be examined.

For example, in *The History of Madness*, Foucault ([1961] 2006) considers how madness is made an object of knowledge and traces historical transformations in conceptions of insanity. He maintains that in the seventeenth and eighteenth centuries, with the development of scientific reason, sanity and madness became increasingly polarised. Insane individuals came to be seen as beyond Reason. In the nineteenth and twentieth centuries, a shaping influence was psychiatry which formed madness as an illness subject to cure and normalisation.

Later, in *The Birth of the Clinic: An Archaeology of Medical Perception*, Foucault ([1963] 2003) examines the origins of modern medicine from the late 1700s. He suggests there was a shift in the structure of knowledge. This change was from a taxonomic period (concerned particularly with classifications) to an 'organic historical' period, allowing the possibilty of a discourse about disease. Anatomy, often assumed to be an uncomplicated empirical science gradually recognising what was 'real', can be seen from Foucault's perspective as more a product of a new structuring of knowledge.

One of Foucault's themes is 'power-knowledge'. Seeing every relationship as a site of power, he regards resistance as part of a related fabric. Foucault is concerned with the power relations which inform the discursive formations that make knowledge possible. Power is understood as an integral part of knowledge which enters discourses and attitudes and everyday life (Foucault, 1980, p. 30).

In *Discipline and Punish: The Birth of the Prison*, Foucault ([1975] 1991) examines changes in Western penal systems in modern times. Concentrating on issues of power and of the human body, he maintains that prison is a new form of technological power, that of discipline. This power is also evident in hospitals and schools.

Foucault traces evidence of a move from a penology where there were clear links between crime and punishment to one in which the principal feature is overall surveillance. Discipline creates conforming bodies for the new industrial age which function in various settings. These disciplinary institutions have to constantly observe the bodies they seek to control. They have to ensure discipline is internalised as the bodies are moulded through observation. Foucault emphasises the intimate relationship between power relations and knowledge. He states, 'there is no power relation without the correlative constitution of a field of knowledge, nor any knowledge that does not presuppose and constitute at the same time power relations' (ibid. p. 27).

Relatedly, he suggests, 'The subject who knows, the objects to be known and the modalities of knowledge', must be regarded as effects of 'the fundamental implications of power-knowledge and their historical transformations' (ibid. pp. 27–28). Also, the processes and struggles that traverse and make up power-knowledge determine the 'forms and possible domains of knowledge' (ibid.).

In summary then, Foucault seeks to identify and explore epistémès with reference to various developments, including medicine, punishment and discipline, and to show how power and knowledge are closely related in such processes.

Evaluation of historical epistemology

In Foucault's writings his ideas are illustrated by widely ranging evidence, sometimes from obscure and vivid sources. These are sometimes interpreted in a refreshingly original way, provoking a rethinking of well-established views.

For example, where many have taken the view that penology has progressed and become more enlightened since the eighteenth century as terrible tortures have been replaced by incarceration, Foucault is more circumspect. In *Discipline and Punish: The Birth of the Prison*, Foucault ([1975] 1991) points out the direct link between crimes and punishments that were typified by torture. For example someone who had committed murder could have the hand that wielded the murder weapon cut off or mutilated before being executed (ch. 1). By comparison, the perpetual surveillance of prisoners seems not just to punish the body but to take over an individual's identity.

Foucault seems to be rarely satisfied that he has reached a settled position and frequently questions his own ideas, either as they arise or in later works, as indicated by his injunction 'Do not ask me who I am and do not ask me to remain the same' (Foucault, [1969] 2002, p. 19). His arguments are the more convincing because counter-arguments the reader might want to raise are often anticipated and examined by the author.

Armstrong (2003, pp. 8–19), drawing on Foucault's ideas and interpretations, presents an outline in which the development of special education is related to historical change in Europe in the past five hundred years. It is stated that, in medieval Europe, 'religious communities cared for the severely handicapped' (ibid.). There are also examples of 'the social inclusion of disabled people in pre-industrial societies' (ibid. p. 9). Foucault ([1961] 2006) is referred to as describing how in the middle ages, insanity and idiocy were part of everyday life and 'fools and madmen walked the streets'. Then the reader is told that 'The fifteenth century marked the beginning of new attitudes in Europe to disability' (Armstrong, 2003, p. 9). Extensively referring to Foucault, Armstrong (2003, p. 9) maintains that normality came to be no longer defined by the certainty of religious and social order but by the management of self. The social meaning of disability was changed through the notion of treatment into the management of self. Referring to Foucault's ([1975] 1991) *Discipline and Punish*, Armstrong (2003, p. 10) writes of the 'great confinement' of the poor, the unemployed and the 'defective'.

However, critics question the coherence and validity of Foucault's epistémès, and his choice and interpretation of historical facts. Piaget criticises Foucault's book ([1966] 2002) *The Order of Things: An Archaeology of the Human Sciences*. For Piaget ([1968] 1971), Foucault's book 'seems in the end to be nothing but a search for conceptual archetypes, chiefly tied to language' (p. 129). Foucault views the human sciences as 'merely a momentary outcome' of epistémès and their sequence 'has no rationale' (ibid.). Man became an object of study only in the nineteenth century and human sciences will perish 'as surely as they came into existence'. We cannot know what epistémè will emerge. Foucault's programme lacks a method. Piaget maintains that Foucault, 'instead of inquiring under what conditions one may speak of the reign of a new epistémè and what are the criteria by which to judge the validity or invalidity of alternative interpretations of the history of science, he relies on intuition and substitutes speculative improvisation for methodical procedure' (ibid. p. 132).

Incredulity has been expressed about the all-encompassing nature of epistémès. Steiner (1971) in an early review states, 'the whole idea of a visible "consciousness" appearing on Monday mornings or at the start and end of centuries, is a fatal simplification'.

Foucault's interpretation of historical trends and historical facts is questioned, for example by Lawrence Stone (1982) in a review in the *New York Times Review of Books*, and by Porter ([1987] 1990) in the book *Mind-Forg'd Manacles*. Shorter (1997) makes extensive criticisms of the historical accuracy and therefore the historical interpretations in Foucault's ([1961] 2006) *The History of Madness*. He takes issue with Foucault's claim that the notion of mental illness is essentially 'a social and cultural invention of the eighteenth century' (Shorter, 1997, p. 274).

Shorter (1997) presents national statistics for England demonstrating only minimal numbers of individuals were admitted to private or public asylums. He states that to call this period of the history of madness, as does Foucault, some kind of grand confinement 'would be nonsense' (p. 5). In France, both Philippe Pinel, the founder of modern psychiatry, and Jean-Etienne-Dominique Esquirol, who advocated what would become social and community psychiatry, had extensive experience with private clinics. If the main thrust of the birth of psychiatry came from private clinics where the wealthy paid to be rid of their manic relatives, this hardly supports the notion of a grand confinement (pp. 16–17, paraphrased).

Shorter (1997) caricatures Foucault's position as the notion that psychiatry 'was born in some kind of fiendish alliance between capitalism and the central state, enlisting psychiatrists in the larger game of confining deviant individuals in order to instil work discipline into an unmotivated traditional population' (p. 16). Some founders of psychiatry were capitalist entrepreneurs. William Battie, founding medical officer of St Luke's Hospital in London, was the owner of two large private madhouses. Benjamin Rush, the Philadelphia physician, was a further representative of the emerging capitalist economy. But Vincenzio Chiarugi, who established a very early therapeutic asylum, was from late eighteenth-century Florence, then far from capitalistic. Grand Duke Leopold was not extending the 'state-making writ of the Austrian monarchy' to the 'Tuscan mental health system'. Viennese money had no interest in Tuscany at this time. To argue otherwise would be 'farcical' (ibid.).

Historical epistemology and special education

Foucault in the context of disability

Foucault's influence has been evident in interrogating views of impairment as a natural phenomenon. Among sources of ideas relating to impairment and disability are *The Birth of the Clinic: An Archaeology of Medical Perception* (Foucault, [1963] 2003) and *The History of Sexuality, Volume 1: The Will to Knowledge* (Foucault, [1976] 1998).

Tremain (2002) draws on these and other sources. Foucault, she states, sees the materiality of the body as associated with the 'historically contingent practices that bring it into being'. It is these practices that make impairment an object of knowledge. They 'objectivize' impairment in this sense (p. 34). The materiality of impairment and impairment itself are 'naturalised *effects* of disciplinary knowledge/power' (ibid., italics in original). 'Impairment' has circulated in discursive and concrete practices as 'non-historical (biological) matter of the body'. This biological matter, it is said, is 'moulded by time and class'. It is 'culturally shaped' or it is seen as the matter on which culture is 'imprinted' (ibid. pp. 34–35).

Consequently, impairment has stayed as an unexamined underpinning of discourse and is seen as politically neutral. In challenging this one can 'identify and resist the ones that have material-*ized* it' (Tremain, 2002, p. 35, italics in original).

In Foucault's analysis, historically shaped modern perceptions of the body emerged in the eighteenth century. These led to the creation of the modern body as 'the effect and object of medical examination, which could be used, abused, transformed and subjugated' (Tremain, 2002, p. 35). The clinical exam-ination procedure led to the passivity of this 'object'. The investigative gaze 'fixed and crystallized' the phenomena it perceived as 'the body' (ibid.). For Foucault ([1976] 1998) this objectification of the body contributed to the new regime of power (biopower). Through such regimes recent forms of power/ knowledge lead to increasingly comprehensive mangement of life.

The objectivisation of the body interacted with 'dividing practices' (Foucault, [1963] 2003) instituted in the compartmentalisation of ninetenth-century clinics, and with categorising, distributing and manipulating subjects. By a process of division within themselves or from others, subjects are 'objectivised' as disabled, sick or mad. Through objectifying procedures these supposed attrib-utes become attached to personal and social identity.

From the eighteenth century, procedures and operations or 'technologies' coalesced around the objectivication of the body. One of these, 'discipline', includes instruments, techniques and procedures of power to produce a body that can be used, transformed and improved. This exercise of power involves guiding the possibilities of conduct. However, it is self-concealing, allowing 'the naturalisation and legitimation of the discursive formation in which they circulate' (Tremain, 2002, p. 36). Influential are hegenomic power structures, maintaining power while (because of their pervasiveness) remaining invisible to those held down. They are made possible through the production of apparent acts of choice by the subject. Normality and normalisation are central to biopower allowing the identification of subjects by others and themselves in ways that make them governable.

Tremain (2002) applies Foucault's notions of the developments that Foucault argued led to the human body being perceived as an object of knowledge. Because these are seen as historically contingent, they can be questioned and dismissed or accepted. As they are intimately related to knowledge and power, that power can be challenged, and the knowledge with which it is bound can be questioned. Time, class and culture are all seen as contributors to the perceptions of the body as an object of knowledge (ibid. pp. 34–35). The objectivising and separating practices (Foucault, [1963] 2003) that were applied to madness, sickness and disability can be challenged. The way the subject is colluded into accepting the perceptions of others as part of their own identity can also be questioned.

Tremain (2002) questions the separation of impairment and disability proposed by the social model to theorise the nature of impairment and biomedical practices. The social model accepts impairment as an 'objective, transhistorical and transcultural entity which biomedicine accurately represents' (p. 34) rather than a 'historically contingent effect of modern power' (ibid.). Tremain argues that impairment is a 'discursive object', but exclusionary practices make it appear that impairment precedes discourse. That is, 'Disciplinary practices in which the subject is inducted and divided from others produce the illusion of impairment as their "prediscursive" antecedent in order to multiply, divide and expand their regulatory effects' (ibid. p. 42).

Tremain (2002) maintains, 'The testimonials, acts and enactments of the disabled subject are *performative* in so far as the "prediscursive" impairment which they are purported to disclose or manifest has no existence prior to, or apart from, those very constitutive performances' (ibid.). Impairment is claimed to be the 'embodiment of a natural deficit or lack'. But this obscures the 'fact' that 'the constitutive power relations' defining and circumscribing impairment 'have already delimited the dimensions of its reification' (ibid. pp. 42–43). Tremain rejects the view that disablement and impairment are separable because this ignores that the category of impairment emerged and partly persists 'to legitimise the disciplinary regime that generated it in the first place' (ibid. p. 43).

Foucault in the context of special education

Whereas Tremain (2002) is concerned with the concept of disability and its implications, Brantlinger (2006) seeks to apply Foucault's ideas in the context of special education. Brantlinger (2006, p. 217) interprets Foucault ([1975] 1991) as theorising that 'middle level bureaucrats' in schools and elsewhere use the disciplinary instruments of 'hierarchic surveillance, normalising sanctions, and examination'. These she maintains are mechanisms that are recognisable in components of the 'accountability and standards movement', which include the adoption of high stakes testing (Brantlinger, 2006, p. 217).

Allan (1996) also relates Foucault's ideas to special education. She contends that research into special children educated in mainstream schools tends not to indicate very much about their school experiences. Foucault's methodology of examining discourses provides alternatives. His analysis of medicine and madness are examples. Allan maintains that Foucault can provide strategies for understanding how discourses on 'special needs' construct pupils' experiences in mainstream schools and constructs their identities as 'subjects and objects of knowledge' (ibid.).

Allan draws on Foucault's ([1975] 1991) notions of surveillance through hierarchical observation (ibid. pp. 170–177), normalising judgement (pp. 177–184), and the examination (pp. 184–194). She suggests (Allan, 1996) that in special education, hierarchical observation can be identified in the higher staffing ratios that special children attract which allow closer scrutiny. Normalising judgements are thought to be apparent in the way special children are 'defined in relation to normality' (p. 223). The 'examination' is seen as relating to assessment in special education, determining whether a child has a disability or disorder, leading to entitlement to special educational provision. Allan suggests Foucault's view of power relationships provide the opportunity of looking for special pupils 'challenging the identities they are given' or choosing 'alternative experiences' (ibid. p. 225).

More recently, a study by Benjamin (2002, pp. 10-11 and *passim*) appears to employ a Foucault-type understanding of discourse. It concerned how 'special educational needs' identities might be influenced by discourses in a girls' secondary (high) school in England. The study explores tensions between the requirement that pupils reach certain expected standards and the aim of 'including' all pupils in school life and learning (ibid. p. 1). The researcher recognises the material reality of disabilities and disorders, but also examines the role of narratives in shaping as well as reflecting identity. It is suggested there is 'intellectual subordination' of pupils related to unequal relations (ibid. p. 6). The same study relates the discourses to power through having 'dominant' discourses about examination success.

Evaluation of historical epistemology in special education

If Tremain's (2002) arguments are taken in isolation, which is difficult as they are clear applications of Foucault, they are essentially based on a social construction of reality. This is hardly surprising as much of Foucault's writings assume a social construction of 'reality' traced through certain perceived historical changes. The objectivisation of the body is seen as a function of historical, class and cultural practices, as such can be challenged and changed.

Such views gain credibility to the extent that Foucault's interpretations of historical trends and his choice of facts to support them are credible. As has been indicated earlier, these interpretations have not gone unquestioned (Shorter, 1997). Foucault's idea that there are radical changes that can be traced across many areas of knowledge, it is said, is over-simplified (Steiner, 1971). To the extent that Foucault's interpretations are open to question, so are Tremain's (2002) applications.

Also, Foucault showed reluctance to set out political agendas derived directly from his work, although ethical implications do emerge, especially in some of his later writings such as the later volumes of *History of Sexuality*. Similarly, it is unclear what steps would be taken if Tremain's position is correct. How would ways of perceiving and forming knowledge be changed if they are so all-pervasive? If they relate to great historical trends, who can effect such trends and on what factors are they influenced? Such issues remain unclear. One response might be trying to resist identity potentially malignly shaped by others, as Allan (1996) suggests.

Allan (1996), focusing on the perceived power-knowledge fabric of special education, argues that individuals should show resistance to counter the possibility of assuming an identity shaped by others. There are however, other power-knowledge structures and fabrics around special children.

Some lobby groups, researchers and academics, 'critical' psychiatrists and psychologists and others press to mainstream special children. They may seek to dismantle what is seen as an oppressive system of identification and provision in special education, whether in special or mainstream schools. Allan does not make it clear why the power considered to pervade special education might be resisted rather than the power that might pervade efforts to encourage 'integration'.

In her discussion of the 'examination', Allan (1996) makes a bold claim. This claim is that, when a formal assessment is made there is often little doubt about the 'special educational need' although 'the notion of difference is itself socially constructed' (p. 224). She states that the multidisciplinary assessment gathering information about the child and his home background is 'primarily a political and social process' (ibid.). No justification is provided in the body of the article for these statements. It could instead be argued that such assessment processes and the provision of special education might be helpful and lead to the child experiencing better progress and development, rather than being simply 'marked out for perpetual surveillance' (ibid.).

More generally, if the matrix of power-knowledge pervades every aspect of social life, there needs to be some further justification of why one set of power-knowledge relationships might be challenged rather than others. If a set of power-knowledge relationships is considered malign, commentators might explain why or produce evidence of ill-effects. The belief that everything is 'socially constructed' does not constitute a form of criticism. Nor does it allow preferences to be identified about which aspects of socially constructed reality might be modified and which left unchallenged.

Benjamin (2002) seems to be critical that special education does not make all pupils attain equally. In the context of requirements that pupils reach certain standards and the aim of 'including' all pupils, some pupils achieve less well than others, giving rise to unequal relations. But it is difficult to see how the analysis of discourses leads to the conclusion that this is 'intellectual subordination' (p. 6). Is this suggesting that the special pupils are being kept down rather than that they have 'real' difficulties in learning? Is this a comment on the school's (or society's) valuing of pupils of different abilities rather than of special education itself? These are questions requiring further explanation that are left unexamined.

Nevertheless, studies drawing on aspects of Foucault's views may point to a greater awareness of discourse and power-knowledge structures where these can be identified. Awareness of power/knowledge relationships might encourage professionals to more fully recognise the importance of pupils' views. A trend in this direction is evident in the interest in so-called pupil 'voice'. This concerns ensuring – through systems and procedures as well as through support and openness – that pupils' views are sought and listened to.

Implications for thinking and practice of historical epistemology in special education

Someone supporting a historical epistemological view of special education may question the views of impairment as a natural phenomenon. She may regard impairment and other material aspects of bodily identity as relating to historically contingent practices that brought it into being, making it an object of knowledge. She may relate this to the effects of knowledge and power. She may question the apparent neutrality of the notion of impairment and challenge those who have made it objective and material.

The areas of curriculum and assessment, pedagogy, resources, and therapy are less relevant to a historical epistemological view of special education than the area of organisation. This is because the main thrust of a historical epistemological view concerns the spread and use of power that permeates relationships and organisations.

Someone holding a historical epistemological view of special education is likely to see the organisation supporting it as much wider than any individual school. The organisation would encompass a network of professionals supporting the special education system.

As historical epistemological notions are intimately related to knowledge and power, she may consider it important to challenge that power and question the knowledge with which it is related. She may challenge the objectivising and separating practices applied to disability, as well as questioning the way the subject is colluded into accepting the perceptions of others as part of their own identity. She may argue against the view that disablement and impairment are separable because this ignores that the category of impairment emerged to legitimise the 'disciplinary regime' that generated it.

With regard to special education, someone with a historical epistemological perspective may take the view that school bureaucrats use hierarchic surveillance, normalising sanctions, and examination, evident in the accountability and standards movement and high stakes testing. She may consider it important to examine how discourses on 'special needs' construct pupils' experiences in mainstream schools and constructs their identities as subjects and objects of knowledge.

She may consider that in special education, hierarchical observation can be identified in the higher staffing ratios that special children attract which allow closer scrutiny. Normalising judgements may be thought to be apparent in the way special children are 'defined in relation to normality'. She may regard the 'examination' as relating to assessment in special education determining whether a child has a disability or disorder leading to entitlement to special educational provision. She might argue that a historical epistemological view of power relationships provides the opportunity of looking for special pupils 'challenging the identities they are given' or choosing 'alternative experiences'. She might be interested in how 'special educational needs' identities might be influenced by discourses in a school and how narratives might shape as well as reflect identity. She may consider that 'intellectual subordination' of pupils reflects unequal relations.

Thinking points

- Might aspects of postmodern thought have the effect of reducing or denying a sense of agency for a special child and, if so, can this be avoided within a postmodern perspective?
- How would you set about identifying power/knowledge relationships in a school and how might developing awareness of any such power/knowledge relationships encourage professionals to more fully recognise the importance of pupils' views?

Key texts

Postmodernism

Lyotard, F. ([1979] 1984) *The Postmodern Condition: A Report on Knowledge* (translated from the French by G. Bennington and B. Massumi), Manchester: Manchester University Press. An often quoted source of postmodern thought on science.

Sokal, A. and Bricmont, J. ([1997] 1998) *Intellectual Impostures: Postmodern Philosophers' Abuse of Science* (translated from the French by the authors), London: Profile Books. An entertaining and informative book dismantling some of the excesses of postmodern pseudoscientific posturing. The hilarious spoof article, 'Transgressing the Boundaries: Towards a Transformative Hermeneutics of Quantum Gravity', is reproduced with commentary.

Historical epistemology

Allan, J. (1996) 'Foucault and Special Educational Needs: A 'Box of Tools' for Analysing Children's Experiences of Mainstreaming', *Disability and Society* 11, 2, 219–233. One of the few attempts to relate some of Foucault's ideas directly to special education, rather than, for example, 'disability'.

Foucault, M. ([1975] 1991) *Discipline and Punish: The Birth of the Prison* (translated from the French by Allan Sheridan), New York and London: Penguin. A vividly written example of Foucault's work, tracing developments in penology before and after the Enlightenment. The perspective of 'discipline' extends to schools and other institutions.

Foucault, M. ([1969] 2002) *The Archaeology of Knowledge* (translated from the French by A. M. Sheridan-Smith), London: Routledge. A theoretical account of the processes of discovering historically underpinning modes of thought.

Tremain, S. (2002) 'On the subject of impairment' in Corker, M. and Shakespeare, T. (Eds.) *Disability/Postmodernity: Embodying Disability Theory*, London: Continuum. A well-argued case for a Foucault-type perspective of impairment.

Chapter 11

Taking stock
Positivist special education and other perspectives

Positivist criticisms of other perspectives in special education

For some, the answer to the question, 'What can positivism learn from other perspectives?' seems to be 'Very little'. Kauffman and Sasso (2006) take the view that postmodernism is 'intellectually bankrupt', whether it is referred to as '"poststructuralism", "hermeneutics", "critical theory", "cultural studies", "deconstruction", or other label' (p. 65). Postmodern research, it is said, considers objective research to be naive because 'all forms of knowledge are exercises in power' (ibid.). Postmodernists see science merely as a 'social construction'. Postmodernism, 'reduces all things to discourse'. Its effect on special education has been 'uniformly negative' (ibid. p. 66).

Postmodern pessimism about establishing truth or effective interventions 'undermine efforts to see that teachers can contribute to a more equitable life for people with disabilities through the effective application of willed effort and objective thought' (Kauffman and Sasso, 2006, p. 67). The postmodern perspective, incompatible with a scientific view, is that 'truth floats or is always constructed to suit the interests of those in power, especially in education or in any other applied social science' (ibid.). Arguments that science has its limitations may leave room for debate about the nature of those limitations. However, the view that science has 'no particular advantage over other ways of knowing' does not leave room for debate (ibid. p. 68).

Kauffman and Sasso (2006) argue against 'scientism', the idea that science can give answers to everything. They also reject what they regard as the opposite extreme, which they associate with postmodernism, that 'science provides clearly superior answers to nothing' (p. 68). Postmodernism 'invites demagoguery and oppression by its denial that truth exists independent of the power to "invent" history, events, facts, or relationships' (p. 69). Postmodernism is a 'rejection of the fact that education requires applying science to problems in teaching and learning' (p. 71). It 'substitutes self-absorption and useless mind games for the practical help that teachers and others who are serious about helping students with disabilities need most desperately' (ibid.).

Kauffman and Sasso (2006) maintain that the various perspectives such as hermeneutics and critical theory all espouse 'philosophical relativism' and criticise 'truth and objectivity' (p. 113). But as Gallagher (2006, p. 94) points out, to lump together perspectives including hermeneutics and critical theory misses the differences between them.

In support of positivism, Kauffman and Sasso (2006) argue that 'celebrating uncertainty does not reduce it'. Furthermore, 'Tearing down ideas about how we establish what we know without replacing them with better rules for establishing knowledge is, in our judgement, an evasion of responsibility' (p. 113). Once postmodernists embrace 'even a weak version of objectivity, they are forced to compete against the objective enterprise of science and logical enquiry' (p. 117). It is then clear 'their program lacks the intellectual resources to answer even the most basic questions regarding how to teach and help children with disabilities'. This is because 'they have no systematic means of reducing doubt, only a philosophy acknowledging its existence' (ibid.).

In brief then, criticisms of other perspectives from the positivist standpoint are various. Postmodernism incorrectly regards science as a social construction and reduces everything to discourse. It diminishes efforts to apply objective thought to improve the lives of special children. Truth is seen as a reflection of the views of those in power. The advantages of a scientific approach are not recognised. Postmodernism is unable to offer anything to replace the positivist position it criticises. For Kauffman (private communication, 2010) differences between postmodernism, hermeneutics, poststructuralism and critical theory are not significant with regard to their implications for special education, for which all of them have negative implications.

Although Kauffman and Sasso (2006) make strong points, they do overlook some of the differences between various perspectives. For example, it is said postmodern research considers objective research to be naive because 'all forms of knowledge are exercises in power' (p. 65). However, this applies more to critical theory (and historical epistemology which is not mentioned) and less to deconstruction, which is more concerned with the slipperiness of meaning. Not all perspectives that might be considered postmodern see science merely as a social construction. Not every postmodernism perspective reduces everything to discourse. The effects of postmodernism on special education may not be completely negative if, for example, one includes work derived from the writings of Merleau-Ponty ([1945] 1982; [1964] 1968).

In grouping together several threads of postmodern thought (postmodernism, hermeneutics, poststructuralism, critical theory and deconstruction) Kauffman and Sasso (2006, p. 65) miss these differences and are therefore unable to consider the relationship of each perspective to positivism. Consequently, some of the weaknesses and strengths of the different positions are overlooked. In the remainder of this chapter, the various perspectives will be considered in relation to positivism.

Relationships between positivism and other perspectives

Phenomenology

Phenomenology, in offering subjective insights, contrasts to the objectivity sought by positivism. The transcendental phenomenology of Husserl ([1900–1901] 2001; [1913] 1982; [1913] 1989; [1913] 1980), the hermeneutic phenomenology of Heidegger ([1927] 1962; [1975] 1982) and especially later developments by Merleau-Ponty ([1945] 1982; [1964] 1968) have all influenced thinking about special education. Disability in relation to sexuality and subjectivity has been considered (Shildrick, 2009) drawing partly on the work of Merleau-Ponty. In exploring possible motivations for discrimination, devaluation and alienation of disabled people, and in seeking to 'rethink' notions of the embodied self and different modes of 'inter subjectivity' Shildrick's standpoint differs markedly from positivism.

Iwakuma (2002), drawing more directly on Merleau-Ponty's ideas, explores possible interpretations of embodiment in relation to the experience of 'phantom' limbs and the extension of faculties through physical and sensory aids. For Iwakuma (2002), Merleau-Ponty's work can help one understand 'disability experiences', especially becoming a 'fully fledged' person with a disability and may aid 'the emergence of disability consciousness' (p. 85). Using phenomenological approaches focusing on 'lived experience', attempts have been made to illuminate meanings for educational phenomena. Carrington, Papinczak and Templeton (2003) examined the social expectations and perceptions of a friendship group of teenagers with Asperger's Syndrome. Tutty and Hocking (2004) looked at the experiences of teacher aides working with students requiring high levels of support. The focus on meaning and perceptions in such research differentiates it from positivist attempts to seek replicable findings.

Yet within special education, teachers and others can reflect on the speculations associated with phenomenology and recognise the thinking behind, for example, a person with a physical disability being 'fully fledged' as an individual. The nature of being fully fledged seems to relate to acceptance as a person and not being seen exclusively in terms of a disability. This is an attitude towards individuals with a disability or disorder quite compatible with a positivist approach to special education because it is less concerned with evidence than with attitude. Teachers can and do respond to a special child in terms of what a disability or disorder requires educationally, and at the same time they can recognise that the disability is not the whole child.

Hermeneutics

Hermeneutics as a theory of knowledge does not apply to scientific method, nor does it provide causal explanations bringing individual instances under general laws. Instead it strives to produce knowledge through interpretation. Indeed, hermeneutics – and especially the philosophical hermeneutics of Gadamer ([1960 and later editions] 2004); [various dates from 1960 to 1972] 1976; [1976, 1978, 1979] 1981) – have informed criticisms of a positivist perspective in special education.

Iano (2004) considers scientific method out of place in social sciences and special education because, for him, the subject matter of social sciences is a solely human creation. Iano regards positivist research in education as a 'natural science-technical model' (Iano, 2004, p. 73). Similarly, Gallagher's philosophical hermeneutics perspective (Gallagher *et al.*, 2004) emphasises the importance of interpretation and rejects a 'correspondence theory' of truth whereby statements are taken to be true if they correspond to or represent reality.

In special education, the tension between a positivist view and practice and a hermeneutic perspective is difficult to resolve. Hermeneutics has tended to criticise positivism rather than suggest a vision of what hermeneutically informed special education would look like. Perhaps the intention is that special education is misguided in its application. However, for those children who thrive because of special education, this would seem difficult to justify. A philosophical position seeing knowledge as produced through interpretation does not seem quite enough to counter what, to some, is practical evidence that the knowledge and skill associated with special education can transform the lives of special children.

Historical materialism

As an aspect of Marxism (Marx, [1867] 1992; [1885] 1993; [1894] 1993; [1859] 1981; Marx and Engels, [1848] 1996), historical materialism is part of a comprehensive attempt to explain how society has developed and to predict future trends. With regard to disability, Oliver (1990) develops a historical-materialist account of disablement and a social model of disability. In this, disabled people are presented as experiencing disability as 'social restriction' (p. xiv) owing to factors such as 'inaccessible built environments' and 'hostile public attitudes' (ibid.). It is said differences in the treatment of disabled people are produced culturally 'through the relationship between the mode of production and the central values of the society concerned' (ibid. p. 23).

For Barnes (1998) the social model of disability distinguishes between impairment as 'biological characteristics of the body and mind' and disability as 'society's failure to address the needs of disabled people'. The knowledge and practice of the social model concerns the 'political project of emancipation' (Corker and Shakespeare, 2002a, p. 3). Similarly, Thomas's understanding of the nature of social and cultural systems is informed by 'historical materialist premises' (Thomas and Corker, 2002, p. 19). Gleeson (1999) theorises historical-geographical relationships that have 'conditioned the social experience of disabled people in Western societies' and seeks to explain disabled people's social experiences 'in specific historical–geographical settings' (p. 3). Historical and geographical organisation of cultural-material life, it is argued, 'shapes all social experiences, including disability' (ibid. p. 8). Links have for a long time been made between disability and limitations on integration and participation, or exclusion (e.g. Despouy, 1991).

Marxism itself sought to be a scientific theory based on evidence and making predictions. However, a historical materialist theory of disability proposes a model and points to its advantages for disabled people – for example, that if their position is one of oppression, the model might be emancipatory. Supporters of a social model may point to evidence that some special children may not have progressed well in special schools (Oliver, 1996, p. 80; Barnes, 1991, pp. 43–46). Yet it is not always clear they are prepared to recognise evidence where special children are demonstrated to make better progress and develop better in a special school than in an ordinary school (Farrell, 2006, *passim*). It has been argued that social model theorists may spurn such contrary evidence as running counter to a pre-agreed position (Clarke, Dyson and Millward, 1998). Where those advocating a social model call for the closure of special schools (Oliver, 1996, pp. 93–94) when it is clear many children thrive in them, it is difficult to maintain they are oppressive. On the other hand, special education can respond to the notion of barriers to education and well-being that the social model points up. These are often physical barriers, which schools can and do seek to minimise. Awareness of attitudinal barriers such as low expectations of some special children is also important.

Critical theory

Critical theory (Adorno, 1931; Horkheimer, [1937] 2002; Marcuse, [1937] 1972; Adorno and Horkheimer, [1947] 2002, Habermas, 1971; [1973] 1976; [1962] 1989) differs from positivism regarding objects of knowledge. A positivist approach makes objects of knowledge so as to arrange the external world using objective reason. Critical theory however does not make objects of knowledge in this sense and is said to be non-objectifying (Geuss, 1981). It does not externalise objects of knowledge but remains critical of the circumstances in which the theory is developing. In this way, critical theory aims to avoid a situation where the objective reason of scientific theory is distorted into a subjective reason in which rationality is regarded only in terms of consumer needs. The reason for this avoidance is that such consumer needs are seen as false needs defined by the functioning of a consumer society.

Following in the footsteps of Tomlinson (1987), Brantlinger (2006c, 2006a, 2006b, 2006c) has developed critical theory approaches in special education. This has included a consideration of the politics of textbook production and sales, the 'ideological and economic reasons behind textbook decisions' and how 'official knowledge' is produced (Brantlinger, 2006a, pp. 67–68). The theme of hidden ideology, hegemony and unrecognised forces shaping events to their own ends while appearing to provide benefits to others is clearly evident in Brantlinger's (2006b) interpretations. Brantlinger (2006b) argues that the obvious beneficiaries of special education – learners with disabilities and disorders – are not the only ones. They also include test producers, transglobal capitalists, media moguls, politicians and political pundits, advocates of school privatisation, school superintendents, and the educated middle class. In the tradition of emancipatory critical theory, Brantlinger (2006b, pp. 222–224) concludes that society should become more egalitarian and there should be more emphasis on redistributive justice.

In special education, factors such as the motivations of school superintendents and the educated middle class are not within the remit of positivism. Such observations are not so much undisputed facts as suspicions that all is not what it seems. If there were clear evidence of abuse – for example, of the corruption of media moguls – the theory would no longer be a theory but a description of events. Yet the point of critical theory is that such corruption is hidden from view. Such a standpoint faces the same problem that critical theory generally faces, that of explaining how anyone from within the fabric of society can take a position that reveals these abuses. Yet, at the very least, critical theory can suggest a healthy scepticism towards special education. To the extent that critical theory in special education might support a more egalitarian society or redistributive justice, a special educator might freely agree or disagree with such a position. In working with special children however, and in aiming to help them learn and develop to the full, special educators may already see themselves as being part of egalitarian efforts.

Holism

Holism does not contradict positivism but rather sees a scientific approach as embedded within a natural tendency toward wholes. Hegel's ([1812, 1813, 1816] 1969) holism is intensely rational although ultimately spiritual. For Smuts (1927) holism is 'a fundamental factor operative towards the creation of wholes in the universe' (p. 88), that is a 'whole making . . . tendency' (ibid. p. 101). Nature cannot be explained in purely mechanical terms. Although there is a 'mechanistic concept of Nature' this has its place and can be justified 'only in the wider setting of holism' (ibid. p. 89). In the social sciences, holism regards the object of the human sciences as structures and systems. The study of individual social agents is not the proper object of study and the structures and systems cannot be reduced to these individual social agents. Ecosystemic studies in the social sciences sometimes imply a unity whose parts are interdependent.

In special education the compatibility of holism with positivism is sometimes missed because constructivist views are emphasised. Heshusius (1989 and in Gallagher et al., 2004; Heshusius, 2004b) views holistic education as understanding human behaviour as 'constructive, self-organising, and self-regulating'

(Heshusius, 2004a, p. 50). Learning is seen as understanding relations rather than 'pieces of knowledge'. It is the personal, social and cultural 'construction of meaning' by the child, based on who the child is and what he knows (ibid.). Progress is seen as 'transformative' and occurring when concepts are seen in new ways' (ibid. p. 51). For Heshusius (2004b), the problem with the positivist paradigm is a need to 'reduce all complexity to simple units of measurement', 'reduce wholes to no more than the sum of parts', 'see the act of knowing as identical to the act of control' and to regard oneself as being 'a privileged knower' with its attendant prestige (ibid. p. 212). Heshusius (2004b, pp. 181–182) considers that a positivist approach puts curriculum content first and uses it to measure a pupil's performance, while meaning and 'real-life purpose' is added afterwards. In a holistic perspective, real-life meaning is seen as coming first with 'learning engagements' emerging from meaning (ibid. p. 181). Kauffman and Sasso (2006) associate holism with a constructivist philosophical position. They maintain that, in teaching and learning reading, holism could suggest that language cannot be meaningfully analysed or taught in component parts and that words should not be segmented. This might be contrasted to direct instruction in sound and symbol correspondence (ibid. p. 73).

In special education, it is unclear why these approaches are presented as dichotomies. Whether one takes a positivist or holistic approach, the content of the curriculum includes content that has to take account of what society considers valuable – reading, for example. The positivist might prioritise externals, such as phonic reading, and supplement this by reading in context and for meaning. The intention is to educate the child to read for meaning but in parallel to learn the mechanics. The holistic educator might focus more on sight vocabulary but would presumably have to supplement this by working on the mechanics of reading. The first approach can build a child's confidence as he can quickly learn to read phonetically regular words, but it has to be supplemented by reading for meaning. The second approach conveys early that reading is for meaning, but needs to be supplemented by phonetic learning. In practice, teachers can combine both approaches. Holism may sometimes misleadingly be presented as contrary to a positivist perspective, but in practice in special education, implications of taking a perspective informed by holism or positivism are compatible and indeed can be complementary.

Constructivism

In constructivism, the relationship with positivism seems equivocal, as though constructivists seek to reject positivism but cannot quite do so. Piaget (1970; Piaget and Inhelder, [1966] 1969) held a constructivist theory of cognitive and affective development, seeing development as involving a process of adaptation to the environment. More influenced by positivism perhaps, 'neo-Piagetian' perspectives, (Morra et al., 2007) tend to be informed by neuropsychology. They take a constructivist approach to cognitive development, but tend to relate increasingly complex stages with the child's information-processing system rather than with logical properties. Vygotsky emphasises the importance to intellectual development of a child interacting with more advanced thinkers (Vygotsky, [various dates] 1978; [1925–1926] 1993; [n.d.] 1993); [1924] 1993); [1927] 1993). His work informs debates on the relative contribution of individual factors and social and cultural factors in special education (Minick, 1987; Wertsch, 1985). Vygotsky's view of psychology and special pedagogy highlights cultural influences on development (Knox and Stevens, 1993, p. 5, translators' introduction). For Gergen (1995) a social constructionist view assumes that language primarily has a communal function; and meaning in language is achieved through social interdependence and is dependent on context, so children are socialised into already existing meanings and languages (pp. 17–40). Yet Vygotsky accepted that individual difference and biological and psychological factors were important for special pedagogy.

For some, constructivist research regards data as inseparable from the theorising agent or theory, in the sense of 'the construction that interprets and gives the data meaning'. Objectivity is not possible and indeed is not always 'a desirable goal' (Paul, Kleinhammer-Tramill and Fowler, 2009, p. 4). Constructivism has been defined as 'a nonpositivist perspective grounding several qualitative approaches to research' (ibid.). Constructivism, associated with qualitative methods, has been contrasted to positivist approaches and related quantitative methods. Nevertheless, it has been maintained there is much common ground in constructivism and positivist methods (Padgett, 2004, pp. 5–7).

In special education, Poplin (1988a, 1988b) initially argued against a 'reductionist' positivist perspective that emphasised behavioural learning theory. She favoured an approach based on structuralist philosophy, constructivist theory and holistic beliefs. Poplin suggested schools concentrate on helping students 'develop new meanings in response to new experiences' instead of learning meanings created by others (Poplin, 1988a, abstract). More recently, Poplin and Cousin (1996) have argued for an eclectic approach, drawing on both constructivist and positivist insights. Danforth and Smith (2005) seek a constructivist approach to 'troubling students', using a constructivist interpretation of Piaget's work (pp. 36–38), social constructionism (pp. 38–39) and critical theory (pp. 44–48). They refer to this as 'critical constructivism' (pp. 6–7, and *passim*). For Danforth and Smith (2005) constructivist/constructionist pedagogy emphasises cognitive structures, and learning is seen as a continuing process of 'interaction between self and environment' involving a 'qualitative change in the learner's thinking' (p. 40). Instead of searching for a single right answer, learners explore the extent to which something is 'right' within a certain context, for a particular person or people, and at a particular time (p. 44). But this makes it difficult for a constructivist position to demonstrate the moral basis on which some constructed meanings and truths are preferred to others. The reluctance to draw on positivist notions of truth and meaning is either unsustainable or comes at a high price. This suggests that constructivism, in its more radical form, depends on positivism at key points and that, in special education practice, a sharp separation between the two perspectives cannot be maintained.

Structuralism

There are senses in which structuralism appears to contrast with positivism (regarding Jacobson and Lévi-Strauss) and others in which structuralist theory uses and is developed through scientific method (with regard to Piaget). In Jacobson's structural perspective, language is organised around the poles of metaphor and metonymy (Jacobson and Halle, 1956). The structuralist view of language differs from a positivist one where it might be assumed to be a means of expression at the will of the speaker. For the structuralist, language is not a tool to express the speaker's thoughts, but a precondition of thought and social existence. Structuralism looks for forms and concepts not routinely available to observers and of which even participants may be unaware. Lévi-Strauss ([1958] 1977) seeks a level of conceptualising that allows structures to be pinpointed. Once these concepts are identified, it becomes possible to see structures of which even participants may be unconscious. For Lévi-Strauss, 'The term "social structure" has nothing to do with empirical reality but with models that are built up after it' (ibid. p. 279). Structure is a method to be applied to any kind of social studies.

Piaget ([1968] 1971) regards the notion of structure in terms of three key ideas: wholeness, transformation and self-regulation (p. 5). He drew on structuralism as a method in his psychology but is sometimes described as a constructivist in the sense that for him, construction is a precondition of structure. Piaget's work provides insights into cognitive impairment. He describes typical development of children, specifying usual chronological ages when certain indications of development are often noted and can be assessed. These indicators of development can help inform understanding of the development of children who have cognitive impairments. Exact parallels are not assumed, but such information can be useful and may help establish suitable pedagogy.

For Piaget ([1968] 1971), structuralism is essentially a method (p. 136). It is not exclusive, and does not suppress other dimensions of investigation (p. 137). It is intimately associated with construction (p. 140). Piaget's theories were based on extensive observation of the development of children and experimental evidence in good scientific tradition. Using the same positivist methods, other researchers have questioned the age at which some of Piaget's stages are said to emerge. For example, within the sensorimotor stage, the age at which infants develop cognitive representations has been shown to be much earlier than Piaget could demonstrate (Goswami, 2008, chs 1 and 2). Neo-Piagetian perspectives (Morra et al., 2007) tend to be informed by neuropsychology, linking increasingly complex stages with the child's information–processing system.

Poststructuralism

Poststructuralism prioritises language and signification in an attempt to destabilise meaning, including scientific meaning. Poststructuralism is reluctant to ground discourse in any theory with metaphysical origins. Enlightenment thinking is regarded with suspicion, and poststructuralism is sceptical about scientific approaches, viewing meaning as unstable and plural. These features may lead to criticisms of positivism. Deconstruction involves a close analytic reading of a text to demonstrate it is not a coherent entity. Derrida frequently uses deconstruction to examine internal contradictions of philosophical discourse ([1967] 1973; [1967] 1997; [various dates and 1967] 1978). Binary oppositions such as speech and writing are considered problematic. Derrida views language as a system of differences, where meaning is conveyed not by some quality of a single word but by its difference from other words ([1967] 1997, p. 23).

Poststructuralism can be regarded as an over-concentration on discourse. Consequently, the human body and sense experience can be reduced to a collection of discursive significations. The symbol can become more important than bodily experience and how the body is constituted. A phenomenological perspective might be diminished if one were to focus only on discourse. Deconstruction may concentrate on showing inconsistencies in positions and discourses. In many respects, poststructuralism seems the antithesis of positivism. Yet, it has been proposed, Derrida is not denying the existence of relatively determinate truths or meanings. Rather, he seeks to see such things as the effects of a deeper history of language and the unconscious (Eagleton, 1996a, p. 128). On the other hand, Derrida's writings have been roundly criticised. They may have been feted by literary theorists but are, in their lack of clarity and reluctance to define basic terms, more like 'counterfeit philosophy' (Kenny, 2008, p. 96).

Danforth and Rhodes (1997) suggest the acceptance of the concept 'disabled' hinders moves towards more inclusive schooling, partly because the concept assumes the identification and separation of one group of children from another. The authors regard disability as a social construct and state that in failing to contest the 'disability construct' those who would wish to support mainstreaming are effectively supporting the 'devaluation and stigmatization' of these students (ibid. p. 357). By developing an approach questioning the term 'disability', it becomes possible to better advocate inclusion. For Danforth and Rhodes (1997), deconstruction offers 'a strategic, political means to promote local change in daily professional work' (pp. 359–360). If society 'somehow' lost the vocabulary of mental retardation, 'the constructed reality of mental retardation would no longer continue in its present form' (p. 360). This position is the opposite of positivist approaches, in that it does not seek evidence for example that some children might receive a poorer education in either special or mainstream education. The concern is to try to change the use and meaning of words to gain a particular end: mainstreaming. However, Silvers (2002) suggests that 'normalcy' and 'disability' need not be antithetical. Plurality in regarding disability can lead to recognition of different perspectives, including positivist ones, but also ones that take account of personal interactions in mapping out disability. As Titchkosky (2002) says, 'In this diversity, it is possible to map disability as opposition, as a medical thing'. However, it is also possible to map disability as 'an interactional accomplishment' (ibid. p. 109), which might open up the possibility of viewing disability as an accomplishment, instead of always regarding it as a difficulty.

Pragmatism

Pragmatism developed through the work of Peirce (1877 and 1878 in Moore, Peirce and Fisch, 1986), James ([1907] 1995; [1912] 2003) and Dewey (e.g. [1910] 2009). It is a form of philosophy centrally concerned to argue for a particular theory of meaning and truth. This theory is that a proposition is true if holding it to be true is advantageous or practically successful. Accordingly, a true belief is one that leads to successful action. The instrumentalism of pragmatism seems to spurn usual notions of truth and breaks the relationship between a belief and the facts that would be said to verify it. It appears to support a conception that depends on inquiry being guided by an unacknowledged Hegelian metaphysic. Neo-pragmatism (Rorty, 1989) is more at odds with positivist conceptions of truth and reality. For Rorty (1989), 'Truth cannot be out there, cannot exist independently of the human mind, because sentences cannot so exist, or be out there. The world is out there, but descriptions of the world are not'. Rorty (1979) argues that the problems of epistemology relate to picturing the mind as seeking to mirror an independent, external reality. A foundationalist has to accept that some beliefs are foundational because if one belief only depends on another and so on, we have a problem of infinite regress. Rorty suggests we have to discard the metaphor of the mind as mirroring nature. He denies that knowledge has objective foundations that can be described by a theory of knowledge. For him, knowledge does not comprise ideas that faithfully mirror the external world but is judged by the accuracy of its representations, and in this sense is seen as what works for us (Rorty, 1979).

Albrecht (2002) suggests that pragmatism has influenced disability studies because it offered 'a conceptual framework for thinking about the critical issues confronting social scientists' (p. 20). Albrecht (2002) maintains that neo-pragmatism has moved towards 'recognition of the importance of subjective experience, relativistic and culturally different conceptions of behaviour, paradigm shifts in the gathering and interpreting of information and competing communities of discourse' (p. 23). Skrtic (1995) employs 'critical pragmatism' to investigate presumptions he believes have constrained professional discourse and practice. He argues that the adhocratic approach makes possible certain organisational conditions necessary to educate diverse pupils. More recently

Skrtic (2004) has elaborated on some common features of critical pragmatism and broad critical theory, aiming to be interdisciplinary and to integrate philosophy and empirical science (p. 358). The approach seeks social change and draws on ethical and social theory informing 'norms of justice, liberty . . . and participatory democracy' (ibid.). In Skrtic's view, critical pragmatism requires 'a particular form of historical reflection'. This is reflection that 'avoids both the transhistorical stance of traditional foundationalism and the relativism of pure contextualism' (p. 359). The concern here is that where traditional foundationalism is the touchstone, a view is taken that tries to rise above historical context. Where 'pure' contextualism is adopted, there is a danger of over-subjectivism. Skrtic aims to avoid both of these positions but his approach seems to miss opportunities afforded by broadly applied evidence-based practice, which has led to useful interventions (Farrell, 2008, *passim*; Fonagy *et al.*, 2005).

In special education, pragmatism, despite its supposed focus on what 'works', seems to miss the opportunity to use evidence-based findings and instead concentrate on perpetual exploratory pedagogy. Yet pragmatism and evidence-based practice share a concern with outcomes. Pragmatism looks to consequences of holding beliefs to inform its view of truth seen as instrumental. Evidence-based practice in special education looks to the outcomes of interventions, not to determine their truth but to judge their efficacy.

Symbolic interactionism

For symbolic interactionists, reality is mainly a social product. The sense of self, society and culture emerge from symbolic interactions and are dependent on symbolic interactions for their existence. The physical environment is interpreted through symbolic systems in the way it is made relevant to human behaviour. Cooley's ([1902] 1983) notion of the 'looking glass self' suggests that individuals in part regard themselves as they believe others see them. Self-concept and our own feelings emerge from how individuals believe other people see and evaluate them. Mead ([1934] 1967) considers how individual minds and selves arise from social processes. He regards social processes as prior to the processes of individual experience. Mind arises within the social processes of communication. Communication processes involve the 'conversation of gestures', which have an unconscious effect, and language, in which communication takes place through significant symbols.

In special education, Bogdan and Kugelmass (1984) report a project drawing on symbolic interactionism. Finding variations in who were considered to require special education provision and why, the authors maintain that perceptions were crucial (p. 175). Within symbolic interactionism, they state that objects, people, situations and behaviour 'do not produce their own meaning'. Objects might be wheelchairs, people would include resource teachers and special education students, situations might be mainstreaming, and behaviour would include reading and writing. In all these instances, meaning is not produced, but 'bestowed upon them' (p. 182). The authors do not deny 'that a child that is blind cannot see' (p. 183). But they argue that these concepts 'need to be understood' by examining the interplay between how different people 'come to define' these children in specific situations (ibid.). Bentley (2005) links symbolic interactionism with a 'Foucauldian genealogy' to investigate disability and inclusion, and the interactions and meanings attached to them. Excluding and including interactions were identified within self-described inclusive practices.

Symbolic interactionism has informed medical sociology and qualitative research methods. It has been used to examine questions such as the subjective experiences of individuals with disabilities and the perceptions of disability of others who are not disabled. Related social construction views of disability similarly focus on subjective concerns. Albrecht (2002) considers social interactionism to be equipped to analyse 'how social problems, behaviour and institutions are socially constructed' (p. 28). Work informed by, among other things, 'the social construction of disability' is believed to contribute to the understanding of disability, 'on the societal and structural levels' (p. 31). The difficulty of extending such approaches beyond the perspectives and subjective experiences reported may limit the wider applicability of any findings.

Psychoanalysis: Freud

Psychoanalysis (Freud, S. 1909; [1940] 2003; [1940] 2002) is a theory concerned with unconscious motivation in which libidinal and aggressive drives are considered the prime movers of mental life and behaviour. Others contributing to understanding analysis with children include Anna Freud (1936; 1945; [various dates] 1998); Klein (1932; [various dates] 1964; [1957] 1975); Winnicott (1958, 1965) and Bowlby (1965, 1969, 1973, 1980).

The psychoanalytic model has a flexibility and subtlety necessary to depict the enormously complicated nature of mental life and behaviour, but the criterion of positivist evidence may not be applicable to theories developed by Freud and others. Freud saw his work as scientific and amenable to examination and confirmation. However, scepticism towards psychoanalytic perspectives has been expressed – for example, the difficulty in testing meaningful hypotheses relating to outcomes. Still, there is some evidence of the effectiveness of specific psychodynamic approaches, such as focal dynamic psychotherapy (Muratori et al., 2002). Webster (2007) criticises Freud for being apparently in the thrall of charismatic healers such as Charcot and afterwards insufficiently interrogating their ideas. Freud's theories are said to be, from the beginning, based on likely misdiagnoses of hysteria. The mechanisms that Freud uses to describe the apparent functioning of the psyche are considered little more than pseudo-science, unknowingly immersed in the traditions of Judeo-Christian religious culture (ibid. pp. 168–181 and *passim*). The development of psychoanalysis as a movement is presented in terms of religious dogma rather than a scientific movement. A possible alternative theory that scientifically begins to explain human behaviour without recourse to mysterious forces and pseudo-science might emerge from neo-Darwinism, argues Webster (2007).

Marks (1999) relates aspects of psychoanalytic theory to disability, mainly drawing on various psychoanalytically related 'defences' such as projection (pp. 18–24). Such suspicions are perhaps speculative correctives to the opposite assumption that every helping professional is driven by purely selfless motives. Music therapy, art therapy, drama therapy, movement therapy and play therapy may draw on psychodynamic perspectives. Where possible, the effectiveness of psychotherapies is evaluated in line with evidence-based practice. There is a perceived dichotomy between attempting to use objective approaches to assess the efficacy of art therapies and the more fluid nature of therapeutic encounters. However, the ways in which drama therapists ascertain whether the client is 'getting any better' have been examined (Valente and Fontana, 1997, p. 29). In art therapy, evaluation may involve a review of pictures with the client, which may uncover previously unconscious connections (Schaverien, 1995, p. 28). In some very specialist settings psychodynamic interpretations are used in day-to-day living and individual sessions. The Mulberry Bush School, England draws on the work of psychotherapist Barbara Dockar-Drysdale (1991, 1993) who followed Winnicott (1958, 1965). In ordinary school settings, the development of early intervention 'nurture groups' (Boxall, 2002) influenced by Bowlby's attachment theory. Where psychoanalytic perspectives have had an impact on special education, the evidence of their suitability has been difficult to demonstrate. Professional judgement and personal testimony has often taken the place of research evidence.

Psychoanalysis: Lacan

Lacan ([various dates and 1966] 2006) reconsiders Freudian theories and their relationships with language with reference to structuralist and poststructuralist theories of discourse. For example, in Freudian theory the child after the Oedipal phase is conflicted between the repressed desires of the unconscious and the executive functions of the ego. In Lacan's theory, the child leaves the full imaginary possession of the mother's body and his unified self. He leaves this for the empty world of language in the symbolic order where there is nothing but an endless chain of absence and difference. The metaphorical mirror world is traded for the metonymic world of language.

Lacan's working out of the implications of pre-Oedipal and Oedipal stages and their interpretation in relation to language (Lacan, [various dates and 1966] 2006) has provided fertile ground for speculation about a range of areas. Sokal and Bricmont (1998) demonstrate that Lacan's use of mathematical symbols is meaningless. Sokal and Bricmont ([1997] 1999), after providing examples of his misuse of mathematical and scientific concepts, criticise Lacan for the privilege he accords theory rather than observation and experiment. They state:

> After all, psychoanalysis, assuming that it has a scientific basis, is a rather young science. Before launching into vast theoretical generalisations, it might be prudent to check the empirical adequacy of at least some of its propositions. But, in Lacan's writings, one finds mainly quotations and analyses of texts and concepts.
>
> (Sokal and Bricmont [1997] 1998, p. 34)

It is not convincing to argue that Lacan uses mathematic terminology metaphorically or that one ought not to expect clear meanings from him, as Fink (2004, p. 130) has claimed.

Shildrick (2009) draws on Lacan's ideas (Lacan, [1966] 2006; [1949 and 1966] 2006; [1948 and 1966] 2005) to explore possible sources of responses to disability. Her discussion is focused on sexuality and subjectivity in relation to disability. However, her more generalised suggestions indicate a possible starting point for understanding negative and positive responses to disability in terms of early infantile experience and states. Shildrick herself however finds an impasse in the further development of Lacan's ideas in the context of her exploration of disability, subjectivity and sexuality. Some but not all of Lacan's theorisings begin with a recognisable basis in Freud's thought, and Lacan considered that a return to Freud was desirable. Shildrick's concentration on the fragmented and discontinuous early imaginary therefore picks out an aspect of Lacan that does not appear to build on Freud. It is difficult to envisage any basis on which a judgement could be made about the credibility of such speculations.

Postmodernism

Postmodernism draws attention to the perceived limitations of philosophy and of discourse in a self-referential way. It attempts to move away from perceived problems with modernism, in particular relating to the values and aspirations of the Enlightenment. These are values and aspirations related to principles that inform positivism. Lyotard ([1979] 1984) argued that scientific knowledge appeared to have supplanted narrative knowledge because scientific knowledge embraced an overarching narrative reflecting the values of humanism, which legitimated modern society. The prestige of scientific thinking and the search for legitimation relate to philosophical narratives emerging from German idealism and political narratives stemming from the French Enlightenment. Yet scientific knowledge depends for its legitimation on philosophical and political narratives, which in the view of science do not constitute knowledge at all. This contradiction shows that science is interrelated to other discourses over which it has no privileged status. Because scientific knowledge depends for legitimacy on German idealism and French Enlightenment thinking, which are declining in credibility, this weakens the legitimacy principle of knowledge, blurring distinctions between different areas of science. Postmodern science concerns 'undecidables' and paradoxes, and evolves in a discontinuous way. Its 'model of legitimation' (Lyotard, [1979] 1984, p. 60) is based on reasoning that contradicts logical rules. It is counter to usual and established ways of reasoning.

Postmodernism intends to challenge traditional views of perception and reality, so that established ways of seeing the world may be opened up to a new scrutiny. But this requires that cogent arguments are put forward to undermine those positions and, ideally, that alternative interpretations are put forward that can in their turn be challenged. Where this is lacking, postmodernism is criticised. For Habermas (1980, 1985) postmodernism deserts the aspirations of modernity, which in his view have not been fulfilled and adopts an eclectic irrationalism. It has been described as a form of 'antirealist doctrine' antipathetic towards 'objectivity and knowledge' (Sasso, 2001, p. 178). Postmodernism is said to mistrust logical positivism and science and to give equal credence to 'alternative ways of knowing or constructing truth' (Kauffman, 1999, p. 248). It is characterised by rejection of the rationalist tradition of the Enlightenment, theoretical discourses unconnected with empirical tests, and a view that science is a social construction (Sokal and Bricmont, 1998). Sokal and Bricmont ([1997] 1999) identify in Lyotard's writing a mixture of statements that are banal, others that are incorrect, and others that are meaningless.

Postmodernism maintains that special education is shaped by social and historical influences (Gerber, 1994, p. 371). Heshusius (1991) criticises curriculum-based assessment and direct instruction, suggesting that their underlying assumptions are parallel to a flawed 'mechanistic, Newtonian paradigm'. Heshusius (2004a, p. 205) argues that scientific procedures are a human construction developed in a historical setting and in a certain social context, not a universal, detached set of practices. Special education fails to recognise the limitations of positivism. What appear to be disinterested and impartial scientifically based findings in special educational research, she argues, are historically and socially constructed. Postmodernism challenges 'the hegemony of normativism' (Corker and Shakespeare, 2002a, p. 14). With reference to special children, normatism may lead to viewing the usual as inevitable and superior. Typical levels and types of development become privileged over others. Consequently, individuals different to the norm can be viewed as lesser individuals instead of different. The norm is simply accepted as the natural course of things that some ways of being are better than others (ibid.). However, it is suggested, aspects of postmodern thought could have the effect of reducing or denying a sense of agency for a disabled individual (Scully, 2002, p. 58). Gross (1998, p. 48) argues that, in the past, science may have offered 'false universals'. But these have been overthrown only by better science. For Kauffman and Sasso

(2006) postmodernism, if applied to special education, could lead to 'malpractice' (abstract, p. 65) and could support extremes of whole-language reading (pp. 73–78), radical multiculturalism (pp. 78–82) and discredited facilitated communication (pp. 82–84).

Historical epistemology

Historical epistemology characterises the work of Foucault ([1961] 2006; [1963] 2003). Foucault examines the conditions that allowed the possibility of ways of knowing and the historically contingent practices that shaped them. Concerned with periodic changes in perception and knowledge and the relationships between knowledge and power, he analysed the historical development of forms of knowledge regarding sexuality, punishment, medicine, the humanities and madness. Foucault ([1963] 2003) suggests there was a shift in the structure of knowledge from a taxonomic period to an 'organic historical' period, allowing the possibilty of a discourse about disease. Anatomy, often assumed to be an uncomplicated empirical science gradually recognising what was 'real', is seen as more a product of a new structuring of knowledge. Seeing power as all-pervading, Foucault regards resistance as part of a related fabric. He is concerned with power and its relationship with discursive formations that make knowledge possible. Power is understood as that which controls individuals and their knowledge, and which enters discourses and attitudes and everyday life (Foucault, [various dates] 1980, p. 30). Foucault ([1975] 1991) examines changes in Western penal systems in modern times, concentrating on issues of power and of the human body. He maintains that prison is a new form of technological power – that of discipline – and that this power is also present in hospitals and schools.

In special education, Foucault's influence has been evident. Armstrong (2003, pp. 8–19) links the development of special education to historical change in Europe. Tremain (2002) argues that impairment is not the 'embodiment of a natural deficit or lack' but a 'discursive object'. But exclusionary practices make it appear that impairment precedes discourse, obscuring that 'the constitutive power relations' defining and circumscribing impairment 'have already delimited the dimensions of its reification' (ibid. p. 42–43). For Brantlinger (2006, p. 217) bureaucrats in schools and elsewhere use the disciplinary instruments of 'hierarchic surveillance, normalising sanctions, and examination'. These mechanisms are recognisable in components of the 'accountability and standards movement', which include adopting high stakes testing. Allan (1996) considers how discourses on 'special needs' construct pupils' experiences in mainstream schools and construct their identities as 'subjects and objects of knowledge'. This involves notions of surveillance through hierarchical observation, normalising judgement, and the examination. Benjamin (2002) examines how 'special educational needs' identities might be influenced by discourses in a girls' secondary (high) school. She suggests an 'intellectual subordination' of pupils related to unequal relations (p. 6) and relates discourses to power through having 'dominant' discourses about examination success.

Although Foucault appears to be examining evidence and presenting historically accurate accounts, from a positivist position critics question the coherence and validity of epistémès, and Foucault's choice and interpretation of historical facts. Piaget criticises Foucault's ([1966] 2002) *The Order of Things* as 'nothing but a search for conceptual archetypes, chiefly tied to language' (Piaget, [1968] 1971, p. 129). Foucault is said to depict human sciences as 'merely a momentary outcome' of epistémès whose sequence 'has no rationale' and his programme lacks a method (ibid.). Piaget maintains that Foucault does not inquire 'under what conditions one may speak of the reign of a new epistémè'. He does not seek 'criteria by which to judge the validity or invalidity of alternative interpretations of the history of science'. Instead Foucault 'relies on intuition and substitutes speculative improvisation for methodical procedure' (ibid. p. 132). Incredulity has been expressed about the all-encompassing nature of epistémès (Steiner, 1971). Foucault's interpretation of historical trends and historical facts is questioned (Stone, 1982; Porter, [1987] 1990). Shorter (1997) challenges Foucault's ([1961] 2006) historical accuracy and historical interpretations, dismissing his claim that the notion of mental illness is essentially 'a social and cultural invention of the eighteenth century' (Shorter, 1997, p. 274).

Thinking points

* What is your interpretation of the relationship of other perspectives to that of positivism?
* How might other perspectives inform a positivist view?

Chapter 12

Different thinking and reviewing provision

Implications for special education of different perspectives

Different ways of thinking

Given that special education is predominantly positivist, some perspectives suggest quite a different way of thinking about disabilities and disorders.

Phenomenology draws attention to immersion in the world and inter-activity. Bodies including disabled ones may be understood as referring to biological, social and communicative levels. Apparently individual bodies may be seen as immersed in the world in such a way that they interweave with other bodies to bring into reality personal and social identity. Consequently, bodies can be open to one another, not just physically, but also perceptually and emotionally. Perception – including general limitations in perception, such as those associated with autism – can also be considered a form of 'embodiment' or a way of being in the world. 'Disability experiences' may be understood in terms of the process of becoming a 'fully fledged' person with a disability. Not being able to walk influences not only an individual's physical condition, but also relationships, self-image, their worldview and sense of time. Ideas such as these might influence one's behaviour, intentions and sensitivities.

Hermeneutics is deeply concerned with responses to others, so apparent external facts are not always what they seem. The nature of human beings and physical reality are seen as quite different. Interpretation may be seen as integral to understanding, implying that individuals are dependent on their pre-judgements to make the most correct interpretations of experiences. These pre-judgements form the basis from which understanding takes place. Disability is seen not just as difference but how others interpret and interact with perceived difference. Researchers cannot achieve theory-free observation, and objectivity is elusive. Naturalistic or ethnographic research may be valued where pedagogical settings are studied in the round, including their developing contexts.

Someone taking a historical materialist view may represent 'disability' as experienced by disabled people as a social restriction. The identification of disabilities and disorders and assumptions around medicalisation and normality would be questioned. Teacher training and professional development might be changed to help the inclusion of disabled students through raising awareness and knowledge about inclusion. Potentially negative attitudes may hinder greater inclusion. Negative attitudes about the capabilities of special pupils could reduce expectations of their progress and development. Negative attitudes to children with non-visible disabilities might be influenced by distorted notions of intelligence and social competence. Important aspirations would be a welcoming school ethos, teachers becoming committed to inclusion, and celebrating difference.

A critical theorist in special education may emphasise the influence of hidden ideology, hegemony and unrecognised forces selfishly shaping events while they appear to provide benefits to others. Accordingly, she may identify people benefiting from special education, other than special students. Professionals who support special pupils may attract suspicion because they benefit from increased numbers of pupils being identified and from categories of supposed disabilities being expanded. A critical theorist may suspect schools of being complicit in such expansion. If test producers benefit from special education, the motivation for testing might be suspected. Attempts would be made to ensure assessments benefit students. High stakes testing, such as that which determines places in schools and progress within schools, may be criticised.

Someone taking a holistic view may be critical of a perceived overly scientific view of special education. She may see holistic principles as offering a different way of looking at relations that make up life and learning, leading to different educational practices, relations and pedagogies.

Someone influenced by structuralism might take a dynamic view of learning. What is perceived may be regarded as modified by existing structures of knowledge through 'assimilation', and knowledge structures are themselves modified to 'accommodate' the perceptions. A structuralist may take a sequential view of child development reflecting Piaget's stages. She may modify such a view according to later findings in child development but may maintain the essential notion of progressive development integrating earlier stages.

A constructivist may see reality as interpreted by individuals. Meaning would be seen as made in the interaction between our minds and that on to which we project our meaning. She may view knowledge as being actively made. Learning might be seen as offering a foundation for social change by making conscious the ways in which knowledge is socially constructed and by highlighting our participation in constructing the truths that structure our social realities.

A poststructuralist may seek to 'deconstruct' terms associated with special education. Contrasts such as 'normalcy' and 'disability' do not necessarily imply that all the experience of disability has to be constituted as a negation of ability. Plurality might illuminate different perspectives, including positivist ones and ones that take account of personal interactions in mapping out disability. Disability as an interactional phenomenon may focus on accomplishment rather than difficulty. Concepts such as 'disabled' hinder more inclusive schooling because it assumes the identification and separation of one group of children from another. 'Ability' and 'disability' may have moral and political implications, so deconstruction might open up the binary logic supporting the separation of children into such categories. Rejecting the terminology of 'mental retardation' could lead to greater respect for children previously so labelled, allowing disability to be socially constructed in a more respectful and egalitarian way. Different forms of disability are seen as social designations made by individuals in interaction and relationships. Deconstruction may promote local change in daily professional work. Analysis might indicate that documents apparently supportive of mainstreaming adopt the language and concepts associated with separate education, unrecognised by those drafting such documents.

A pragmatist may take the view that the only foundation for ethical and political ideals is the 'history of their meaning' and being 'sensitive to context'. In special education, she might focus on possible reasons for separate provision. She may understand special education as concerning not only separate special schooling but also students educated separately for substantial amounts of time in ordinary school. Special education may be seen as responding to a failure of ordinary schools to educate all children. Special education is only required because of deficiencies in mainstream schooling: inflexible school organisation, and rigid professional culture and practice.

A symbolic interactionist could emphasise subjective experience and the interpretation of social reality. She might be interested in the nature of the subjective experience of disability and how others perceive, define and react to disabled people. She may be interested in variations in who supposedly requires special education provision and why, taking into account the ways children are perceived. Concepts would be best understood by examining the interplay between how different people come to define special children in specific situations. Areas for investigation would be disability and inclusion, and the interactions and meanings attached to them. Excluding and including interactions could be identified within self-described inclusive practices. She may favour qualitative research methods.

Someone supporting a psychoanalytic viewpoint may consider processes such as projection important. In a school or elsewhere, she may consider a 'disturbed' pupil may be the repository for rebellious feelings within the institution. Mental health professionals may also be projecting some of their own rage, shame or vulnerability on to clients, misdiagnosing them and remaining disconnected from their own feelings.

Lacanian ideas could suggest how hidden (because unconscious) motives lead some people to view disabled individuals negatively or with anxiety. Lacanian views may show how unconscious processes influence the way able-bodied individuals perceive impairment and how people with impairments perceive each other. Language and perception would be of interest, as well as unconscious processes. The early imaginary and its fragmented images of the body may be related to images sometimes associated with physical disability. Such fantasies have to be suppressed so a child can achieve the stability of normative embodiment, but they can re-emerge in the form of aggressiveness. Where a (physically disabled) body continues as a form of disunity it may become a repository of anxiety, perhaps evoking a violent response. An individual responding to a disabled person may feel endangered by the putative failure of his own boundaries of distinction and separation. This could explain why disabled bodies are culturally constructed as 'lacking' and how aesthetic anxieties emerge associated with disability in a culture that takes the able-bodied as its norm. She may consider how anxieties are involved in the way disabled people might be excluded by the built environment. 'Normality' may be so highly prioritised over 'impaired' through deep linguistic structures that their paired link is broken. Any possibility of relationship of the impaired to the normal is repressed in the unconscious as the imaginary. The concept of identity takes place through this repression of impairment, so that people with impairments cannot affirmatively identify with others like themselves.

A postmodernist may see special education as shaped by social and historical influences. Schooling, teacher education and education law and policy may be seen as rigidly hierarchical, in line with a focus on standards and a linear view of learning which differentiates learners and excludes some. Science may be regarded as a human construction that is historically socially exclusive. She may champion a multifaceted model for thinking about learning and inclusion that can subvert and invent. Learning should involve the undecided, the incalculable, and the unpredictable and might encourage lateral thinking and active bodily learning. Mainstreaming would be preferred to separate special schooling, and the whole identification and assessment of special children may be questioned. The apparent inevitability of views of normality may be challenged by drawing attention to diversity rather than unanimity. With regard to special children, 'normatism' may lead to viewing the usual as inevitable and superior, so that typical levels and types of development become privileged over others. She could try to avoid ways of thinking that reflect hierarchical forms of knowledge and that might lead to unhelpful concepts such as 'exclusion' and 'disability'. Instead, she may seek more decentred and non-hierarchical ways of thinking, allowing resistance and change in response to rigid modes of thought and perception. A postmodernist might argue for shifting power and altering the way people can interact.

Someone supporting a historical epistemological perspective may question the views of impairment as a natural phenomenon. She may regard impairment and other material aspects of bodily identity as relating to historically contingent practices that brought it into being, making it an object of knowledge. She may relate this to the effects of knowledge and power and challenge the apparent neutrality of the notion of impairment and those who have made it objective and material.

Where aspects of these positions – or indeed the whole drift of their think-ing – may be incompatible with positivism, the implications of some of these perspectives are not always as different as may be at first supposed. It is to these practical implications that this chapter now turns.

Implications for provision

Not all perspectives have the same amount to say about different aspects of special education. Some have more to say, for example, about pedagogy than about organisation, while for others the reverse is true. However, the implica-tions can be considered in relation to the main elements of special education:

- curriculum and assessment
- pedagogy
- resources
- organisation
- therapy.

Curriculum and assessment

The implications of phenomenology are that the curriculum can contribute to pupils' self-image and relationships. This might suggest encouraging per-sonal, social and health education and recognising the importance of social and friendship groups in school clubs and leisure time.

Under the influence of hermeneutics, students may be given opportunities to examine the extent to which interpretations influence views of difference, discussing this in a wide range of contexts – in history, for example. Personal and social development might involve understanding cultures different to one's own as well as interpretations of others different to oneself in terms of gender, ethnicity or disability.

In line with historical materialism, curriculum materials would be made as accessible as possible for special pupils. Any negative expressions of disability could be questioned. Forms of assessment would show what students could do, as well as what they could not. Equally important would be: teamwork; developing good literacy, numeracy and computer skills; and offering work experiences and opportunities to get to know the world of work. Careers edu-cation would be very important for students, to try to avoid exclusion from the labour market.

A holistic curriculum would stress interdependence among concepts and areas of study and among individuals and the wider world. In the child-centred curriculum, real-life meaning would be primary, and learning engagements would emerge from that. Holistic assessment would take account of how the child thinks and reasons, focusing on what children do over a period of time in natural, interactive settings. Assessment would document real-life processes and accomplishments, perhaps through continuous assessment and portfolio work.

For a constructivist, curriculum content might be more diverse than usual and conveyed in a more exploratory way. Different student views and opinions – about music or art, for example – may be accepted rather than closing exploration too early by conveying the teacher's own preferences. Assessment may be ongoing, reflecting the gradual development of knowledge and skill.

A structuralist may consider that Piagetian indicators of development can help inform understanding of the development of special children. This may inform developmental aspects of the curriculum, showing very small changes in development and learning that are reflected in small-steps assessments. Such an approach to the curriculum for students with profound cognitive impairment may be found in special schools.

A pragmatist may take the view that flexibility would help assure responsiveness to the particular learning requirements of different students. New programme development would draw together aspects of creative responses that worked and apply them in what appeared to be similar situations. This would be part of overall problem solving, flexibility, innovation and further programme development.

From a psychoanalytic view of special education, several of the arts subjects may be considered relevant as modes of communication. The curriculum might encourage more open communication from pupils and provide activities that may be communicative and expressive, such as drama, aspects of physical education, and play. These could be assessed through subject progress in skills and knowledge but also through a judgement about the contribution to well-being and general communicativeness. In a mainstream or special school where therapy is provided it would be planned into the whole curriculum. The curriculum would be viewed as a whole, to balance therapy and education. Also, careful thought will be given to transition times, as a pupil moves from a lesson to a therapy session or vice versa.

A postmodern view suggests a broad curriculum which takes full account of all areas of development. As with a holistic curriculum, ongoing and portfolio-type assessments might be more acceptable than single-time high stakes examinations and testing or curriculum-based assessment.

It will be seen that many of the above suggestions for the curriculum and assessment can be embraced by positivist special education. The key test is that they encourage learning and development. A real difference arises with regard to the holistic and the postmodern view that assessment might be formative rather than summative. However, there is no reason that both forms of assessment could not be used – formative as well as summative.

Pedagogy

In phenomenology, the teacher might be particularly aware of the social expectations, perceptions and different perspectives of friendship groups of individuals with particular disabilities or disorders, and use such insights when helping students develop social skills. Such skills might be seen not so much as skills within a person or demonstrated by a person but as a shared way of interrelating with others, in which others form a crucial part of the social skills interaction.

Someone taking a hermeneutic view will be likely to encourage pupils to explain and describe their understandings to see how they interpret their world. The teacher will explore with pupils possibly different interpretations and understandings as well as the context. There will be opportunities for discussion and debate in a free, open and non-coercive manner, where individuals taking opposing perspectives try to understand others' points of view.

In a historical materialist view of special education, pedagogy is likely to focus on removing barriers so that the concentration is on the teacher and the pedagogy rather than the things the student might find difficult. If a student finds an activity difficult, the task might be modified so that it is achievable and leads to the same learning outcome.

In critical theory, the teacher may avoid assuming any difficulties in learning or development are predominantly with the student rather than the school. It may not be immediately assumed that a student has behaviour problems. A school's ability to manage behaviour well or build good relationships might be considered an alternative explanation. There may be caution labelling a student as having a disability or disorder because of its potentially negative effects. An individual/medical view of disabilities and disorders may be regarded as an unexamined ideology.

For a holistic educator, instruction might be allowed to emerge dialectically from the teacher coming to understand students better and helping them become empowered as individuals. Learning would involve working with the students' previous experiences and debating and confirming them. Learning would be seen as the personal, social and cultural construction of meaning by the child, based on who the child is and what he knows. Progress would be seen as transformative and occurring when concepts are seen in new ways, suggesting that teachers make use of children's natural curiosity and natural interests. For teaching reading, whole-word strategies might be preferred. Behaviour and its context might be seen in a 'systems' way, considering components of a school system that may sustain unacceptable conduct and trying to modify them.

A constructivist educator may wish to help students develop new meanings in response to new experiences, ensuring that instruction is from students' perspectives. Students would have opportunities to construct meanings and share these constructions, while the teacher would be a sort of mediator of learning. Pupils would be encouraged to actively make connections between existing knowledge and new learning. The teacher may see learning as occurring through engagement, facilitated by language. Learning through group discussions is likely to be valued. A constructivist may value diverse meanings, cultures, perspectives and ways of learning and might emphasise relationships, contexts and cultures.

Someone advocating pragmatism would be likely to work in a mainstream school and use problem solving, innovation, flexibility, and new programme development. She may apply problem solving to the real everyday situations in which teachers find themselves. The creativeness of such problem solving would typify pedagogy. Problem solving would relate to innovation as solutions are found. Flexibility would emerge as teachers adapted to challenges, aware that there is no uniform approach.

For a symbolic interactionist, literacy, numeracy, and social and personal skills are considered as forms of behaviour, each with their own meanings. Building confidence in social skills is likely to be viewed as a student gradually investing with meaning various types of behaviour and coming to understand them in an interactive social context. This might suggest a social observational approach to encouraging social skills rather than a behaviour approach.

Postmodernism would tend to reject didactic teaching.

A structuralist might encourage pupils to be engaged in activities suggested by a developmental view, drawing on fine gradations of learning and development.

A positivist approach could agree with much of the above ideas about pedagogy. For example, care does need to be taken in identifying special children and there are indications that some apparent disorders are over-identified – attention deficit hyperactivity disorder, for example. Open discussion and listening to the views of others are already features of good provision. The importance of supporting the development of personal and social skills is widely accepted. Many of these suggestions concern the tone of teaching and the importance of strong mutually respectful relationships between teacher and pupil, with which positivists might be very comfortable.

Resources

A phenomenologist may extend the notion of the body to include physical aids to bodily mobility and perception. For example, for someone using a cane for mobility the object seems to become almost part of that individual's body. Technology may be important, not just in aiding communication or mobility, but as helping expand an individual's horizons and self-image.

From a hermeneutic view, resources may be seen as materials that contribute to understanding. Resources provided for the student to examine and interpret can be a powerful way of learning in a wide range of subjects. Resources can be presented to encourage prejudgement and interpretation so that a student's initial understanding can be compared with the findings of others. Pupils would be given time to explore and see that various alternatives can be productive.

A historical materialist would see resources as conducive to improving accessibility and removing barriers. A wide range of Braille reading material would be available for blind students. The school community might learn sign language to communicate with deaf students. If resources were increased, segregation might be reduced.

A critical theorist might be critical of textbooks, questioning the possible political and economic reasons influencing their production and sale, and the way official knowledge is produced by others. She might see in textbooks on special education evidence of oppressive negative constructions of special pupils so as to retain social hierarchies that benefit dominant groups.

In a holistic perspective, resources and their use may reflect a view of learning as whole. In the teaching of reading this would suggest a resistance to phonics resources and an emphasis on whole-word reading and reading for meaning. In mathematics, resources might be aimed at developing insights rather than learning step-by-step techniques.

For a constructivist, resources and their use would reflect the view that meanings are made. The environment would be rich in learning resources that would be fully used to help the student build their own meanings. There would tend to be less telling and more experiencing and discussing.

Resources associated with a structuralist view – of profound cognitive impairment, for example – are likely to reflect the importance of responses at very early stages of development. These may include sensory rooms, computer-operated switches, or aids to very early communication, such as objects of reference.

For a pragmatist, resources would serve the flexibility and innovation necessary for mainstream schools to provide for special pupils. Resources in the wide sense would include flexible staffing, and opportunities to collaborate and develop new and ongoing responses to the requirements of students. Learning resources associated with special schooling would be available within mainstream schools as necessary. These might include aids to communication, and support services such as audiology for deaf children. Such services and support could be provided peripatetically at certain times during the week.

To a symbolic interactionist, resources such as wheelchairs or aids to communication would have different meanings for different people. To one person a wheelchair may be a helpful aid; to another it may be a reminder of restrictions. Considering people as resources, roles such as resource teachers or psychologists would imply creating networks of meaning that influence the way others – special children, for example – are seen.

A psychoanalytic approach to special educational provision suggests items for play therapy, costumes or other materials for drama therapy, and instruments for music therapy.

A positivist approach to resources would be compatible with many of these suggestions. For example, using local and wider surroundings to learn, and exploring resources to develop one's own ideas as part of learning through experience is conversant with a positivist view. The exploration would lead, it would be hoped, to learning and development and would not be predominantly for its own sake. In an echo of debates in the 1960s about child-centred education, a balance would be found between, on the one hand, using resources for aimless exploring and, on the other hand, using over-didactic methods that might stifle pupils' interest.

Organisation

With a phenomenological view, the body may be seen in terms of social 'bodies', and 'bodies' emerging from the way people communicate. Individual bodies may be seen as immersed in the world so that they interweave with other bodies to create personal and social identity. The school will be especially aware that social groupings, friendship groups, and groupings for learning are likely to influence notions of the individual body and the self.

In a historical materialist perspective, disabled people might be considered to be devalued socially and culturally, and marginalised in society and in different environmental spaces. Integration and full participation in the community for disabled people may be an aim. The special education system, and special schooling, may be regarded as a segregated system that has the effect of excluding disabled people from the education process and from mainstream social life. In a mainstream school context, attempts would be made to minimise physical barriers in and around the building and grounds and with regard to classroom furnishings.

For a constructivist, organisation would tend to be more democratic than typical. Students may be invited to participate with others in creating meaning, choosing aspects of the curriculum, and influencing decisions affecting the class. The school may support peer mentoring and close and supportive partnership with families, and approaches such as Circle of Friends that encourage networks of social support in general education classes.

In a structuralist perspective, students with profound cognitive impairment may work in a 'responsive environment' (Ware, 2003), in which pupils 'get responses to their actions, get the opportunity to give responses to the actions of others, and have the opportunity to take the lead in interaction' (p.1). 'Room management' may be used in which groups of pupils and adults are assigned to one of three roles: individual helper, group activity manager, or mover (Lacey, 1991).

A pragmatist may seek to change rigid organisation so as to include pupils presently outside the mainstream. Public education could be for all children if mainstream schools were 'adhocratic' in their organisation. Interdisciplinary working would be valued to try to bring ethical positions and social views together with empirical evidence.

From a symbolic interactionist view, students should be able to express their views and be listened to. Some 'voices' are excluded from special educational debate and theorising. Where there are significant differences in views and interpretations of reality, social interaction may provide the rational structures for their mediation and resolution. This could help ensure that special students have their perspectives heard and taken into account.

A historical epistemologist may see organisation as a network of professionals supporting the special education system. Educators may question the power and knowledge associated with special education. School bureaucrats may be seen as exerting forms of control relating to accountability, standards, and high stakes testing. Special needs discourses are considered to construct pupils' experiences in mainstream schools and construct their identities as subjects and objects of knowledge. Higher staffing ratios for special children may be seen negatively as allowing closer scrutiny. She may question the way special children are defined in relation to normality and be suspicious of assessments leading to entitlement to special educational provision. Special pupils may be encouraged to challenge their allocated identities or choose alternative experiences. Unequal relations may be considered to be a reflection of intellectual subordination of pupils.

A critical theorist may see reasons for student failure in the social, economic and political structures of a society and may question institutional and professional interests in special education. Differences in power may be critically examined, so that they can be reduced or eliminated in educational practice. This might suggest a school organisation in which students have a greater say than is typical and where staff organisational structures are flatter than usual.

Positivism would not go along with some of the above organisational suggestions. It would be critical of the historical materialist aspiration of ending special schooling, where there is evidence that pupils learn and develop well in special schools and when parents and children value them so highly. It would be dubious about pragmatic claims that mainstream schools could provide for all children through creative organisation or 'adhocracy'.

However, a positivist view of organisation could recognise the importance of social groupings, friendship groups, and groupings for learning and their influence on self and self-esteem. Opportunities for pupils to participate in school life and to express their views are common features of good schools.

Therapy

Psychotherapy might sit quite comfortably in a range of provision for special children for someone taking a phenomenological view. The openness of 'bodies' to one another perceptually and emotionally can be seen as one of the foundations of therapy.

The general views of hermeneutics as deeply concerned with responses to others, and as seeing interpretation as integral to understanding, seems compatible with psychotherapy. In cognitive psychotherapy interpretations are examined and sometimes challenged, with an underlying implication that perception can be as influential as possible reality. Different ways of thinking may be encouraged where present patterns appear dysfunctional.

In a historical materialist view, psychotherapy is little mentioned, conversant with the emphasis on social rather than psychological factors. However, removing barriers might be seen as a key function of physical therapy, which may be seen as enabling movement and enskilling with a functional purpose.

A critical theorist may be suspicious of those providing therapy, as they are beneficiaries of special education. Apparently rising numbers of certain conditions supposedly requiring therapy may be treated sceptically.

Therapy might fit into a holistic view of educational provision. Psychodynamic psychotherapy might be seen as exploring past events and present behaviour, and as building a relationship with a therapist. There may be an expectation that, at various points in the therapy, holistic insights will illuminate past and present concerns and behaviour.

A constructivist might be reluctant to see emotional or behavioural disorders as being largely within the individual. She might wish to draw on a range of support services to link preventative efforts across school, home and other settings. She may try to link interventions between individuals and their families to changes in environment and systems. Agents of change might include teachers and other class members. She might see individual and family functioning in terms of interactions between and among the broader social environments. The teacher's way of influencing the world around the child (classroom, teachers' attitudes, and teachers' practice) would be important.

For a structuralist, therapy for students with profound cognitive impairment is likely to be closely integrated with other aspects of provision. Speech and language therapy, physiotherapy, and occupational therapy are likely to be an integral part of provision for learning and development.

Someone taking a pragmatic view of special education might see therapy as part of the flexibility and innovation that should be developed in mainstream schools. She might therefore seek to develop provision for therapy within the flexible organisation of the mainstream school.

For a symbolic interactionist, provision for therapy and what it means may not be considered innocent. Questions would be raised about the requirement of therapy, who decides, the meaning of therapy for the special child, and whether the requirement of therapy reflects a negative view of the child. Nevertheless it may be considered that, within psychodynamic psychotherapy, subjective experience and the interpretation of social reality can be usefully explored, leading to positive outcomes.

Someone advocating a psychoanalytical viewpoint may work in a specialist setting which uses psychodynamic interpretations in day-to-day living and individual sessions. Nurturing experiences may be seen as important, as well as offering children the opportunity for re-experiencing caring and clear relationships with adults and other children. This might be a special school or therapeutic community. Through 'planned environment therapy', group-living opportunities might give the child clear expectations, routines and rules about how to live and get on with others. In ordinary school settings, attachment theory might inform early intervention and 'nurture groups' for children whose emotional, social and behavioural 'needs' cannot be addressed in a mainstream classroom. She may regard focal dynamic psychotherapy as effective with children with mild anxiety disorder or dysthymic disorder. She could take a positive view of psychoanalytically grounded approaches to arts therapies and play therapy. Such interventions might be seen as encouraging healing and well-being.

If in a postmodern view much of the identification of disabilities and disorders is considered spurious, the case for therapy seems to be diminished.

Positivism would take an evidence-based view of therapy. It may have reservations, like some of the perspectives outlined, although the reasons may be different. Where there appears to be a reasoned case for therapy and where there is evidence it helps learning and enhances well-being, a positivist would be supportive.

Conclusion

The previous chapter, 'Positivist special education and other perspectives' illustrated the complexity of the relationships between a predominantly positivist special education and other perspectives. A hermeneutic view in special education appears to be largely critical of a positivist position, although it is difficult to see with what it would wish to replace special education. Lacanian speculation is more difficult to appraise and, again, it is not evident what it could contribute.

However, insights from phenomenology, to the extent that they concern attitudes of mind, are not necessarily incompatible with special education. Symbolic interactionism can highlight the importance of personal perceptions. Historical materialism supports a social model of disability that can raise awareness of physical barriers and negative attitudes where they exist. Critical theory might raise sensitivity to potential distortions of features of special education, such as that the apparently benign motives of others may be open to question.

Holism seems compatible with a positivist view of special education, while constructivism has a more equivocal relationship. Aspects of structuralism in relation to special education appear to rely on positivist findings. Poststructuralism allows a mapping of disability that may be, in different interpretations, either in line with or different to positivist notions. Attempts to draw on pragmatism may lead to similar interventions in special education to evidence-based practice, but pragmatism seems to require reinventing what works rather than extrapolating what has previously worked to new situations.

Developments from Freudian theory have contributed to interventions that appear to benefit special children, although the evidence is difficult to interpret. Postmodernism can encourage one to reflect on the assumption that normal always means better, but it can also lead to misguided special education approaches. Historical epistemology might provide insights into power-knowledge relationships in special education, especially where they are considered in the light of direct evidence and not based on assumptions that Foucault's work can be applied uncritically.

This chapter has explored the implications of different perspectives in relation to different ways of thinking and different aspects of special education provision: curriculum and assessment, pedagogy, resources, organisation and therapy. The response of a mainly positivist special education might be to reject any perspective that differs. The various positions are not, of course, immune from criticism themselves. However, it is hoped that this book has demonstrated that to reject all other perspectives than positivism would be to miss some interesting insights. It would deny the opportunity to engage with views which can lead to re-examining convictions that may have gone unquestioned. Even if the outcome is that one's views remain essentially unchanged and strengthened, such a questioning can be useful in testing long-held assumptions. At the same time, the different perspectives in ways quite compatible with positivism can provide insights that can further inform the way one thinks and acts with regard to special children and special education.

Bibliography

Achenbach, T. M. and Edelbrock, C. S. (1983) *Manual for the Child Behaviour Checklist and Revised Child Behaviour Profile*, Burlington: University of Vermont.

Adorno, T. W. (1931) 'The Actuality of Philosophy', *Telos* 31, 1997.

Adorno, T. W. and Horkheimer, M. ([1947] 2002) *Dialectic of Enlightenment* (translated from the German by Edmund Jephcott), Stanford, CA: Stanford University Press.

Adorno, T. W., Albert, H., Dahrendorf, R., Habermas, J., Pilot, H. and Popper, K. (1976) *The Positivist Dispute in German Sociology* (translated from the German by Glyn Adey and David Frisby), London: Heinemann.

Albrecht, G. L. (2002) 'American Pragmatism, Sociology and the Development of Disabilty Studies' in Barnes, C., Oliver, M. and Barton, L. (Eds.) *Disability Studies Today*, Cambridge: Polity Press and Malden, MA: Blackwell (pp. 18–37).

Alexander, B. K. (2009) 'Autoethnography: Exploring Modalities and Subjectivities that Shape Social Relations' in Paul, J. L., Kleinhammer-Tramill, J. and Fowler, K. (Eds.) *Qualitative Research Methods in Special Education* Denver, CO: Love Publishing.

Allan, J. (1996) 'Foucault and Special Educational Needs: A 'Box of Tools' for Analysing Children's Experiences of Mainstreaming', *Disability and Society* 11, 2, 219–233.

Allan, J. (2006) 'Failing to Make Progress? The Aporias of Responsible Inclusion' in Brantlinger, E. A. (Ed.) *Who Benefits From Inclusion? Remediating (Fixing) Other People's Children*, Mahwah, NJ and London: Lawrence Erlbaum Associates.

Allan, J. (2008) *Rethinking Inclusion: The Philosophers of Difference in Practice*, Dordrecht: Springer.

Alvarez McHatton, P. (2009) 'Grounded Theory' in Paul, J. L., Kleinhammer-Tramill, J. and Fowler, K. (Eds.) *Qualitative Research Methods in Special Education*, Denver, CO: Love Publishing.

American Psychiatric Association (2000) *Diagnostic and Statistical Manual of Mental Disorders Fourth Edition Text Revision*, Washington, DC: APA.

Antia, S. D., Stinson, M. S. and Gaustad, M. G. (2002) 'Developing Membership in the Education of Deaf and Hard-of-Hearing Students in Inclusive Settings', *Journal of Deaf Studies and Deaf Education* 7, 214–229.

Apple, M. W. (1989) *Teachers and Texts: A Political Economy of Class and Gender Relations in Education*, New York: Routledge.

Apple, M. W. (1995) *Education and Power* (Second edition), New York and London: Routledge.

Apple, M. W. and Christian-Smith, L. (1991) 'The Politics of the Textbook' in Apple, M. W. and Christian-Smith, L. (Eds.) *The Politics of the Textbook*, New York: Routledge (pp. 1–21).

Armstrong, D. (2003) *Experiences of Special Education: Re-evaluating Policy and Practice Through Life Stories*, New York and London: Routledge.

Ayer, A. J. ([1936] 2001) *Language, Truth and Logic* (Penguin Modern Classics), London: Penguin Books.

Bacon, M. (2007) *Richard Rorty: Pragmatism and Political Liberalism*, Lanham, MD: Lexington Books.

Bailey, J. (1998) 'Medical and Psychological Models in Special Needs Education' in Clarke, C., Dyson, A. and Millward, A. (Eds.) *Theorising Special Education*, London: Routledge.

Ballard, K. (1995) 'Inclusion, Paradigms, Power and Participation' in Clarke, C., Dyson, A. and Millward, A. (Eds.) *Towards Inclusive Schools*, London: David Fulton.

Barnes, C. (1998) 'The Social Model of Disability: A Sociological Phenomenon Ignored by Sociologists?' in Shakespeare, T. (Ed.) *The Disability Reader: Social Science Perspectives*, London: Cassell.

Barrow, R. (2001) 'Inclusion vs. Fairness', *Journal of Moral Education* 30, 3, 235–242.

Barrow, R. and Woods, R. (1982) *An Introduction to Philosophy of Education* (Second edition), London: Methuen.

Barton, L. (1995) 'The Politics of Education for All', *Support for Learning* 10, 4, 156–160.

Barton, L. (2005) 'Special Educational Needs: A New Look', unpublished discussion paper.

Bauman, Z. (1978) *Hermeneutics and Social Science*, New York: Columbia University Press.

Bauman, Z. (1992) *Intimations of Postmodernity*, London: Routledge.

Beaton, A. A. (2004) *Dyslexia, Reading and the Brain: A Sourcebook of Biological and Psychological Research*, London: Psychology Press.

Benjamin, S. (2002) *The Micropolitics of Inclusion: An Ethnography*, Buckingham: Open University Press/McGraw-Hill Education.

Benn, S. I. and Peters, R. S. (1959) *Social Principles and the Democratic State*, London: George Allen & Unwin.

Bentley, J. K. C. (2005) 'Symbolic Interaction in Inclusive Fourth- and Fifth-Grade Classrooms: "Can She Pinch Me Goodbye?" (1 January) *ETD Collection for Texas State University*, Paper AAI3172109. http://ecommons.txstate.edu/dissertations/AAI3172109.

Berger, P. and Luckmann, T. (1971) *The Social Construction of Reality*, Harmondsworth: Penguin Books.

Berkeley, G. ([1710] 1982) *A Treatise Concerning the Principles of Human Knowledge* (HPC Classics Series), Indianapolis, IN: Hacket.

Bigge, J. L., Stump, C. S., Spagna, M. E. and Silberman, R. K. (1999) *Curriculum, Assessment and Instructions for Students with Disabilities*, Belmont, CA: Wadsworth.

Blumer, H. (1986) *Symbolic Interactionism: Perspective and Method*, Berkeley: University of California Press.

Bogdan, R. and Kugelmass, J. W. (1984) 'Case Studies of Mainstreaming: An Interactionist Approach to Special Schooling' in Barton, L. and Tomlinson, S. (Eds.) *Special Education and Social Interests* (Croom Helm Series on Special Educational Needs: Policy, Practices and Social Issues), Kent: Croom Helm (pp. 173–190).

Booth, T. and Ainscow, M. with Black-Hawkins, K. (2000) *Index for Inclusion: Developing Learning and Participation in Schools*, Bristol: Centre for Studies for Inclusion in Education.

Bouchard, T. J., Lykken, D. T., McGue, M., Segal, N. L. and Tellegen, A. (1990) 'Sources of Human Psychological Differences: The Minnesota Study of Twins Reared Apart', *Science* 250, 223–228.

Bourdieu, P. (1984) *Distinction*, London: Routledge & Keegan Paul.

Bourke, P. E. (2007) 'Inclusive Education Research and Phenomenology', *Proceedings of the Australian Association for Research in Education*. Research Impacts – Proving or Improving. Fremantle, Western Australia (http://eprints.qut.edu.au).

Bowe, F. (1978) *Handicapping America*, New York: Harper & Row.

Bowlby, J. (1965) *Child Care and the Growth of Love* (Second edition), Harmondsworth: Penguin Books.

Bowlby, J. (1969) *Attachment and Loss Volume 1: Attachment*, London: Hogarth Press.

Bowlby, J. (1973) *Attachment and Loss Volume 2: Separation, Anxiety and Anger*, London: Hogarth Press.

Bowlby, J. (1980) *Attachment and Loss Volume 3: Loss, Sadness and Depression*, London: Hogarth Press.

Boxall, M. (2002) *Nurture Groups in School: Principles and Practice*, London: Paul Chapman.

Brantlinger, E. A. (1997) 'Using Ideology: Cases of Non-Recognition of the Politics of Research and Practice in Special Education', *Review of Educational Research* 67, 425–460.

Brantlinger, E. A. (2000) 'Using Ideology: The Politics of Research and Practice in Special Education' in Ball, S. (Ed.) *Sociology of Education*, Vol. 3, London and New York: Routledge-Falmer (reprint).

Brantlinger, E. A. (2006a) 'The Big Glossies: How Textbooks Structure (Special) Education' in Brantlinger, E. A. (Ed.) *Who Benefits From Special Education? Remediating (Fixing) Other People's Children*, Mahwah, NJ: Lawrence Erlbaum Associates.

Brantlinger, E. A. (2006b) 'Winners Need Losers: The Basis for School Competition and Hierarchies' in Brantlinger, E. A. (Ed.) *Who Benefits From Special Education? Remediating (Fixing) Other People's Children*, Mahwah, NJ: Lawrence Erlbaum Associates.

Brantlinger, E. A. (2006c) 'Conclusion: Whose Labels? Whose Norms? Whose Needs? Whose Benefits?' in Brantlinger, E. A. (Ed.) *Who Benefits From Special Education? Remediating (Fixing) Other People's Children*, Mahwah, NJ: Lawrence Erlbaum Associates.

Bruce, V., Green, P. R. and Georgeson, M. (1996) *Visual Perception: Physiology, Psychology and Ecology* (Third edition), Hove and London: Psychology Press.

Bury, M. (2000) 'A Comment on the ICIDH2', *Disability and Society* 15, 7, 1073–1077.

Carrington, S., Papinczak, T. and Templeton, E. (2003) 'A Phenomenological Study: The Social World of Five Adolescents Who Have Asperger's Syndrome', *Australian Journal of Learning Disabilities* 8, 15–21.

Centre for Studies in Inclusive Education (2003) *Reasons Against Segregated Schooling*, Bristol: Centre for Studies in Inclusive Education.

Charmaz, K. (2006) *Constructing Grounded Theory: A Practical Guide Through Qualitative Analysis*, Thousand Oaks, CA: Sage.

Cheu, J. (2002) 'De-gene-erates, Replicants and Other Aliens: (Re) Defining Disability in Futuristic Film' in Corker, M. and Shakespeare, T. (Eds.) *Disability/Postmodernity: Embodying Disability Theory*, London: Continuum.

Christensen, B. (2000) 'Gadamer' in Mautner, T. (Ed.) *The Penguin Dictionary of Philosophy*, London and New York: Penguin Books.

Clarke, A. E. (2004) 'Situational Analyses: Grounded Theory Mapping after the Postmodern Turn', *Symbolic Interaction* 26, 553–576.

Clarke, C., Dyson, A. and Millward, A. (1998) (Eds.) *Theorising Special Education*, London: Routledge.

Collins, K. M. (2003) *Ability Profiling and School Failure: One Child's Struggle to be Seen as Competent*, Mahwah, NJ: Lawrence Erlbaum Associates.

Commission for Scientific Medicine and Mental Health (2005) 'Statement Criticising Syracuse University's Appointment of Facilitated Communication Promoter Dr. Douglas Bilken, (www.csmmh.org/news/fc_statement.htm).

Comte, A. ([1822] 1998) *Plan de travaux scientifiques nécessaires pour réorganiser la société (Plan of scientific studies necessary for reorganizing society)* in Jones, H. S. (Ed.) *Cambridge Texts in the History of Political Thought: Comte – Early Political Writings*, Cambridge: Cambridge University Press.

Cooley, C. H. ([1902] 1983) *Human Nature and Social Order* (Social Science Classics Series), Piscataway, NJ: Transaction Publishers.

Cooley, C. H. ([1909] 1998) *Self and Social Organisation* (edited by Hans Joachim Schubert), Chicago: University of Chicago Press.

Cooper, P. and O'Regan, F. J. (2001) *Educating Children with AD/HD*, London: RoutledgeFalmer.

Corker, M. and Shakespeare, T. (2002a) (Eds.) *Disability/Postmodernity: Embodying Disability Theory*, London and New York: Continuum.

Corker, M. and Shakespeare, T. (2002b) 'Mapping the Terrain' in Corker, M. and Shakespeare, T. (2002) *Disability/Postmodernity: Embodying Disability Theory*, London and New York: Continuum.

Danermark, B. and Gellerstedt, L. C. (2004) 'Social Justice: Redistribution and Recognition: A Non-Reductionist Perspective on Disability', *Disability and Society* 19, 4, 339–353.

Danforth, S. (2009) *The Incomplete Child: An Intellectual History of Learning Disabilities* (Disability Studies in Education), London: Continuum.

Danforth, S. and Rhodes, W. C. (1997) 'Deconstructing Disability: A Philosophy for Inclusion', *Remedial and Special Education* 18, 357–366.

Danforth, S. and Smith, T. J. (2005) *Engaging Troubling Students: A Constructivist Approach*, Thousand Oaks, CA: Corwin Press/Sage.

Dawkins, R. (1998) 'Postmodernism Disrobed', *Nature* 394, July, 141–143.

Deleuze, G. ([1968] 1994) *Difference and Repetition* (translated by Paul Patton), New York: Columbia University Press.

Deleuze, G. ([1969] 1990) *The Logic of Sense* (translated by M. Lester), London: Athlone Press.

Deleuze, G. and Guattari, F. ([1972] translation 1983) *Anti-Oedipus: Capitalism and Schizophrenia* (translated by Robert Hurley, Mark Seem and Helen R. Lane), New York: Viking.

Deleuze, G. and Guattari, F. ([1976] 1981) *Rhyzome: Introduction* (translated by Paul Foss and Paul Patton in *Ideology and Consciousness*, 8, Spring 1981, 49–71).

Deleuze, G. and Guattari, F. ([1980] 1987) *A Thousand Plateaus: Capitalism and Schizophrenia* (translated by Brian Massumi), Minneapolis and London: University of Minnesota Press.

Deleuze, G. and Guattari, F. ([1991] 1996) *What is Philosophy?* (translated by Hugh Tomlinson and Graham Burchell), New York: Columbia University Press.

Department for Education and Skills (DfES) (2003) *The Report of the Special Schools Working Group*, London: DfES.

Department for Education and Skills (DfES) (2005) *Data Collection by Special Educational Need* (Second Edition), London: DfES.

Derrida, J. ([various dates and 1967] 1978) *Writing and Difference* (translated from the French by Alan Bass), Chicago: University of Chicago Press.

Derrida, J. (1966) 'Structure, Sign and Play in the Discourse of the Human Sciences' in Macksey, R. and Donato, E. (1972) *The Structuralist Controversy: The Languages of Criticism and the Sciences of Man*, Baltimore and London: Johns Hopkins University Press.

Derrida, J. ([1967] 1973) *Speech and Phenomena* (translated from the French by D. B. Allison), Evanston, IL: Northwestern University Press.

Derrida, J. ([1967] 1997) *Of Grammatology* (translated from the French by Gayatri Chakravorty Spivak, corrected edition), Baltimore: Johns Hopkins University Press.

Derrida, J. (1975) 'The Purveyor of Truth' in Derrida, J. (1987) *De L'Esprit: Heidegger et la question*, Paris: Galilée.

Derrida, J. (1991) '"Eating Well", or the Calculation of the Subject: An Interview with Jacques Derrida' in Cadava, E., Connor, P. and Nancy, J-L (Eds.) *Who Comes After the Subject?*, London: Routledge.

Despouy, L. (1991) *Human Rights and Disability*, New York: United Nations Economic and Social Council.

Dewey, J. ([1899] 1976) 'The School and Society' in Boydston, J. A. (Ed.) *John Dewey: The Middle Works 1899–1924 Vol. 1*, Carbondale: Southern Illinois University Press.

Dewey, J. ([1899, revised 1943] 2001) *The School and Society and the Child and the Curriculum*, Mineola, NY: Dover Publications.

Dewey, J. ([1910] 2009) *How We Think*, General Books LLC.

Dewey, J. ([1916] 1997) *Democracy and Education: An Introduction to the Philosophy of Education*, New York: Free Press.

Dilthey, W. ([1883] 1991) *Wilhelm Dilthey: Selected Works, Volume 1: Introduction to the Human Sciences* (edited by Rudolph A. Makkreel and Frithjof Rodi), Princeton, NJ: Princeton University Press.

Dilthey, W. ([1900] 1972) 'The Rise of Hermeneutics' (translated from the German by Frederic Jameson), *New Literary History* 3, 2.

Dockar-Drysdale, B. (1991) *The Provision of Primary Experience: Winnicottian Work with Children and Adolescents*, London: Free Association Press.

Dockar-Drysdale, B. (1993) *Therapy and Consultation in Childcare*, London: Free Association Press.

Doll, R. C. (1996) *Curriculum Improvement: Decision Making and Process* (Ninth edition), Needham Heights, MA: Allyn & Bacon.

Donaldson, M. (1978) *Children's Minds*, London: Routledge.

Dosse, F. (1967) *History of Structuralism: Volume 1: The Rising Sign 1945–66* (translated from the French by Deborah Glassman), Minneapolis: University of Minnesota Press.

Dowling, E. and Osborne, E. (Eds.) (1994) *The Family and the School: A Joint Systems Approach to Problems with Children* (Second edition), London: Routledge.

Durkheim, E. ([1895] 1982) *The Rules of Sociological Method and Selected Texts on Sociology and its Method* (translated from the French by W. D. Halls), New York: Free Press.

Dyson, A. (2001) 'Special Needs in the Twenty-first Century: Where We've Been and Where We're Going', *British Journal of Special Education* 28, 1, 24–29.

Eagleton, T. (1996a) *The Illusions of Postmodernism*, Oxford: Blackwell.

Eagleton, T. (1996b) (Second edition) *Literary Criticism: An Introduction*, Oxford and Malden, MA: Blackwell.

Ericson, D. P. and Ellett Jr., F. S. (1982) 'Interpretation, Understanding and Educational Research', *Teachers College Record* 85, 1, 497–513.

Evans, D. (1996) *Introductory Dictionary of Lacanian Psychoanalysis*, London: Routledge.

Farrell, M. (1999) *Key Issues for Primary Schools*, London and New York: Routledge.

Farrell, M. (2000) 'Educational Inclusion and Raising Standards', *British Journal of Special Education*, 21, 1, 35–38.

Farrell, M. (2001) *Standards and Special Educational Needs: The Importance of Standards of Pupil Achievement*, London and New York: Continuum.

Farrell, M. (2004) *Inclusion at the Crossroads: Special Education – Concepts and Values*, London: David Fulton.

Farrell, M. (2005) *Key Issues in Special Education: Raising Standards of Pupils' Attainment and Achievement*, New York and London: Routledge.

Farrell, M. (2006) *Celebrating the Special School*, London: David Fulton

Farrell, M. (2008) *Educating Special Children: An Introduction to Provision for Pupils with Disabilities and Disorders*, New York and London: Routledge.

Farrell, M. (2009) *Foundations of Special Education: An Introduction*, New York and London: Wiley & Sons.

Farrell, M. (2010) *Debating Special Education*, New York and London: Routledge.

Farrell, M., Kerry, T. and Kerry, C. (1995) *The Blackwell Handbook of Education*, Oxford and Cambridge, MA: Blackwell.

Fink, B. (2004). *Lacan to the Letter*, Minneapolis: University of Minnesota Press.

Fletcher, J. M., Morris, R. D. and Lyon, G. R. (2003) 'Classification and Definition of Learning Disabilities: An Integrative Perspective' in Swanson, H. L., Harris, K. R. and Graham, S. (Eds.) (2003) *Handbook of Learning Disabilities*, New York: Guilford Press.

Fletcher, J. M., Shaywitz, S. E. and Shaywitz, B. A. (1999) 'Comorbidity of Learning and Attention Disorders: Separate but Equal', *Paediatric Clinics of North America* 46, 885–897.

Fonagy, P., Target, M., Cottrell, D., Phillips, J. and Kurtz, Z. (2005) *What Works for Whom? A Critical Review of Treatments for Children and Adolescents*, New York: Guilford Press.

Forest, M. and Lusthaus, E. (1989) 'Promoting Educational Equality for All Students: Circles and Maps' in Stainback, W. and Forest, M. (Eds.) *Educating All Students in the Mainstream of General Education*, Baltimore: Paul H. Brookes (pp. 443–457).

Foucault, M. ([1961] 2006) *The History of Madness* (translated from the French by Jonathan Murphy and Jean Khalfa), London and New York: Routledge.

Foucault, M. ([1963] 2003) *The Birth of the Clinic: An Archaeology of Medical Perception* (translated from the French by A. M. Sheridan-Smith), London and New York: Routledge.

Foucault, M. ([1966] 2002) *The Order of Things: An Archaeology of the Human Sciences* (translated from the French by an unnamed translator), New York and London: Routledge.

Foucault, M. ([1969] 2002) *The Archaeology of Knowledge* (translated from the French by A. M. Sheridan-Smith), London: Routledge.

Foucault, M. ([1975] 1991) *Discipline and Punish: The Birth of the Prison* (translated from the French by Allan Sheridan), New York and London: Penguin Books.

Foucault, M. ([1976] 1998) *The History of Sexuality, Volume 1: The Will to Knowledge* (translated from the French by Robert Hurley), London and New York: Penguin Books.

Foucault, M. ([various dates] 1980) *Power/Knowledge: Selected Interviews and other Writings 1972–1977* (edited by Gordon, C. and translated from the French by Gordon, C., Marshall, L., Mepham, J. and Soper, K.), New York: Pantheon Books.

Freiberg, H. J. (1999) *Beyond Behaviourism: Changing the Classroom Management Paradigm*, Boston: Allyn & Bacon.

Freud, A. ([various dates] 1998) *Selected Writings – Anna Freud* (edited by Richard Ekins and Ruth Freeman), London: Penguin.

Freud, A. (1936) *The Ego and the Mechanisms of Defence*, London: Hogarth Press and the Institute of Psychoanalysis.

Freud, A. (1945) 'Adolescence', *The Psychoanalytic Study of the Child* 13, 255–278.

Freud, S. (1909) 'Analysis of a Phobia in a Five-Year-Old Boy', *Standard Edition* 10: 1–149.

Freud, S. ([1923] 1960) *The Ego and the Id* (Standard Edition, edited by James Strachey), New York: W. W. Norton.

Freud, S. ([1940] 2002) *An Outline of Psychoanalysis* (translated from the German by Helena Ragg-Kirkby), London: Penguin Books.

Fulcher, G. (1995) 'Excommunicating the Severely Disabled: Struggles, Policy and Researching' in Clough, P. and Barton, L. (Eds.) *Making Difficulties: Research and the Construction on SEN*, London: Paul Chapman.

Gabbard, C. LeBlanc, B. and Lowry, S. (1994) *Physical Education For Children: Building the Foundation* (Second edition), Upper Saddle River, NJ: Prentice-Hall.

Gadamer, H-G. ([1960 and later editions] 2004) *Truth and Method* (revised translation from the German by Joel Weinsheimer and Donald G. Marshall), New York: Continuum.

Gadamer, H-G. ([1976, 1978, 1979] 1981) *Reason in the Age of Science* (translated from the German by Frederick G. Lawrence) Cambridge, MA: MIT Press.

Gadamer, H-G. ([1976] 1993) 'Hermeneutics as a Practical Philosophy' in Gadamer, H-G. ([1976, 1978, 1979] 1981) *Reason in the Age of Science* (translated from the German by Frederick G. Lawrence), Cambridge, MA: MIT Press (pp. 88–112).

Gadamer, H-G. ([various dates from 1960 to 1972] 1976) *Philosophical Hermeneutics* (translated from the German and edited by David E. Linge), Berkeley: University of California Press.

Gadamer, H-G. (1966) 'The Universality of the Hermeneutic Problem' in Gadamer (1976) in Gadamer, H-G. ([various dates from 1960 to 1972] 1976) *Philosophical*

Hermeneutics (translated from the German and edited by David E. Linge), Berkeley: University of California Press.

Gallagher, D. J. (1998) 'The Scientific Knowledgebase of Special Education: Do We Know What We Think We Know?', *Exceptional Children* 64, 493–502.

Gallagher, D. J. (2001) 'Neutrality as a Moral Standpoint, Conceptual Confusion and the Full Inclusion Debate', *Disability and Society* 16, 5, 637–654.

Gallagher, D. J. (2004a) 'Entering the Conversation: The Debate Behind the Debates in Special Education' in Gallagher, D. J., Heshusius, L., Iano, R. P. and Skrtic, T. M. (2004) *Challenging Orthodoxy in Special Education: Dissenting Voices*, Denver, CO: Love Publishing.

Gallagher, D. J. (2004b) 'Moving the Conversation Forward: Empiricism versus Relativism Reconsidered' in Gallagher, D. J., Heshusius, L., Iano, R. P. and Skrtic, T. M. (2004) *Challenging Orthodoxy in Special Education: Dissenting Voices*, Denver, CO: Love Publishing.

Gallagher, D. J. (2006) 'If Not Absolute Objectivity, Then What? A Reply to Kaufman and Sasso', *Exceptionality* 14, 2, 91–107.

Gallagher, D. J., Heshusius, L., Iano, R. P. and Skrtic, T. M. (2004) *Challenging Orthodoxy in Special Education: Dissenting Voices*, Denver, CO: Love Publishing.

Gallagher, J. M. and Reid, D. K. (1981) *The Learning Theory of Piaget and Inhelder*, Belmont, CA: Brooks/Cole.

Gartner, A. and Lipsky, D. K. (1989) 'New Conceptualisations for Special Education', *European Journal of Special Needs Education* 4, 1, 16–21.

Gerber, M. M. (1994) 'Postmodernism in Special Education', *The Journal of Special Education* 28, 3, 368–378.

Gergen, K. (1985) 'The Social Construction Movement in Modern Psychology', *American Psychologist* 40, 3, 266–275.

Gergen, K. J. (1995) 'Social Construction and the Educational Process' in Steffe, L. P. and Gale, J. (Eds.) *Constructivism in Education*, Hillsdale, NJ: Lawrence Erlbaum (pp. 17–40).

Geuss, R. (1981) *The Idea of a Critical Theory: Habermas and the Frankfurt School*, Cambridge: Cambridge University Press.

Glaser, B. G. and Strauss, A. (1967) *The Discovery of Grounded Theory*, Chicago: Aldine.

Gleeson, B. (1999) *Geographies of Disability*, London: Routledge.

Glendon, M. (1991) *Rights Talk: The Impoverishment of Political Discourse*, New York: Free Press.

Goodley, D. (2001) '"Learning Difficulties", the Social Model of Disability and impairment: Challenging Epistemologies', *Disability and Society* 16, 2, 207–231.

Goodley, D. (2007) 'Becoming Rhizomatic Parents: Deleuze, Guattari and Disabled Babies', *Disability and Society* 22, 2, 145–160.

Goswami, U. (1998) *Cognition in Children*, Hove: Psychology Press.

Goswami, U. (2008) *Cognitive Development: The Learning Brain*, New York and Hove: Psychology Press.

Gottlieb, J. (1986) 'Mainstreaming: Fulfilling the Promise?' *American Journal of Mental Deficiency* 86, 2, 115–126.

Gould, S. J. (1997) 'The Positive Power of Skepticism', Foreword in Shermer, M., *Why People Believe in Weird Things: Pseudoscience, Superstition and other Confusions of our Time*, New York: Freeman (pp. ix–xii).

Government of South Australia Department of Education and Children's Services (2007) *Disability Support Programme 2007 Eligibility Criteria*, Adelaide: Government of South Australia.

Gross, P. R. (1998) 'The Icarian Impulse', *The Wilson Quarterly* 22, 39–49.

Gurman, A. S. and Messer, S. B. (Eds.) (2003) *Essential Psychotherapies: Theory and Practice*, New York: Guilford Press.

Haack, S. (1996) 'Pragmatism' in Bunnin, N. and Tsui-James, E. P. (Eds.) *The Blackwell Companion to Philosophy*, Oxford: Blackwell (pp. 643–661).

Habermas, J. ([1962] 1989) *Structural Transformation of the Public Sphere: An Inquiry into a Category of Bourgeois Society* (translated from the German by T. Burger and F. Lawrence), Cambridge: MA: MIT Press.

Habermas, J. (1971) *Knowledge and Human Interest*, Boston: Beacon Press.

Habermas, J. ([1971] 1974) *Theory and Practice* (translated from the German by John Veirtel), London: Heinemann.

Habermas, J. ([1973] 1976) *Legitimation Crisis* (translated from the German by Thomas McCarthy), London: Heinemann.

Habermas, J. (1980) 'Modernity versus Postmodernity' (translated from the German by Seyla Ben–Habi), *New German Critique* 22.

Habermas, J. (1983) 'Interpretive Social Science v Hermeneutics' in Haan, N. *et al.* (Eds.) *Social Science as Moral Inquiry*, New York: Columbia University Press (pp. 251–269).

Habermas, J. (1985) *The Philosophical Discourse of Modernity: Twelve Lectures* (translated from the German by Frederick G. Lawrence), Cambridge: Polity Press.

Hallward, P. (2006) *Out of this World: Deleuze and the Philosophy of Creation*, London: Verso Books.

Hegel, G. F. W. ([1812, 1813, 1816] 1969) *The Science of Logic* (translated from the German by A. V. Miller), London: George, Allen & Unwin.

Heidegger, M. ([1927] 1962) *Being and Time* (translated from the German by John MacQuarrie and Edward Robinson), Oxford: Basil Blackwell.

Heidegger, M. ([1975] 1982) *The Basic Problems of Phenomenology* (translated from the German by Albert Hofstader), Bloomington and Indianapolis: Indiana University Press.

Herman, N. J. and Reynolds, L. T. (1995) *Symbolic Interaction: An Introduction to Social Psychology*, New York: General Hall.

Heshusius, L. (1984) 'Why Would They and I Want to Do It? A Phenomenal-Theoretical View of Special Education Learning', *Learning Disability Quarterly* 7, 363–368.

Heshusius, L. (1989) 'The Newtonian Paradigm, Special Education, and Contours of Alternatives: An Overview', *Journal of Learning Disabilities* 22, 403–415.

Heshusius, L. (1991) 'Curriculum-based Assessment and Direct Instruction: Critical Reflections on Fundamental Assumptions', *Exceptional Children* 57, 315–329.

Heshusius, L. (2004a) 'The Newtonian Paradigm, Special Education, and Contours of Alternatives: An Overview', the 1989 article reproduced in Gallagher, D. J., Heshusius, L., Iano, R. P. and Skrtic, T. M. (2004) *Challenging Orthodoxy in Special Education: Dissenting Voices*, Denver: Love Publishing.

Heshusius, L. (2004b) 'From Creative Discontent Toward Epistemological Freedom in Special Education: Reflections on a 25-year Journey' in Gallagher, D. J.,

Heshusius, L., Iano, R. P. and Skrtic, T. M. (2004) *Challenging Orthodoxy in Special Education: Dissenting Voices*, Denver: Love Publishing.

Horkheimer, M. ([1937] 2002) 'Traditional and Critical Theory' (translated from the German by Mathew J. O'Connell) in Horkheimer, M. ([various dates] 2002) *Critical Theory: Selected Essays*, New York and London: Continuum (pp. 188–243).

Hornby, G., Atkinson, M. and Howard, J. (1998) *Controversial Issues in Special Education*, London: David Fulton.

Hughes, B. and Patterson, K. (1997) 'The Social Model of Disability and the Disappearing Body: Towards a Sociology of Impairment', *Disability and Society* 12, 3, 325–340.

Hume, D. ([1748] 2004) *An Enquiry Concerning Human Understanding* (Dover Philosophical Classics), Mineola, NY: Dover Publications.

Hurst, R. (2000) 'To Revise or Not to Revise?', *Disability and Society* 15, 7, 1083–1087.

Husserl, E. ([1900–1901] 2001) *Logical Investigations* (translated from the German by J. N. Findlay and edited by Dermot Moran), New York: Routledge.

Husserl, E. ([1913] 1982) *Ideas Pertaining to a Pure Phenomenology and to a Phenomenological Philosophy, First Book: General Introduction to a Pure Phenomenology* (translated from the German by F. Kersten), The Hague: Nijhoff.

Husserl, E. ([1913] 1989) *Ideas Pertaining to a Pure Phenomenology and to a Phenomenological Philosophy, Second Book: Studies in the Phenomenology of Constitution* (translated from the German by R. Rojcewitcz and A. Schuwer), Dordrecht: Kluwer.

Husserl, E. ([1913] 1980) *Ideas Pertaining to a Pure Phenomenology and to a Phenomenological Philosophy, Third Book: Phenomenology and the Foundations of the Sciences* (translated from the German by T. E. Klein and W. E. Pohl), Dordrecht: Kluwer.

Husserl, E. ([1954] 1970) *The Crisis of European Science and Transcendental Phenomenology* (translated from the German by David Carr), Evanston, IL: Northwestern University Press.

Hutcheon, L. (1988) *A Poetics of Postmodernism: History, Theory, Fiction*, New York and London: Routledge.

Iano, R. P. (2004) 'The Study and Development of Teaching: With Implications for the Advancement of Special Education' in Gallagher, D. J., Heshusius, L., Iano, R. P. and Skrtic, T. M. (2004) *Challenging Orthodoxy in Special Education: Dissenting Voices*, Denver: Love Publishing.

Iwakuma, S. (2002) 'The Body as Embodiment: An Investigation of the Body by Merleau-Ponty' in Corker, M. and Shakespeare, T. (2002a) (Eds.) *Disability/Postmodernity: Embodying Disability Theory*, London and New York: Continuum.

Jacobson, R. and Halle, M. (1956) 'Fundamentals of Language', *Janua Lingarum* 1.

James, W. ([1907] 1995) *Pragmatism: A New Name for Some Old Ways of Thinking*, Mineola, NY: Dover Publications.

James, W. ([1912] 2003) *Essays in Radical Empiricism*, Mineola, NY: Dover Publications.

Jenks, C. (1977) *The Language of Postmodern Architecture*, London: Academy Editions.

Jenks, C. (1996) *What is Postmodernism?* London: Academy Editions.

Jones, P. (2005) *The Arts Therapies: A Revolution in Healthcare*, Hove: Brunner-Routledge.

Karkou, V. (1999a) 'Art Therapy in Education: Findings from a Nationwide Survey in Arts Therapies', *Inscape* 4, 2, 62–70.

Karkou, V. (1999b) 'Who? Where? What? A Brief Description of DMT: Results from a Nationwide Study', *E-motion* XI, 2, 5–10.

Kauffman, J. M. (1999) 'Commentary: Today's Special Education and its Messages for Tomorrow', *The Journal of Special Education* 32, 4, 244–254.

Kauffman, J. M. and Sasso, G. M. (2006) 'Toward Ending Cultural and Cognitive Relativism in Special Education', *Exceptionality* 14, 2, 65–90.

Kavale, K. A. and Mostert, M. P. (2003) 'River of Ideology, Islands of Evidence', *Exceptionality* 11, 4, 191–208.

Kenny, A. (2008) *A New History of Western Philosophy Volume 4: Philosophy in the Modern World*, Oxford and New York: Clarendon.

Klein, M. (1932) *The Psychoanalysis of Children*, London: Hogarth Press.

Klein, M. ([1957] 1975) *Envy and Gratitude*, New York: Delacorte Press.

Klein, M. ([various dates] 1964) *Contributions to Psychoanalysis, 1921–1945*, New York: McGraw-Hill.

Knox, J. E. and Stevens, C. B. (1993) 'Translators' Introduction' in Rieber, R. W. and Carton, A. S. (Eds.) *The Collected Works of L. S. Vygotsky Volume 2: The Fundamentals of Defectology* (Abnormal Psychology and Learning Disabilities) (translated by Knox, J. E. and Stevens, C. B.), New York: Plenum Press.

Kohl, H. (1994) *I Won't Learn From You, and Other Thoughts on Creative Maladjustment*, New York: New Press.

Köhler, W (1947) *Gestalt Psychology* (Second edition), New York: Liveright.

Kumar, P. and Clark, M. (Eds.) (2005) *Clinical Medicine*, New York and London: Elsevier Saunders.

Kundera, M. (1991) *Immortality*, London: Faber & Faber.

Kurtz, P. D., Harrison, M. Neisworth, J. T. and Jones, R. T. (1977) 'Influence of "Mentally Retarded" Label on Teachers' Non-Verbal Behaviour Towards Pre-School Children', *American Journal of Mental Deficiency* 82, 204–206.

Lacan, J. ([1948 and 1966] 2006) 'Aggressiveness in Psychoanalysis: Theoretical Paper Presented in Brussels in Mid-May 1948 at the Eleventh Congress of French-Speaking Psychoanalysis' in Lacan, J. ([1966] 2006) *Écrits* (translated from the French as *Écrits: The First Complete Edition in English* by Bruce Fink in collaboration with Héloïse Fink and Russell Grigg), New York and London: W.W. Norton (pp. 82–101).

Lacan, J. ([1949 and 1966] 2006) 'The Mirror Stage as Formative of the I Function as Revealed in Psychoanalytic Experience (Delivered on July 17, 1949, in Zurich at the Sixteenth International Congress)' in Lacan, J. ([1966] 2006) *Écrits* (translated from the French as *Écrits: The First Complete Edition in English* by Bruce Fink in collaboration with Héloïse Fink and Russell Grigg), New York and London: W.W. Norton (pp. 75–81).

Lacan, J. ([1955 and 1966] 2006) 'Seminar on "The Purloined Letter"' in Lacan, J. ([1966] 2006) *Écrits* (translated from the French as *Écrits: The First Complete Edition in English* by Bruce Fink in collaboration with Héloïse Fink and Russell Grigg), New York and London: W.W. Norton (pp. 6–33; supplementary material follows this seminar in *Écrits*).

Lacan, J. ([1955–1956 and 1966] 2006) 'On a Question Prior to Any Possible Treatment of Psychosis' (drawing on a seminar given in the first two terms of the academic year 1955–1956) in Lacan, J. ([1966] 2006) *Écrits* (translated from the French as *Écrits: The First Complete Edition in English* by Bruce Fink in collaboration with Héloïse Fink and Russell Grigg), New York and London: W.W. Norton (pp. 445–488).

Lacan, J. ([various dates and 1966] 2006) *Écrits* (translated from the French as *Écrits: The First Complete Edition in English* by Bruce Fink in collaboration with Héloïse Fink and Russell Grigg), New York and London: W.W. Norton.

Lacey, P. (1991) 'Managing the Classroom Environment' in Tilstone, C. (Ed.) *Teaching Pupils with Severe Learning Difficulties*, London: David Fulton.

Larkin, D. and Cermac, S. A. (2002) 'Issues in Identification and Assessment of Developmental Coordination Disorder' in Cermak, S. A. and Larkin, D. *Developmental Coordination Disorder*, Albany, NY: Delmar Thompson Learning.

Lévi-Strauss, C. ([1955] 1961) *Tristes Tropiques* (translated from the French by John Russell), New York: Criterion Books.

Lévi-Strauss, C. ([1958] 1977) *Structural Anthropology* (translated from the French by Claire Jacobson and Brooke Grudfest Schoepf and originally essays published from 1944 to 1957), Harmondsworth and New York: Penguin Books.

Lewis, A. and Norwich, B. (2001) 'A Critical Review of Systematic Evidence Concerning Distinctive Pedagogies for Pupils with Difficulties in Learning', *Journal of Research in Special Educational Needs* 1, 1, 1–13.

Lindsay, G. (2003) Inclusive Education: A Critical Perspective', *British Journal of Special Education* 3, 1, 3–12.

Linge, D. E. (1976) editor's introduction to Gadamer, H-G. ([various dates from 1960 to 1972] 1976) *Philosophical Hermeneutics* (translated from the German and edited by David E. Linge), Berkeley: University of California Press.

Lloyd, G., Stead, J. and Cohen, D. (Eds.) (2006) *Critical New Perspectives on ADHD*, New York: Routledge.

Locke, J. ([1690] 1979) *Essay Concerning Human Understanding* (edited and with an introduction by Peter H. Nidditch), New York: Oxford University Press.

Lyotard, F. ([1979] 1984) *The Postmodern Condition: A Report on Knowledge* (translated from the French by G. Bennington and B. Massumi), Manchester: Manchester University Press.

Macey, D. (1994) 'Thinking with Borrowed Concepts: Althusser and Lacan' in Elliott, G. (Ed.) *Althusser: A Critical Reader*, Oxford: Blackwell.

Macey, D. (2000) *The Penguin Dictionary of Critical Theory*, London and New York: Penguin Books.

MacKay, H. A., Soraci, S., Carlin, M., Dennis, N. and Sawbridge, C. P. (2002) 'Guiding Visual Attention during Acquisition of Matching to Sample', *American Journal of Mental Retardation* 107, 6, 445–454.

MacMillan, D. L., Jones, R. L. and Aloia, G. F. (1974) 'The Mentally Retarded Label: A Theoretical Analysis and Review of Research', *American Journal of Mental Deficiency* 79, 241–261.

Manset, G. and Semmel, M. I. (1997) 'Are Inclusive Programmes for Students with Mild Disabilities Effective? A Comparative Review of Model Programmes', *Journal of Special Education* 31, 2, 155–180.

Marcuse, H. ([1937] 1972) 'The Affirmative Character of Culture' in Marcuse, H. (1965) *Negations: Essays in Critical Theory* (translated from the German by Jeremy J. Shapiro), Harmondsworth: Penguin.

Marks, D. (1999) *Disability: Controversial Debates and Psychological Perspectives*, London: Routledge.

Marston, D. (1996) 'A Comparison of Inclusion Only, Pull-Out Only, and Combined Service Models for Students with Mild Disabilities', *Journal of Special Education* 30, 2, 121–132.

Marx, K. and Engels, F. ([1848] 1996) *The Communist Manifesto*, New York: Signet Classics.

Marx, K. ([1859] 1981) *A Contribution to the Critique of Political Economy* (translated from the German by S. W. Ryazanskaya), Moscow: Progress Publishers and London: Lawrence & Wishart.

Marx, K. ([1867] 1992) *Capital: A Critique of Political Economy, Volume 1* (translated from the German by Ben Fowkes), London and New York: Penguin Books.

Marx, K. ([1885] 1993) *Capital: A Critique of Political Economy, Volume 2* (translated from the German by David Fernbach), London and New York: Penguin Books.

Marx, K. ([1894] 1993) *Capital: A Critique of Political Economy, Volume 3* (translated from the German by David Fernbach), London and New York: Penguin Books.

Maus, M. ([1925] 1954) *The Gift: Forms and Functions of Exchange in Archaic Societies* (translated from the French by Ian Cunnison and comprising essays written between 1944 and 1957), London: Cohen & West.

Mautner, T. (Ed.) (2000) *The Penguin Dictionary of Philosophy*, London and New York: Penguin Books.

McDowell, J. (1994) *Mind and World*, Cambridge, MA: Harvard University Press.

Mead, G. H. ([various dates] 1932) *The Philosophy of the Present* (edited by Arthur E. Murphy), La Salle, IL: Open Court.

Mead, G. H. ([various dates and 1934] 1967) *Mind, Self and Society: From the Standpoint of a Social Behaviourist* (*Works of George Herbert Mead, Volume 1*) (edited by Charles W. Morris), Chicago and London: University of Chicago Press.

Mead, G. H. ([various dates] 1936) *Movements of Thought in the Nineteenth Century* (edited by Merritt H. Moore), Chicago: University of Chicago Press.

Meighan, R. and Harber, C. with Barton, L., Siraj-Blatchford, I. and Walker, S. (2007) *A Sociology of Educating* (Fifth edition), London and New York: Continuum.

Merleau-Ponty, M. ([1945] 1982) *Phenomenology of Perception* (translated from the French by Colin Smith), New York: Routledge.

Merleau-Ponty, M. ([1948] 1973) *Sense and Non-sense* (translated from the French by Hubert Dreyfus and Patricia Allen Dreyfus), Evanston, IL: Northwestern University Press.

Merleau-Ponty, M. ([1964] 1968) *The Visible and the Invisible* (translated from the French by Alphonso Lingis), Evanston, IL: Northwestern University Press.

Michelfelder, D. P. and Palmer, R. E. (Eds.) (1989) *Dialogue and Deconstruction: The Gadamer–Derrida Debate*, Albany, NY: SUNY Press.

Mills, P. E., Cole, K. N., Jenkins, J. R. and Dale, P. S. (1998) 'Effects of Differing Levels of Inclusion on Pre-schoolers with Disabilities', *Exceptional Children* 65, 79–90.

Minick, N. J. (1987) *The Development of Vygotsky's Thought: An Introduction to Thinking and Speech* (edited and translated by Minick), New York: Plenum: reprinted in Daniels, H. (Ed.) *An Introduction to Vygotsky* (Second edition), New York: Routledge (pp. 33–57).

Minogue, K. (1995) *Politics: A Very Short Introduction*, Oxford: Oxford University Press.

Mitchell, D. (Ed.) (2004a) *Special Educational Needs and Inclusive Education: Major Themes in Education Volume 1: Systems and Contexts*, London and New York: RoutledgeFalmer.

Mitchell, S. A. and Black, M. J. (1995) *Freud and Beyond: A History of Psychoanalytic Thought*, New York: Basic Books.

Moore, E. C., Peirce, C. S. and Fisch, M. H. (1986) *Writings of Charles S. Peirce: A Chronological Edition, Volume 3: 1872–1878*, Bloomington: Indiana University Press.

Morra, S., Gobbo, C., Marini, Z. and Sheese, R. (2007) *Cognitive Development: Neo-Piagetian Perspectives*, New York and Hove: Psychology Press.

Mostert, M. P. and Kavale, K. (2001) 'Evaluation of Research for Usable Knowledge in Behavioural Disorders: Ignoring the Irrelevant, Considering the Germane', *Behavioural Disorders* 27, 53–68.

Muratori, F., Picchi, L., Casella, C., Tancredi, R., Milone, A. and Patarnello, M. G. (2002) 'Efficacy of Brief Dynamic Psychotherapy for Children with Emotional Disorders', *Psychotherapy and Psychosomatics* 71, 28–38.

National Center on Inclusive Education and Restructuring (1995) *National Study of Inclusive Education*, New York: City University of New York, NCIER.

Norwich, B. (2008) 'Perspectives and Purposes of Disability Classification Systems: Implications for Teachers and Curriculum Pedagogy' in Florian, L. and McLaughlin, M. J. (2008) *Disability Classification in Education: Issues and Perspectives*, Thousand Oaks, CA: Corwin Press.

Nussbaum, M. (2000) *Women and Human Development: The Capabilities Approach*, Cambridge: Cambridge University Press.

Oliver, M. (1990) *The Politics of Disablement*, Basingstoke: Macmillan.

Oliver, M. (1996) *Understanding Disability: From Theory to Practice*, Basingstoke: Macmillan.

Oliver, M. (1999) 'Capitalism, Disability and Ideology: A Materialist Critique of the Normalisation Principle' in Mitchell, D. (Ed.) *Special Educational Needs and Inclusive Education: Major Themes in Education Volume 1: Systems and Contexts*, London and New York: RoutledgeFalmer.

Oliver, M. (2004) 'The Social Model in Action: If I Had a Hammer' in Barnes, C. and Mercer, G. (Eds.) *Implementing the Social Model of Disability: Theory and Research*, Leeds: Disability Press.

Oliver, M. and Barnes, C. (1998) *Disabled People and Social Policy*, London: Longman.

Padgett, D. K. (2004) 'Introduction' in Padgett, D. K. (Ed.) *The Qualitative Research Experience*, Toronto: Wadsworth.

Paul, J. L., Kleinhammer-Tramill, J. and Fowler, K. (2009) 'Qualitative Research in Special Education' in Paul, J. L., Kleinhammer-Tramill, J. and Fowler, K. (Eds.) *Qualitative Research Methods in Special Education*, Denver: Love Publishing.

Peetsma, T., Verger, M., Roeleveld, J. and Karsten, S. (2001) 'Inclusion in Education: Comparing Pupils' Development in Special Education and Regular Education', *Education Review* 53, 2, 125–135.

Peirce, C. S. (1877) 'The Fixation of Belief' in Moore, E. C., Peirce, C. S. and Fisch, M. H. (1986) *Writings of Charles S. Peirce: A Chronological Edition, Volume 3: 1872–1878*, Bloomington: Indiana University Press.

Peirce, C. S. (1878) 'How to Make Our Ideas Clear' in Moore, E. C., Peirce, C. S. and Fisch, M. H. (1986) *Writings of Charles S. Peirce: A Chronological Edition, Volume 3: 1872–1878*, Bloomington: Indiana University Press.

Peters, R. S. (1966) *Ethics and Education*, London: Allen & Unwin.

Piaget, J. ([1968] 1971) *Structuralism* (translated from the French by Chaninah Maschler), London: Routledge & Keegan Paul.

Piaget, J. (1970) 'Piaget's Theory' in Mussen, P. H. (Ed.) *Manual of Child Psychology*, London: Wiley.

Piaget, J. and Inhelder, B. ([1966] 1969) *The Psychology of the Child* (translated from the French by Helen Weaver), London: Routledge & Keegan Paul.

Pine, E. (1990) *Drive, Ego, Object and Self*, New York: Basic Books.

Poplin, M. (1988a) 'The Reductionistic Fallacy in Learning Disabilities: Replicating the Past by Reducing the Present', *Journal of Learning Disabilities* 21, 389–400.

Poplin, M. (1988b) 'Holistic/Constructivist Principles of the Teaching/Learning Process: Implications for the Field of Learning Disabilities', *Journal of Learning Disabilities* 21, 401–416.

Poplin, M. and Cousin, P. (Eds.) (1996) *Alternative Views of Learning Disabilities: Issues for the 21st Century*, Austin, TX: Pro-Ed.

Popper, K. ([1934] 2002) *The Logic of Scientific Discovery*, New York and London: Routledge.

Popper, K. (1959) *The Logic of Scientific Discovery* (translated from the German by the author with the assistance of Julius Freed and Lan Freed), London: Hutchinson.

Porter, R. ([1987] 1990) *Mind-Forg'd Manacles: A History of Madness in England from the Restoration to the Regency*, Harmondsworth: Penguin.

Powers, S., Gregory, S. and Thoutonhoofd, D. (1999) 'The Educational Achievement of Deaf Children', *Deafness and Education International* 1, 1, 1–9.

Qualifications and Curriculum Authority (1999) *Shared World – Different Experiences: Designing the Curriculum for Pupils who are Deafblind*, London: QCA.

Qualifications and Curriculum Authority (2001a) *Planning, Teaching and Assessing the Curriculum for Pupils with Learning Difficulties: English*, London: QCA.

Qualifications and Curriculum Authority (2001b) *Planning, Teaching and Assessing the Curriculum for Pupils with Learning Difficulties: Mathematics*, London: QCA.

Qualifications and Curriculum Authority (2001c) *Planning, Teaching and Assessing the Curriculum for Pupils with Learning Difficulties: Personal, Social and Health Education and Citizenship*, London: QCA.

Reiser, R. and Mason, M. (1992) *Disability Equality in the Classroom: A Human Rights Issue*, London: Disability Equality in Education.

Reynolds, L. T. (1995) 'Intellectual Antecedents' in Herman, N. J. and Reynolds, L. T. *Symbolic Interaction: An Introduction to Social Psychology*, New York: General Hall (pp. 6–24).

Richardson, K. (1999) *The Making of Intelligence*, London: Weidenfeld & Nicolson.

Ricoeur, P. ([n.d.] 1970) *Freud and Philosophy: An Essay on Interpretation* (translated from the French by D. Savage), New Haven, CT and London: Yale University Press.

Ricoeur, P. ([various dates] 1969) *The Conflict of Interpretations: Essays in Hermeneutics* (edited by Don Ihde), Evanston, IL: Northwestern University Press.

Rorty, R. (1979) *Philosophy and the Mirror of Nature*, Princeton, NJ: Princeton University Press.

Rorty, R. (1989) *Contingency, Irony and Solidarity*, Cambridge: Cambridge University Press.

Rousseau, J. J. ([1769 and published posthumously in 1782] 2005) *The Confessions of Jean-Jacques Rousseau* (translated from the French by J. Cohen), London and New York: Penguin.

Rousseau, J. J. ([n.d. and posthumously published in 1781] 1986) *Essay on the Origin of Languages* in *Two Essays of the Origin of Languages* (translated from the French by John H. Moran) Chicago: University of Chicago Press.

Russell, B. ([1912] 2001) *The Problems of Philosophy*, Oxford: Oxford University Press.

Russell, B. ([1946] 1996) *History of Western Philosophy*, New York and London: Routledge.

Sabournie, E. J. (2006) 'Preface – Philosophy of Education', *Exceptionality* 14, 2, 63–64.

Salend, S. J. and Duhany, L. M. G. (1999) 'The Impact of Inclusion on Students with and Without Disabilities and their Educators', *Remedial and Special Education* 20, 2, 114–126.

Sartre, Jean-Paul ([1947] 1957) *Existentialism and Humanism* (translated from the French by Phillip Malet), London: Methuen.

Sasso, G. M. (2001) 'The Retreat From Inquiry and Knowledge in Special Education', *The Journal of Special Education* 34, 4, 178–193.

Saussure, F. de ([1915] 1966) *Course in General Linguistics* (derived from student notes on lecture courses delivered by Ferdinand de Saussure between 1906 and 1911; edited by Charles Bally and Albert Sechehaye in collaboration with Albert Riedlinger; translated from the French by Wade Baskin), New York and London: McGraw-Hill.

Schaverien, J. (1995) 'Researching the Esoteric: Art Therapy Research' in Gilroy, A. and Lee, C. (Eds.) *Art and Music Therapy Research*, London: Routledge.

Schleiermacher, F. ([1808] 1998) *Hermeneutics and Criticism and Other Writings* (*Cambridge Tests in the History of Philosophy*) (edited and translated from the German by Andrew Bowie), Cambridge and New York: Cambridge University Press.

Schopler, E. (1997) 'Implementation of TEACCH philosophy' in Cohen, D. and Volkmar, F. (Eds.) *Handbook of Autism and Pervasive Developmental Disorders* (Second edition), New York: Wiley.

Scruton, R. ([1995] 2002) *A Short History of Modern Philosophy from Descartes to Wittgenstein* (Second edition), London and New York: Routledge.

Scully, J. L. (2002) 'A Postmodern Disorder: Moral Encounters With Molecular Models Of Disability' in Corker, M. and Shakespeare, T. (2002) *Disability/Postmodernity: Embodying Disability Theory*, London and New York: Continuum.

Sen, A. (1992) *Inequality Re-examined*, Oxford: Oxford University Press.

Sen, A. (1997) *Inequality Re-examined*, Oxford: Clarendon Press.

Shakespeare, T. (2006) *Disability Rights and Wrongs*, London and New York: Routledge.

Shildrick, M. (2009) *Dangerous Discourse of Disability, Subjectivity and Sexuality*, London: PalgraveMacmillan.

Shorter, E. (1997) *A History of Psychiatry: From the Era of the Asylum to the Age of Prozac*, New York and Chichester: John Wiley.

Silvers, A. (2002) 'The Crooked Timber of Humanity: Disability, Ideology and the Aesthetic' in Corker, M. and Shakespeare, T. (2002) *Disability/Postmodernity: Embodying Disability Theory*, London and New York: Continuum.

Simeonson, R. J., Simeonson, N. E. and Hollenweger, J. (2008) 'International Classification of Functioning, Disability and Health for Children and Youth' in Florian, L. and McLaughlin, M. J. *Disability Classification in Education: Issues and Perspectives*, Thousand Oaks, CA: Corwin Press.

Simpson, R. L. (2005) 'Evidence-based Practices and Students with ASD', *Focus on Autism and Other Developmental Disabilities* 20, 3, 140–149.

Singer, J. (1999) '"Why Can't You Be Normal for Once in Your Life?" From a problem with no name to the emergence of a new category of difference' in Corker, M. and French, S., *Disability Discourse*, Buckingham: Open University Press.

Skidmore, D. (2004) *Inclusion: The Dynamic of School Development*, Buckingham: Open University Press/McGraw-Hill Education.

Skrtic, T. M. (Ed.) (1995) *Disability and Democracy: Reconstructing (Special) Education for Postmodernity*, New York: Teachers College Press.

Skrtic, T. M. (2004) 'Critical Disability Studies' in Gallagher, D. J., Heshusius, L., Iano, R. P. and Skrtic, T. M. (2004) *Challenging Orthodoxy in Special Education: Dissenting Voices*, Denver: Love Publishing.

Skynner, R. (1991) *Institutes and How to Survive Them: Mental Health Training and Consultation*, London: Routledge.

Sleeter, C. E. (1995) 'Radical Structural Perspectives on the Creation and Use of Learning Disabilities' in Skrtic, T. M. (Ed.) *Disability and Democracy: Reconstructing (Special) Education for Postmodernity*, New York: Teachers College Press.

Smith, M. D. and Fowler, K. M. (2009) 'Phenomenological Research' in Paul, J. L., Kleinhammer–Tramill, J. and Fowler, K. (Eds.) *Qualitative Research Methods in Special Education*, Denver: Love Publishing.

Smuts, J. C. ([1926] 1999) *Holism and Evolution: The Original Source of the Holistic Approach to Life* (edited by Sanford Holst), Thousand Oaks, CA: Sierra Sunrise Books.

Smuts, J. C. (1927) *Holism and Evolution* (Second edition), London: Macmillan.

Soanes, C. and Stevenson, A. (Eds.) (2003) *Oxford Dictionary of English* (Second edition), Oxford: Oxford University Press.

Sokal, A. and Bricmont, J. ([1997] 1999). *Intellectual Impostures: Postmodern Philosophers' Abuse of Science*, London: Profile Books.

Sokal, A. and Bricmont, J. (1998) *Fashionable Nonsense: Postmodern Intellectuals' Abuse of Science*, New York: Picador.

Spear-Swerling, L. and Sternberg, R. J. (2001) 'What Science Offers Teachers of Reading', *Learning Disabilities Research and Practice* 16, 51–57.

Staley, C. E. (1991) *A History of Economic Thought: From Aristotle to Arrow*, Cambridge, MA and Oxford: Blackwell.

Stangvik, G. (1998) 'Conflicting Perspectives on Learning Disabilities' in Clark, C., Dyson, A. and Milward, A. (Eds.) *Theorising Special Education*, London and New York: Taylor & Francis.

Stanovich, P. J., Jordan, A. and Perot, J. (1998) 'Relative Differences in Academic Self-Concept and Peer Acceptance Among Students in Inclusive Classrooms', *Remedial and Special Education* 19, 2, 120–126.

Steiner, G. (1971) 'The Mandarin of the Hour – Michel Foucault', *New York Times*, 28 February.

Stone, L. (1982) 'Madness', *New York Review of Books*, 16 December.

Stuhr, J. J. (Ed.) (2000) *Pragmatism and the Classical American Philosophy: Essential Readings and Interpretive Essays* (Second edition), New York: Oxford University Press.

Swanson, H. L., Harris, K. R. and Graham, S. (Eds.) (2003) *Handbook of Learning Disabilities*, New York: Guilford Press.

Terzi, L. (2005) 'Beyond the Dilemma of Difference: The Capability Approach to Disability and Special Educational Needs', *Journal of Philosophy of Education* 39, 3, 443–459.

Tharp, R. (1993) 'Institutional and Social Context of Educational Practice and Reform' in Forman, A. E., Minick, N. and Stone, C. A. (Eds.) *Contexts for Learning: Sociocultural Dynamics in Children's Development*, Oxford: Oxford University Press.

Thomas, C. and Corker, M. (2002) 'A Journey around the Social Model' in Corker, M. and Shakespeare, T. (2002) (Eds.) *Disability/Postmodernity: Embodying Disability Theory*, London and New York: Continuum.

Thomas, G. and Loxley, A. (2007) *Deconstructing Special Education and Constructing Inclusion* (Second edition), Maidenhead: Open University Press/McGraw-Hill.

Titchkosky, T. (2002) 'Cultural Maps: Which Way to Disability?' in Corker, M. and Shakespeare, T. (2002) *Disability/Postmodernity: Embodying Disability Theory*, London and New York: Continuum.

Tomlinson, S. (1987) 'Critical Theory and Special Education', *CASTME Journal* 7, 2, 33–41.

Townsend, D. (1997) *An Introduction to Aesthetics*, Oxford, and Malden, MA: Blackwell.

Tremain, S. (2002) 'On the Subject of Impairment' in Corker, M. and Shakespeare, T. (Eds.) *Disability/Postmodernity: Embodying Disability Theory*, London: Continuum.

Tutty, C. and Hocking, C. (2004) 'A Shackled Heart: Teachers Aides' Experience of Supporting Students with High Support Needs in Regular Classes', *Kiararanga* 5, 2, 3–9.

United States Department of Education (1999) 'Assistance to States for the Education of Children with Disabilities Program and the Early Intervention Program for Infants and Toddlers with Disabilities: Final Regulations', *Federal Register*, 64, 48, (CFR Parts 3000 and 303).

Valente, L. and Fontana, D. (1997) 'Assessing Client Progress in Drama Therapy' in Jennings, S. (Ed.) *Dramatherapy: Theory and Practice 3*, London: Routledge.

Vanheule, S., Lievrouw, A. and Verhaeghe, P. (2003) 'Burnout and Intersubjectivity: A Psychoanalytical Study from a Lacanian Perspective', *Human Relations* 56, 3, 321–338.

Vaughan, S. and Klinger, J. K. (1998) 'Students' Perceptions of Inclusion and Resource Room Settings', *Journal of Special Education* 32, 2, 79–88.

Vlachou, A. D. (1997) *Struggles for Inclusive Education: An Ethnographic Study*, Buckingham: Open University Press/McGraw-Hill Education.

Vygotsky, L. S. ([1924] 1993) 'The Psychology and Pedagogy of Children's Handicaps' (originally published in *Questions of Education of the Blind, the Deaf-Mute and Mentally Retarded Children*, edited by Vygotsky, 1929) in Rieber, R. W. and Carton, A. S. (Eds.) (1993) *The Collected Works of L. S. Vygotsky, Volume 2: The Fundamentals of Defectology (Abnormal Psychology and Learning Disabilities)* (translated from the Russian by Knox, J. E. and Stevens, C. B.), New York: Plenum Press.

Vygotsky, L. S. ([1925–1926] 1993) 'Principles of Education for Physically Handicapped Children' (based on a report of the same title prepared for the Second Congress on the Social and Legal Protection of Minors, 1924) in Rieber, R. W. and Carton, A. S. (Eds.) (1993) *The Collected Works of L. S. Vygotsky, Volume 2: The Fundamentals of Defectology (Abnormal Psychology and Learning Disabilities)* (translated from the Russian by Knox, J. E. and Stevens, C. B.), New York: Plenum Press.

Vygotsky, L. S. ([1927] 1993) 'Defect and Compensation' (a version was published as 'Defect and Overcompensation' in *Retardation, Blindness and Deafness*, 1927) in Rieber, R. W. and Carton, A. S. (Eds.) (1993) *The Collected Works of L. S. Vygotsky, Volume 2: The Fundamentals of Defectology (Abnormal Psychology and*

Learning Disabilities) (translated from the Russian by Knox, J. E. and Stevens, C. B.), New York: Plenum Press.

Vygotsky, L. S. ([n.d.] 1993) 'The Blind Child' in Rieber, R. W. and Carton, A. S. (Eds.) *The Collected Works of L. S. Vygotsky, Volume 2: The Fundamentals of Defectology (Abnormal Psychology and Learning Disabilities)* (translated by Knox, J. E. and Stevens, C. B.) New York: Plenum Press.

Vygotsky, L. S. ([various dates] 1978) *Mind in Society: The Development of Higher Psychological Processes* (edited by Cole, M., John-Steiner, V., Scribner, S. and Souberman, E.), Cambridge, MA: Harvard University Press.

Wade, J. (1999) 'Including All Learners: QCA's Approach', *British Journal of Special Education*, 26, 2, 80–82.

Ware, J. (2003) *Creating a Responsive Environment for People with Profound and Multiple Learning Difficulties*, London: David Fulton.

Warnock Report (1978) *Special Education Needs: Report of the Committee of Enquiry into the Education of Handicapped Children and Young People*, London: Her Majesty's Stationery Office.

Warnock, M. (2005) 'Special Educational Needs: A New Look' (*Impact No. 11*), London: The Philosophy of Education Society of Great Britain.

Webster, R. (2007) *Why Freud Was Wrong: Sin, Science and Psychoanalysis*, Oxford: Orwell Press.

Wertsch, J. V. (1985) *Vygotsky and the Social Formation of Mind*, Cambridge, MA: Harvard University Press.

Wiggerhaus, R. ([1986] 1995) *The Frankfurt School: Its History, Theories and Political Significance* (translated from the German by Michael Robertson), Cambridge, MA: Massachusetts Institute of Technology.

Wilton, R. D. (2003) 'Locating Physical Disability in Freudian and Lacanian Psychoanalysis: Problems and Prospects', *Social and Cultural Geography* 4, 3, 369–389.

Winnicott, D. W. (1958) *Through Paediatrics to Psychoanalysis*, London: Hogarth Press.

Winnicott, D. W. (1965) *The Maturational Process and the Facilitating Environment*, London: Hogarth Press.

Wittgenstein, L. ([1945] 2001) *Philosophical Investigations* (German text with English translation by G. E. M. Anscombe), Oxford: Blackwell.

Wolitzky, D. L. (2003) 'The Theory and Practice of Traditional Psychoanalytic Treatment' in Gurman, A. S. and Messer, S. B. (Eds.) *Essential Psychotherapies: Theory and Practice*, New York: Guilford Press.

Wood, D. (1998) *How Children Think and Learn* (Second edition), Oxford: Blackwell.

World Health Organisation (2001) *ICF-International Classification of Functioning, Disability and Health*, Geneva: WHO.

World Health Organisation (2002) *International Classification of Functioning, Disability and Health: Towards a Common Language for Functioning, Disability and Health*, Geneva: WHO.

World Health Organisation (2007) *International Classification of Functioning, Disability and Health: Children and Youth Version*, Geneva: WHO.

Young, I. M. (2002) 'Foreword' in Corker, M. and Shakespeare, T. (2002) (Eds.) *Disability/Postmodernity: Embodying Disability Theory*, London and New York: Continuum.

Index